HOLLYWOOD EAST

Hong Kong Movies and the People Who Make Them

STEFAN HAMMOND

foreword by Michelle Yeoh

CB

CONTEMPORARY BOOKS

Library of Congress Cataloging-in-Publication Data

Hammond, Stefan.
    Hollywood East : Hong Kong movies and the people who make them / Stefan
Hammond ; foreword by Michelle Yeoh.
        p.   cm.
    Includes index.
    ISBN 0-8092-2581-6
    1. Motion pictures—China—Hong Kong.   2 Motion picture producers and
directors—China—Hong Kong.   3. Motion picture actors and actresses—
China—Hong Kong.   I. Title.
PN1993.5.H6H25   2000
791.43´095125—dc21

                                                                    99-16578
                                                                        CIP

Cover design by Todd Petersen
Front-cover photographs courtesy of Fitto Movie Co. Ltd. (left), Mei Ah (top right), and
Fung Ping Films (bottom right)
Back-cover photograph courtesy of Gai Ngap Films
Interior design by Hespenheide Design

Published by Contemporary Books
A division of NTC/Contemporary Publishing Group, Inc.
4255 West Touhy Avenue, Lincolnwood (Chicago), Illinois 60712-1975 U.S.A.
Printed in the United States of America
International Standard Book Number: 0-8092-2581-6

00 01 02 03 04 VL 19 18 17 16 15 14 13 12 11 10 9 8 7 6 5 4 3 2 1

for keiko

contents

foreword

Over the course of the 17 films I've had the pleasure of making in Hong Kong, I have gained a sense of what we have that is unique to our corner of the film world. The particular blend of fantastic stories, gritty and realistic action, pulled together in a strikingly fast pace of production by a dedicated and talented group of artists, directors, and technical film creators has an appeal that extends far beyond Hong Kong and Asia. Film fans around the world appreciate our finished product, even though many of them do not realize the extent to which Hong Kong films truly differ from those made elsewhere.

My education in the Asian film industry, working in Hong Kong, was a nonstop school where swirling smoke was made not by machines but by men burning bundles of joss sticks in metal cans, creating a thick and aromatic atmosphere. Many of these sets were devoid of trailers, and I did my hair and makeup outdoors, using a mirror propped up against a wall. Script pages were produced at the last possible moment, and stunt sequences were created with real and dangerous action, not with computers and green screens. The spontaneity gets in your blood.

There are many career highlights but I am most proud of *Yes! Madam*, where I first made the transition into playing action roles, proving that a woman could be an effective action star. Stunt boys and action choreographers in Hong Kong graciously taught me this craft. Making *Supercop* with Jackie Chan was especially memorable: I got to work in Malaysia and perform some amazing stunts—such as riding a dirt bike onto a moving train. *Supercop* was released in the U.S. in 1996 and I believe that for many U.S. audience members it was their first exposure to HK action movies.

Many of us have made the move to Hollywood, where filmmaking is a slower and more controlled process—but we have not turned our backs on Hong Kong movies. Audiences appreciate the spontaneity of the Hong Kong style, and we hope to bring about a synthesis of these two very different traditions, keeping the best of both worlds. In 1997 I appeared in *Tomorrow Never Dies* with Pierce Brosnan, and we brought Philip Kwok (Kuo Chui) and his stunt boys from Hong Kong to London to choreograph a fight sequence for the movie.

By reading this book you will find out about the many people who have contributed to Hong Kong moviemaking. These are the people who are important to me and HK movie fans around the world.

Michelle Yeoh

acknowledgments

Thanks to my editor, Betsy Lancefield, whose encouragement and support were invaluable, and whose hook kicks cause her opponents to quake in their boots; Danielle Egan-Miller for making this book a reality and understanding the true value of Hex Errors; Todd Petersen for wrangling images; Craig Bolt; Denise Betts; and all the rest of the fine editorial staff at NTC/Contemporary.

Thanks to all the great people at Fitto Movie Company Ltd., including Elliot Tong, Julianne Wong, and Irene Lam Hok-shun.

Special thanks (in no particular order) to Carrie Wong of Golden Network for her invaluable assistance and energy. Almen Wong for her support and for the "Panther Girl" pose. Herman Yau for his good cheer and explanations of ghost culture. Johnnie To and Wai Ka-fai for making thunderously good films—also at Milkyway, thanks to Catherine Chan and a special thank-you to Christina Lee for making it all happen.

The unique Christopher Doyle. Money Lo and Kimmy Shuen of Martini Films. Edwin Kong, one of Hong Kong's more creative film people. Tim Youngs for subediting the manuscript and chasing down data. Frank Djeng and Helen Soo of Tai Seng Video in San Francisco. Michael Wong and his wonderful family: Janet Ma, Kayla, and Irissa. The one and only Jackie Chan and his manager Willie Chan. Angela Tong and all the inspirational folks at the Hong Kong Film Archive. Michelle Yeoh, who rocks the planet. TS Lo, Alice Chan, and Esther Fong at the Hong Kong International Film Festival. Wu Chien-lien, articulate, thoughtful, and a hell of a shot, and Cora Cheng at Right Stone. Bill Jenkins, who needs to visit Hong Kong more often. The terrific Karen Mok and her manager Keenie Ho. Simon Furman and David Barraclough of Titan Books in London. Benny Chia of the Fringe Club in Hong Kong. John Woo, who deserves *all* his accolades, and Terence Chang, underappreciated all too often. Michelle Tsang of the Hong Kong Film Awards. Ringo Lam for his irascibility, for his lack of compromise, and for all my favorite parts of his repertoire. Felix Leung of China Trend Building Press. Glenn Kay for his irrepressible and contagious *bonhomie*. Mike Wilkins for his expertise in hard-diggin' journalism, for his museum-quality collection of PopCult ephemera, and for asking: "What happens to the babies?" Jim Morton for his constant support, encyclopedic knowledge of film, and virtuoso accordion performances. Mike Mallery of World Lithographic Services in San Francisco. DE Hardy, master of muses and a constant inspiration. And all the members of the TST Friday Lunch Club, including Jon Benn, everyone named Mike, TJ, and The Beast.

Thanks also to Richard A. Akiyama, Keith Allison, David Atkinson, Thea Baird, Magnus Bartlett, Bruce Black, Blitz, Pietro Bonomi, Tod Booth, David Bordwell, Carmen Bradley, Jeff Briggs, Diana Bringardner, Jane Jordan Browne, Monte Cazazza, Beverly Chan, Bobo Chan, Shirley Chan, Chan Ka Ho, Gary Chang, John Charles, Alfred Cheung, Roberta Chin, Peter Coe, Bill Connolly, Colin Covert, Stefan Cucos, Diane Davis, Sheila Duignan, David Dunton, Anastasia Edwards, Jill Elsner, Eric and June, Naresh Fernandes, Joseph Fierro, Jane Finden-Crofts, Peter Flechette, Paul Fonoroff, Allison Dakota Gee, Sari Gordon, Tom Gray, Richard Grosse, Fionnuala Halligan, Sandy Hau, Titus Ho, Tim Holmes, Lars-Erik Holmquist, Carol Hui, Ange Hwang, Fiona Jerome, Kent Johnson, Richard Kadrey, Tom Kagy, Bill Kong, Kidai Kwon, Gere Ladue, Mick Lasalle, Bruce Law, Jenny Lee, Rebecca Lee, Mike Leeder, Max Leighton, Simon Li, Felix Lu, Stephen Lu, Brad Masoni, Paul Mavrides, John Minford, Aparna Mukherjee, Ron Murillo, Paul Nerbonne, Richard Norton, Ben Ng, Francis Ng, Hank Okazaki, Kiyomi Ono, Carl Parkes, Charlotte Parsons, Richard Petersen, Kevin Powers, William Henry Pratt, Catherine Reuther, Brad Roberts, Cynthia Rothrock, Keiji Sato, Andrew Scal, Steve and Serin Schechter, Cameron Scholes, Dr. Bob Smith, Douglass St. Clair Smith, Richard A. Spears, Candy Tam, Lursak Thavornvanit, Steve and Joanie Tibbetts, Stanley Tong, Ridley Tsui, Hideo Uchiyama, Uncle Seven, Wendy Van Dusen, Steve Vascik, Nury Vittachi, Matthew Walker, Jeff Wilkins, Sam Wilkins, Bill Wilson, Anthony Wong, Declan Wong, William Woo, Miles Wood, Lambert Yam, Keiko Yoshimoto, Daniel Zilber, William O. Zinsser.

Apologies to anyone I've forgotten or whose name I've misspelled, as if that could possibly happen.

iNtroductioN

For many Western viewers, "Hong Kong films" means "action films"—kung fu epics or double-handed blastfests. But Hong Kong films are an industry, not a genre. The HK film industry produces everything from weepy love stories to social dramas to gambling flicks.

As it's an industry and not a genre, no single book slipping into the Hong Kong movie maelstrom can do more than spin on the surface. The sheer volume and pace of the industry, coupled with the publicity-shy nature of the film companies themselves, make any explication of "Hong Kong films" a Herculean task.

Hong Kong used to be the third-largest film industry in the world, and its recent slippage to number four is a powerful symbol of the industry's decline—a slide that began in 1993. The reasons? First and foremost is Hollywood, a global industry no longer mystified by overseas market share.

The rise of Japanese pop culture as an entertainment vector, the poaching of Hong Kong talent by Hollywood, and rampant video piracy all contribute. The industry's output has fallen from more than 200 features in 1992 to fewer than 90 in 1998. The late 1980s and early 1990s, when so many terrific HK films were made, now constitute an epoch of sorts.

Why are Hong Kong films still worth knowing? Partly because of the breadth and depth of the back catalog. But mostly because the creative power is still here— amazing and unique films continue to stream outta this rock. Films of passion, *murderous* passion. As any Hong Kong *afflictionado* can tell you, the lightning-quick HK vibe—that faster/wilder/weirder thing they do—is a distinction well worth hurdling language or cultural barriers.

There are no guilty pleasures in a Hong Kong flick. These are not films for dissection of languorous symbolism, but cinema of movement and action that grabs you by the scruff of the neck. The richest Hong Kong cinematic experiences are in grimy theaters surrounded by families spitting melon seeds and guffawing at the Cantonese punmanship, not jazz-infested coffeehouses where beret-types blow mocacchino foam, dissecting the hidden subtexts of *Ebola Syndrome*. Hong Kong films are refreshingly apolitical, not to mention politically incorrect. Suffice to say that even some film studies professors have rediscovered their own passion upon exposure to this dynamo, tossing their baked brie in the trash can and becoming infused "with the delusion that they can vault, grave and unflappable, over the cars parked outside the theater"—as Professor David Bordwell of the University of Wisconsin so wonderfully put it.

Counterbalancing the delightful richness of the material is the fluidity of these short-shelf-life films. Hong Kong media react with a speed more suited to the American International films of the 1950s and 1960s than the measured torpor of modern-day Hollywood. When a HK gangster is collared in summertime, his biopic is scripted, shot, and playing HK cinemas by fall. Television dramas (where many film actors moonlight) are presented as five episodes per week rather than one—a 30-episode TV drama runs its course in six weeks, to be supplanted by

another. Entertainment monthlies, weeklies, and dailies, fed by battalions of pushy *paparazzi*, compete Darwin-style on Hong Kong newsstands.

While there's plenty of cross-fertilization, Asian filmmakers should never be lumped together, and neither should their individual cultures, languages, and influences. Chinese directors Zhang Yimou and Chen Kaige are not HK filmmakers; neither is American director Wayne Wang, nor Taiwanese-American director Ang Lee, nor Korean director Kim Ki-young, nor Japanese masters Akira Kurosawa and Seijun Suzuki. Their films may be excellent, but they are not Hong Kong films, which is what this book is about.

Now that the mallrats of America are hip to Jackie Chan, and John Woo has become a U.S. citizen, Hong Kong movie books are becoming commonplace. The one I cowrote with Mike Wilkins, *Sex and Zen & a Bullet in the Head*, was published by Fireside for the United States and Canada and by Titan Books in London for the United Kingdom and Australia/New Zealand markets. If you *sprechen Deutsch*, you'll also want the German-language edition from Heyne Books of Munich: *Sex und Zen und eine Kugel in den Kopf* (take a deep breath and stick http://www.amazon.de/exec/obidos/ASIN/3453140559/o/qid=92 0009289/sr=2-2/t/028-5212200-1004402 in your browser window. *Danke schoen*!).

This new book, from NTC/Contemporary in Chicago, is not intended to be completist, nor an update of *Sex and Zen & a Bullet in the Head.* You won't find chapters on Ringo Lam and Tsui Hark this time around, not because those filmmakers are no longer important, but because the bulk of their work was covered earlier. You will find chapters on John Woo and Jackie Chan this time that go deeper into their work, providing more analysis and insight. And you'll find a lot more on the film culture in Hong Kong itself—a prime ingredient in the vitality, speed, and flexibility of these films.

Portions of this book are sheer rant, born of passion and love for the experience of the Lighted Wall. Abandon the solitary viewing experience of the Haunted Fish Tank and seek out the communion of your fellow HK crazies in theaters that present these films. There is nothing like being a single cell in the unified organism undergoing the collective experience of a rippin' good Hong Kong flick. To know Hong Kong cinema is to delve into an alternative cinematic universe, to discover and savor a richness unsuspected. These films provide conversion experiences.

Stefan Hammond
Hong Kong

Movie advertising Hong Kong style

Stefan Hammond

1

iN ſitu

a polluted, noisy, congested Asian hell on the knife-edge of apocalypse. The crowds: a shoving mass of humanity that packs public transportation to the gills and elbows you off the sidewalk. The food: offensively weird and humiliatingly expensive. In fact, every damn thing: insanely expensive. Nobody speaks English. Over-the-top rudeness and outright chicanery everywhere and watch out they don't sneak dog meat in your fried rice. . . .

It's a great place to live.

Street Hong Kong is not exactly what you've seen in the films. Don't waste time looking for maddened crowds of revenge-crazed youngsters wielding choppers, or cops and robbers slinging lead at each other. If you visit Chungking Mansions in hopes of finding Faye Wong boppin' to "California Dreamin'," you're dreamin'.

Street-real HK lies somewhere between the sterile newness of Seoul and Tokyo and the fertile grime of Bangkok or Manila. With few natural resources but a deep-water port and a hardworking populace dedicated to a better tomorrow, Hong Kong has carved its way from its mid-nineteenth-century "barren rock" status to a financial and service center for the region.

Business is what Hong Kong knows best, but culture is an important and often-overlooked part of the HK success equation. The Chinese film industry was located in Shanghai in the 1920s and 1930s, but the Japanese invasion of 1937 convulsed all of China for a decade or so. When the dust settled, the Nationalists had fled to Taiwan, Mao had founded the People's Republic of China (PRC), and the Brits, somewhat chastened, returned to Hong Kong. A fledgling

Hong Kong's best shopping district: Mongkok

Stefan Hammond

buildings shoehorned into city blocks. Pedestrian traffic provides retail lubrication, and the best arcades are located in well-trampled areas like Mongkok/Yau Ma Tei on the Kowloon side and Wanchai/Causeway Bay on Hong Kong Island. The arcades rent out spaces to individual owners, most of whom are young kids who are also fans—*laissez-faire* capitalism at its best.

The small businesses that have helped make Hong Kong an economic powerhouse define the shopping arcades that cater to movie freaks. And the word *small* is essential. Just as the meaning of *elbow-room* is never fully grasped until you've visited certain areas of Hong Kong, the phrase *enough room to swing a cat* is just an expression until you descend into Mongkok's infamous Sino Centre. If you're not claustrophobic, that may change. Don't bring a backpack, do watch your elbows, and go easy on the Right Guard. And if you go on a weekend, God help you.

What are the arcades like, besides tiny and cramped? Eccentric. Smoky. Although smoking was banned in Hong Kong shopping malls in July of 1998, many people light up anyway, creating a thick haze of foul-smelling, cancerous exhaust. Worse, some casually toss their smoldering butts where they please. Every once in a while, a building in Hong Kong experiences a horrific fire. Then everyone complains about fire doors, or signage, or the fire brigade.

independence movement was mooted by the British government postwar, but sentiment was weak, as most Hong Kongers presciently assumed the colony would revert to Chinese rule sooner or later.

Needless to say, Shanghai never returned to its glory as a celluloid capital, so Hong Kong stepped in to fill the gap, serving as filmmaker to most of the Asian world, as well as Chinatowns worldwide.

But enough of all this. Let's go shopping!

iNto the arcades

Hong Kong film fans want movies and memorabilia, and their horn of plenty spills its bounty in HK neighborhood shopping arcades. These emporia are nothing like the Muzak-stewed malls of American suburbia. In the cramped environs of urban Hong Kong, the arcades inhabit commercial

What's on offer? It changes with the winds. An arcade loaded with VCD shops and poster stores can transform into a multistory fluffy horror (stuffed animals, cutesy plastic models, "Hello Kitty" stickers) overnight. If bootleg VCDs are being sold (see "Avast Ye Swab," page 19), raids by the vigilant Customs and Excise Department can rapidly create shuttered or empty storefronts. Many arcades offer techno gear of the digital and/or analog variety, and these represent some of Hong Kong's best shopping bargains. You may have to crawl over people to get to it, but the arcades are where to go for power strips and phone cords and CD cases and blank media.

The best area to shop is the Mongkok district and its contiguous cousin: Yau Ma Tei. This area, on the Kowloon peninsula just north of the touristed Tsim Sha Tsui district, is the most crowded urban area on Earth. No joke—Mongkok's urban crowding makes Manhattan look like Montana. Steel yourself and get down there.

Also of note on the Kowloon side is the Sham Shui Po district, though this is more useful to residents. On the Hong Kong side, Wan Chai and Causeway Bay are a must. Here's what's current as of this writing, although by the time this book gets into your hands, things will be at least slightly different. Nowhere is the phrase *caveat emptor* more appropriate.

Sai Yeung Choi Street South, Mongkok

If you're primarily looking for movies on VCD and/or DVD, do this *first*: take the MTR to Mongkok Station and take exit E2. This will spit you out on Sai Yeung Choi Street South, and there are three shops between Nelson Street and Shantung Street that will keep you busy for hours. The best of the lot is the Win Win AV Shop.

The surrounding streets are also well worth exploring. Tung Choi Street one block over has an outdoor market called Ladies Street. Fa Yuen Street one block farther has great prices on electronic goods. Farther south, the Temple Street Market is on the tourist trail, but if you approach it from the Yau Ma Tei end, you get to the most interesting stuff first.

Sino Centre, Mongkok

The lowest ceilings. The worst crowds. The tiniest shops. Shop here on a Saturday afternoon and you'll wish your mother had never spawned you. Still, a really great place to buy all kinds of supergroovy junk. Sample at noon on a weekday, though some shops don't open until the kiddies get out of school around three. If you survive, you can always come back later.

We are talking four floors of closet-sized shops, including the basement. Sino Centre changes so much from month to month—depending on PopCult trends,

TEN IMAGINARY HONG KONG DANGERS

1. Triad Trouble. Don't bother peering over your shoulder for that army of chopper-wielding goons. You're unlikely to run into any violent street crime in Hong Kong, organized or not.

2. Godless Communists Crushing Your Personal Freedom under Their Big Black Leather Jackboots. See "Blood! Thunder! Handover!," page 138.

3. The Bird Flu. This mysterious disease freaked out everyone in December 1997, as a virus thought to be poultry-specific turned up in some human bloodstreams. Scorched-earth measures included the banning of live poultry sales and the massacre of bazillions of birds. Although the bird flu killed six people, it has not been heard from since. It's estimated that cigarette smoking kills 4,000 people annually in the SAR, which means that according to that estimate, it takes less than a day for cigs to kill six in HK.

4. The PLA. A garrison of troops from the People's Liberation Army has been stationed in Hong Kong since the handover. My mother didn't like the look of those troops. She saw them on her television arriving via open truck in the rainstorms of the handover and said they looked scary.

   The PLA troops replaced British troops who may or may not have looked scary but had a reputation for getting drunk and whizzing in nearby gardens, which did not endear them to the locals. The PLA troops have not been accused of any such stunts.

   Brits or PLA, you won't see soldiers in the street, as opposed to the Hong Kong Police, who are ubiquitous.

5. The Cops. Hong Kong, like Manhattan, is a walking town. And like their Gotham counterparts, HK cops walk beats, getting to know neighborhoods and keeping the peace.

   The HK police force is professional and well disciplined. The creation of the ICAC in the mid-1970s has dampened (though not eliminated) corruption. The cops will ignore you, so ignore them. Don't expect to be hauled downtown for wearing your "Free Tibet" T-shirt.

6. The Language Barrier. Most people in Hong Kong speak at least a little English, and many speak it very well indeed. It helps to have maps with Chinese characters for taxi drivers and such. Keep your communication simple and point when you need to; you'll be fine.

7. Rudeness. Brusque, loud, abrasive, sure. It's part of the culture. The veneer of rudeness rules in the retail climate, and the zeal of the Customs and Excise Department—that there's no way of knowing exactly what will be available when you visit. If you're a Hong Kong film freak on a pilgrimage, pay homage, though I wouldn't plunge in straight from the airport if I were you.

P.O.V. Bookstore, Yau Ma Tei

The Broadway Cinematheque in the Prosperous Gardens Housing Estate is a

The Hong Kong Police (no longer known as the Royal Hong Kong Police) look smart in their navy blue winter uniforms. Fortunately, this pair posed with Shu Qi, a handy excuse to include another shot of her.

Starlight Entertainment

HK's shops and on its streets. But in terms of concentrated, nasty rudeness, you'll find it quicker in London or New York than you will in Hong Kong. The glaring exception is shopkeepers in the tourist-frequented area of Tsim Sha Tsui, who have seen one tourist too many. Patronizing the electronic-goods shops in this neighborhood is not recommended.

6. Overcharging. Assuming you avoid the TST shops, you won't be peeled whole in HK (as you might be in some other Asian destinations)—unless you're part of a Japanese tour group. Bargain at street markets, but be civil about it. Don't forget that HK is a relatively expensive place.

9. Montezuma's Revenge. No need to brush your teeth with Coca-Cola.

10. Poodle Noodles. Few Hong Kongers chow down on sweet-and-sour dog these days. Not only is it illegal, but dog is considered a medicinal food, eaten as a curative and not because you hanker for a hunk of mastiff.

Yet many Westerners are inexplicably convinced that not only is Fido on the menu, but Chinese chefs delight in sneaking it into dishes intended for *gwailos*. These suspicions are like worrying that McDonald's is slipping peacock tongues into your Big Mac in lieu of beef discs. If *xenophobia gustatorum* strikes, head for the Golden Arches or Dan Ryan's Bar and Grill.

unique movie house (see page 15). Its annex contains this must-visit shop, which sells books and movie software. There's nothing else like it in Asia—shelves of great books on movies, movie soundtracks, VCDs, and DVDs. Owned by HK film critic/filmmaker Shu Kei (not to be confused with actress Shu Qi), P.O.V. is the only VCD store in town where HK films are sorted by director under English name. Pick up Takeshi Kitano's *Violent Cop* on VCD with English subtitles, the soundtrack to Orson Welles's *Touch of Evil*, and a copy of *Sex and Zen & a Bullet in the Head* all at this one-stop wonder.

Allied Plaza, Mongkok

This arcade is part of the Cosmopolitan Centre, at the corner of Nathan Road and Nullah Road, next to the Prince Edward MTR Station. One level up from the street is HK Movie, a one-stop poster, film book, and postcard shop surrounded by a sea of clothing and collectibles.

298 Hennessy Road, Wanchai

The best arcade on the Hong Kong side; look for the huge sign with "298" hanging over the street as you pass by on the tram. 298's dozens of shops change with the seasons. Always worth a visit. There are usually some excellent VCD/DVD stores on the second and third levels—take the escalators.

328 Hennessy Road, Wanchai

A new mall created to cash in on 298's success. Stop on by and browse, but check out 298 first.

Causeway Bay Centre

Grab your tourist map and find Sugar Street, right next to Victoria Park in Causeway Bay. Great name for a street. Too bad it doesn't intersect with Electric Road farther east; then you could meet people at the corner of Sugar and Electric.

Where was I? Oh yes, the Causeway Bay Centre, perhaps the most eccentric shopping mall in HK. You'll find shops dealing in used audio/video software (including some with only Japanese products), wedding apparel, photocopies, plastic models, toys, military apparel, stamps, and coins. Anomaly is the specialty of this dynamite little mall.

The Japanese Vector

Most Americans tend to think of Japan when presented with something Asian. Japan is by far the most prosperous nation in Asia, and Japanese products are household names in the USA. Japan's fascination with American popular culture is legendary, and its exports of both high-brow (Kurosawa) and low-brow (Mecha-Godzilla and Baby Mothra) movies have kept it high in American consciousness for decades. When the Japanese economy was flying high in the mid-1980s, there were even paranoid mutterings that Japanese investors would "buy up America."

The "Japanese Vector" has yet to make much of a dent in Western PopCult, but it has had a tremendous effect on Hong Kong's popular culture. Recent Japanese movies like Suo Masayuki's *Shall We Dance?*, Masakatsu Suzuki's *Bounce Ko Gals*, and Takeshi Kitano's *Hana-Bi* and *Kids Return* are extremely popular. Cantonese-dubbed *anime* fills the local TV channels, and 11-episode Japanese TV dramas are subtitled in Chinese and peddled on VCD. In many other aspects of popular culture—typography, comic books, food packaging—HK designers receive inspiration from Japanese sources. T-shirts with Japanese writing are sold at Mongkok markets—no one can read them, but they look cool. The most popular new chain restaurants in HK today serve conveyor-belt sushi and bowls of Japanese-style ramen noodles rather than burgers and fries.

Why has Japanese pop culture had such a strong influence on Hong Kong? One reason is a lack of strong PopCult rivals: China is too poor, Taiwan too small; Britain and America have had influence but are too Western. The other reason is the appeal of Japanese PopCult—Asia's most potent pop culture. The Japanese Vector is apparent all over new markets in Asia—Thailand, for example, has never been colonized but its television commercials certainly have been.

What has the J-Vector brought to Hong Kong's beleaguered film industry? Japanese fans, like their Western counterparts, have been appreciating HK films more of late.

No need to jet off to Tokyo when you can stroll Wanchai's Japan Street arcade.

Japan Street (HK) Co. Ltd.

1. **Expense.** That whooshing sound is the funnel cloud of banknotes being sucked out of your wallet. Hong Kong is a good place to spend money, but you do tend to part with a fair bit of it. Hong Kong movie maniacs visiting shops here should bring horse-choking rolls of the stuff (but will leave in a euphoric state).

2. **Cigarette Smoke.** It's not as bad as in Japan or Poland, but many HK men fume like chimneys. In the innumerable "greasy chop-stick" joints, it's almost a point of pride; even the *waiters* smoke in these places. However, more and more areas are banning smoking, and people obey these regulations most of the time. The Council on Smoking and Health estimates that 4,000 Hong Kongers die from smoking-related diseases every year.

3. **Crowds.** It helps if you view moving through Hong Kong as a very civilized, subtle, and ongoing rugby scrum. Be civil, don't get irate at the occasional bump, and twist sideways when necessary.

4. **Noise.** A couple of elderly ladies chatting next to you in a restaurant will rattle your fillings. They're not shouting, just *projecting*, at a level Elizabethan actors would envy. It's all in proportion to a generally high ambient noise level.

   On Hong Kong streets, pavement-birds (jackhammers) warble away amid a cacophony of ringing mobile phones, roaring traffic, shouting passersby, and squealing bus brakes. Duck into a restaurant and it's not an imminent gangland tussle at that table, just a group of friends enjoying dim sum, as the waiter crashes the fresh crockery down in front of you, each tink of porcelain reverberating from the polished-mirror walls. It's all part of the experience. Carry earplugs just in case.

5. **Air Pollution.** Along the major thoroughfares of the SAR, you

Although Jackie Chan has enjoyed great popularity since the 1980s, the only other really popular HK genre was, you guessed it, the hopping vampires known as *gyonsi* in Cantonese and *kyonshi* in Japanese. Those cute dead tykes with their rimless Ming dynasty hats were a big hit with Japanese fans.

These days, more and more Japanese stars are finding their way into HK films. There's more crossover as well, spearheaded by Takeshi Kaneshiro, who's a bit of a crossover himself. Half-Taiwanese and half-Japanese, Kaneshiro is known as Gum Sing-mo in Cantonese, and rocketed to fame in Wong Kar-wai's *Chungking Express*, which was very popular in Japan. The shot-in-Tokyo thriller *Sleepless Town* (1998) was described by costar Mirai Yamamoto as "a Hong Kong film made in Japan."

Stuntman and special-effects master Bruce Law made his directorial debut with *Extreme Crisis* (1998), an explosive thriller that featured dialogue in four languages,

may find a thousand particles of diesel exhaust going up your nose. The government is finally starting to implement measures (such as converting the taxi fleet to liquid petroleum gas) to address this problem. In the meantime, do as the locals do—put your index finger under your nose and wrinkle your brow as you cross the street.

6. Claustrophobia. Small spaces and big crowds are facts of life in Hong Kong. Weekdays are your best bet for popular places.

7. Chungking Mansions. Backpackers head like lemmings for this enormous concrete horror in the heart of the Tsim Sha Tsui tourist district, looking for cheap sweatbox rooms. But the neighbors are dealin', the cockroaches are fearless, and the elevators are a nightmare. Fire safety is not guaranteed, and eating paper-plate vindaloo from the curry-in-a-hurry restaurants isn't recommended. If you do stay here, ignore people who say, "Yes sir! What are you looking for?" and padlock your laundry to something solid. The best reason to step into the Mansions, other than rubbernecking, is to pick up VCDs of Hindi movies and Nusrat Fateh Ali Khan remix CDs at the fabulous Zam Zam Music and Video Shop.

8. Pickpockets. In Hong Kong, as anywhere, watch your bag and pockets in crowds and on transport.

9. Mobile Phones and Pagers Going off in Cinemas and Driving Ya Nuts. As they say in the subtitles, "Just take it as peanut."

10. The Orange Sauce. This lamentable emulsion—a translucent reddish-orange gooze concocted from tomatoes, cornstarch, and sugar—is liberally applied atop dubious rice and meat dishes. A plate of rice with a fried porkchop, a chicken wing, and a lukewarm hot dog all blanketed with the Orange Sauce (*fan kei jup* in Cantonese) is much more Hong Kong than eggrolls or sweet 'n' sour pork, but it's not recommended. Get the duck instead.

Japanese funding, and a plot based on an Aum Shinri Kyo–type cult and their nerve-gas canisters. Unfortunately for Law, the film didn't play in Japan due to suspected interference from real cults!

The J-Vector has been ignored by the conventional model, which holds that Western/American PopCult "currency" (McDonald's/Michael Jackson/Michael Jordan, etc.) is the variety worshiped by other countries. Japanese PopCult, as pungent as a styropod of fermented *nattoh*, diffuses across Asian land and sea borders through osmosis.

the festival

Early April is a splendid time to be in Hong Kong. The chill of winter has ebbed, but the summer rains are still weeks away, and the Easter holidays mean everyone has a few days off to nibble on hollow chocolate bunnies.

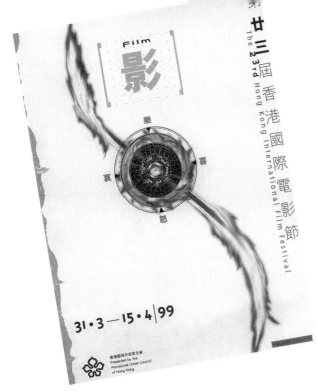

The Hong Kong International Film Festival's 1999 catalog featured a fire-propeller and a *feng shui* compass.

Hong Kong International Film Festival

presents a themed retrospective dedicated to Hong Kong films and filmmakers—this "Hong Kong Cinema Retrospective" section started with the second festival in 1978.

As HKIFF director TS Lo explains, many print-owners are loathe to lend prints outside of Hong Kong. This means that these films often show *only* at the HKIFF—thanks in no small part to the efforts of programmer Law Kar, one of the best-known and most trusted names in Hong Kong film circles. The prospect of seeing long-buried Shaw Brothers films like Chang Cheh's *The Singing Thief* (1969) or *Hong Kong Nocturne* (1967) draws film-lovers to the HKIFF. Other high points for HK fans are the catalogs, featuring interviews with local filmmakers and invaluable contributions from writers like Stephen Teo, Sek Kei, and Li Cheuk-to. For years these catalogs were virtually the only source of English-language information on Hong Kong films.

How worthwhile are these Hong Kong cinema retrospective sections? The retro "Mandarin Musicals" of 1993 presented the transcendent Grace Chang in a series of films from the 1950s and 1960s. A sold-out showing of *Mambo Girl* (1957) caused a phenomenon I've not seen before or since: as the opening scene faded up from black, the audience broke into a spontaneous ovation. The shot (any description makes it sound prosaic, but let's say it involves Chang's shod feet on a checker-

Film fans, though, have only one thing on their minds: the Hong Kong International Film Festival. Annual since 1977, this event is distinct from the world's 300-or-so other film festivals. The HKIFF was the first film festival in East Asia, and the first festival to focus on Asian films.

Many film festival circuit films are included, and since most will not be playing other local venues, it's a great opportunity for Hong Kongers to catch up. But the dedicated festival programmers are not content to simply replicate the Rotterdam or Vancouver program in Asia. Each HKIFF

board-tiled floor), was so perfect that you simply couldn't *not* applaud. The film also included her hit "Jajambo," a catchy Mandarin-dialect ditty that instantly relaunched itself into the PopCult matrix of Hong Kong 1993. In tune with the nostalgia movement evident in the territory that year, celebs cut new versions of the Shanghai-goes-Caribbean tune and it blared from TV/radio airwaves. The audience's enjoyment of these films (many of which were never released with subtitles) has been increased by the use of the Barco system: a below-the-screen computer-driven subtitling system that allows English subtitles to be shown.

The Hong Kong Film Archive has a symbiotic relationship with the HKIFF and has staged mini-festivals and exhibits of film-related artifacts concurrent with the festival. This relationship means that the archive has restored prints for exhibition at the HKIFF, which greatly enhanced retrospectives like "Transcending the Times: King Hu and Eileen Chang."

The festival's measure of support for the local industry has increased in recent years. The HKIFF's opening film for 1998 was Gordon Chan's *Beast Cops*. A sold-out crowd at the Hong Kong Cultural Centre was treated to a prefilm presentation with Chan, Kathy Chow, and Anthony Wong, the latter garbed in ostentatious sunglasses and white shoes. Only in Hong Kong!

The 1999 HKIFF went even further in lauding local films. A "Director-in-Focus" section was added to the Hong Kong panorama and the first director covered was Johnnie To Kei-fung (see *The Unexpected*).

During the festival, films are shown at a number of venues around town, including Hong Kong City Hall in Central, the Hong Kong Cultural Centre in Tsim Sha Tsui (TST), the Science Museum in TST East, and other venues. The exact dates for the HKIFF fluctuate from year to year but hover around Easter. Schedules are available at the Hong Kong Cultural Centre and Hong Kong City Hall early in the year.

Hong Kong International Film Festival:
Tel.: (852) 2734 2888
Fax: (852) 2366 5206
E-mail: hkiff@hkyf.com.hk
http://www.hkiff.com.hk (schedule information appears during the last week of February)

the archive

The term *archive* conjures up images of dusty shelving crammed with crumbling treasures, tended by desiccated denizens bowed double by the weight of history. In the case of the Hong Kong Film Archive, however, this brittle model shatters.

The cast of a television drama, where you'll spot film actors moonlighting.

Starlight Entertainment

The Archive was created in 1993, decades after it was needed to preserve now-lost fragments. The attitude of many HK film studios toward their product has traditionally been one of disposability: crank out the films, wring out the box office, then bin 'em. The perennial focus of HK filmmakers is financial return, and during the gravy years (which ended in 1993 when the apocalyptic footfalls of Spielberg's dinosaurs sent the local industry into its ongoing tailspin), preservation of the product seemed absurd.

Perhaps it was the burgeoning interest among English-speaking fans (ironically, the ascension of this cross-cultural intrigue coincided with the Jurassic stomp of 1993) that served as a catalyst for collation. Perhaps it was the looming handover that tweaked the nostalgia gland and helped spur a fascination with bygone days and Josephine Siao's white plastic go-go boots. Perhaps the headlong rush onto the mobile com/data superhighway spawned the longing for scratchy monochromatic light projecting the electric shadow of Kwan Tak-hing. Whatever the genesis, the creation of the Hong Kong Film Archive is one of the defining events of Hong Kong film history. Its support will ensure that generations to come will remain aware of Hong Kong's celluloid triumphs.

That support has not been slow in coming. The Archive has already collected more than 2,800 film prints and 38,000 items of film-related material. Siao donated a fistful of her awards dating back to the 1960s. Chow Yun-fat, currently riding his Hong Kong popularity into the Hollywood rodeo, donated 16 of his Best Actor awards. The late Chua Boon-hean donated hundreds of the screenplays he approved during his 40 years as Shaw Brothers' Singapore distribution manager. And before his passing in 1996, Kwan Tak-hing donated a trunkful of mementos, including props and costumes from his dozens of appearances as Wong Fei-hong.

The concept of film preservation is not a new one. At the advent of sound in the late 1920s, both the Museum of Modern Art in New York and the Academy of Motion Picture Arts and Sciences in Beverly Hills realized that the films of the silent era might be lost if steps were not taken to preserve them. These organizations began to acquire films selectively for study and appreciation. Throughout the 1930s, the film-archive movement picked up momentum, leading to the founding of the International Federation of Film Archives in 1938. In the 1950s, the Academy laboriously rephotographed 3,300 paper prints from the 1893–1918 period, creating the single greatest resource for the study of early American cinema.

But the pace of cinematic industry evolution in America is not analogous to the pace here in Hong Kong. The American lessons of the benefits of film preservation were not quickly learned. As author Paul Fonoroff tells it in *Silver Light: A Pictorial History of Hong Kong Cinema 1920-1970* (1997): "I realized some time ago that in order to research Hong Kong film history, I would have to amass the primary source materials myself." Indeed, 90 percent of the photos in Fonoroff's unique book are from his private collection.

Why aren't there more prints of old Hong Kong films? The main culprit is the region's heat and humidity. Unless prints are stored in properly chilled and dehumidified conditions, the forces of entropy make quick work of the raw material. Films shrink as a result of loss of moisture, solvents, and plasticizer; when some parts shrink more than others, the film buckles. Sprocket holes

PICTURE PALACES
BY TIM YOUNGS

The term *cinema* is more apt than *movie theater*. Live theater has been around for millennia and is likely to remain forever popular. Motion pictures, on the other hand, have only been here for a century or so. But a century from now, it's possible that the 500-channel cable TV universe will have terminated the experience of sitting en masse in front of a lighted screen.

Nothing complements a good Hong Kong film like a cinema viewing. Audience feedback transforms a great film into an unforgettable experience, and the older cinemas dotting the Hong Kong map add value to your ticket dollar. Hordes of teens gurgle at Leon Lai in between mobile-phone jingles on opening night. A nice-and-sleazy Category 3 thriller at a 10:15 morning show attracts pajama-clad grannies and excited old men who drop their lunchboxes when an actress strips, shrilling their thrills across the cinema. Unlike the megaplexes which shall inherit the earth, no bow-tied creep confiscates your fishball skewers and tetrapak-box of lemon tea on the way in. And when the villain dies, the credits may be curtained, but you exit straight into the thick air of Hong Kong—the movie's vibrant setting. Bliss.

These cinemas would be packaged as retro were they not the real thing. Technicolor-painted billboards and decaying timewarp decor add to the charm. Tickets still bear prices from a decade earlier. Some introduce their films with traditional flute music and "Coming Soon" trailer intros from the 1970s. Local hawkers set up their food stalls outside these cinemas, peddling steaming snacks to the moviegoing faithful. The 1993 smoking ban remains consistently unheeded inside—one side of the cinema used to be the smoking area—and emphysema sufferers need not inform the ushers because they don't care. Got a Partagas Lusitania or a Cohiba Esplendido handy?

Although modern cinemas (often showing Western films) pull the kids and couples, the big local cinemas appeal to all ages. Tastes young and old come together under one peeling roof—the same midday horror comedy pulls cackles from a pocket of old ladies and grumbles from the *Young & Dangerous* set. Some viewers make visiting their local cinema a weekly institution.

But Hong Kong's once-vast network of glorious old auditoria has been decimated in the last decade. Skyrocketing property values, the decline of local cinematic fare, and the ascension of the VCD have stripped Hong Kong of many cinema patrons. Cavernous cinemas still soldier on, wedged under blocks of flats or crammed into a dense city block. These cinemas still have reserved seating (point to a seat on the diagram at the ticket window), and the bathrooms are inside the seating area, marked by groovy glowing signs.

Yet few retain their original form: a huge main auditorium ("stalls" in ticket-window nomenclature) crowned by a pricier "dress circle" upstairs in the balcony. Subdivision has transformed some into duplexes or triplexes with half-size screens. Or, in the case of the enormous Ritz Theatre in San Po Kong, half is simply closed and its ticket box blocked. Many, like the huge Nam Cheong Theatre in Shek Kip Mei, have switched to foreign porn and sit in murky disrepair while others have become churches, shops, or vacant lots. Sadly, some cinemas are virtually devoid of viewers. You can only imagine the buzz decades earlier at a Michael Hui or Cheng Pei-pei film, a cheerful thousand packed to the front corners.

For the Hong Kong movie tourist, the older local cinemas represent a good opportunity to get out among the locals for an authentic experience.

Parting those heavy, musty curtains and entering a pitch-black auditorium for the latest *Sex and Zen* installment is something home entertainment can't emulate. And it may be the last chance to sink into those squeaky plastic seats smoothed by decades of patronage—most of these old cinemas still stand only because the property market slumped in recent years. Deplorably, the fate of many is certain. Photos of many HK cinemas can be found at http://www.hkmdb.com/hkmec/hkcinema/. Here are a few that still do business as of this writing.

Kowloon Side

The South China, corner of Portland and Soy Streets, Mongkok: A popular duplex nestled right into the famed Portland Street, immortalized in gangster flicks like *Prince of Portland Street* and *Portland Street Blues*. With its brothels and saunas, Portland and its surrounds make up the sleazier side of Mongkok. The downstairs auditorium is cavernous and the upstairs section, with its steep-pitch seating and big screen, is a treat. Reduced-price morning shows mean you can catch recent films in the midmornings and also on weekday afternoons. Check the lobby cards for details and join the (mostly retiree) audience inside.

The Broadway Cinematheque, in the Prosperous Garden Housing Estate, Public Square Street and Shanghai Street, Yau Ma Tei: Local distributor Edko Films commissioned this four-screen arthouse cinema for a housing estate. The Cinematheque offers a fascinating mix of films (mostly Japanese, European, and American) in an extremely comfortable environment: cushy seats with the steepest pitch in HK. The award-winning interior design, by Hong Kong's Edge Architects, echoes the urban elements of Mongkok/Yau Ma Tei, using materials like translucent backlit panels made of corrugated plastic (the striking design has been featured on a Hong Kong postage stamp). The Cinematheque also has a library of film-related books, magazines, and software, plus a shop selling movie memorabilia. And don't miss the P.O.V. Bookstore just a couple of doors down.

The Empire, corner of Soy and Fa Yuen Streets, Mongkok: Minutes away from the South China, the Empire boasts a pair of enormous hand-painted billboards looming over passersby. This one hasn't been chopped in two and still offers "dress circle" seating at a modest surcharge. Hawkers are out in force on the weekends serving up steamed corn and roasted chestnuts outside the entrance.

The President in Causeway Bay is a great place to catch a spooky one.

Stefan Hammond

The Newport, corner of Jordan Road and Parkes Street, Jordan: This one draws quite a crowd from its environs, some of whom drift, pajama-clad, into the two-tiered hall for the morning reruns. The screen is enormous—sit well back.

The Ritz, 84 Choi Hung Road, San Po Kong (near Kowloon City): Often frequented by solitary male viewers, the muddy screen makes Elvis Tsui and Yvonne Yung Hung equally pretty. Your kung fu slippers will crunch on melon-seed shards and crusty cigarette butts in the enormous and dilapidated hall.

Hong Kong Side

The President, corner of Cannon Street and Jaffe Road, Causeway Bay: A classic two-tiered hall with plenty of space, a big screen, and green plastic seats. This part of town is always hopping and is best at night when throngs of youngsters mill about on dates, gabbing into mobile phones and shopping for weird shoes. A trip to the upstairs gents' room gives you a classic view of Hong Kong neon through a hallway wall with huge ventilation holes.

The Isis, on Tai Hang Road just south of Causeway Road, east of Causeway Bay and across from Victoria Park: The 1960s green-and-white polka-dot decor is museum-quality—one peek at the lobby and you know you're in for a huge auditorium and big honkin' screen. The Isis often shows the same films as the President, but both cinemas advertise the other's offerings, which is very handy.

Just a couple doors down on Tai Hang Road is the not-to-be-missed Golden House Delicious Foods Snack Shop. Look for the bubbling stainless steel containers in front—the feisty old ladies running the joint don't speak a lick of English, but it doesn't matter. Point to your choice of noodles, vegetables, and other things, which include chicken wings, stewed turnip, and curried squid. Point point point and don't hesitate—if they think you should have the curried fishballs rather than the plain fishballs, they'll just dump them in anyway.

The Sunbeam, corner of King's Road and Shu Kuk Street, North Point: Live Cantonese opera and local films, luckily not within earshot of each other. Often showing films a week or so behind the other cinemas, and offering steep-pitch upstairs seating, it's well worth a visit.

widen or tear, colors fade, and scratches are so common that their patterns are defined as "tramlines" or "rain." Worst of all is the dreaded "vinegar syndrome," in which the acetate emulsion experiences chemical release and separates from the film base, causing irreversible damage. The only sure prevention for this witches' brew of decay is restoration by trained technicians followed by storage under controlled conditions.

This is precisely what the Archive offers. The prints restored by Hong Kong Film Archive technicians have been placed in storage in the Archive's warehouse. Acquisition manager Angela Tong points out that donating prints for storage does not represent abdication of copyright; film companies without their own storage facilities can donate prints (subject to Hong Kong Film Archive approval) and access them for duplication or video transfer as they see fit. The Archive works in concert with commercial interests—it understands that donors want their business interests safeguarded.

Preservation contributes more than good citizenry. The release of films on video is a golden opportunity to include outtakes, additional footage, and trailers, or to allow the director to create a director's cut, which spurs interest in the video release. The new DVD format is a natural medium for an expanded version. But without the raw material, in presentable shape, the opportunity for a rerelease to pump up viewer interest and squeeze more revenue out of preexisting material is lost.

The Archive's temporary office is housed in an Urban Council complex in the heart of Mongkok—a locale more suited to knock-off Reeboks than to limelight grandeur. Altogether, a staff of 20 (including Yu Mo-wan, who has spent 30 years chronicling HK film and is now compiling a multivolume filmography of all HK films) labors to overturn the throwaway mentality that has decimated film-related collections in Hong Kong.

Arguably the Archive's most crucial project is its ongoing Oral History Project. This pressing task involves conducting interviews with Hong Kong film personalities, with the immediate goal of recording their memories before they either pass away or retire into oblivion. In an industry lacking a systematic documentation of materials and events, oral histories are critical. The Archive has interviewed more than 150 industry kingpins (including Shaw Brothers' Chang Cheh and Golden Harvest's Raymond Chow) and plans to publish these interviews in both English and Chinese in the future.

The Archive is dedicated to screening its treasures where possible. It has organized screenings in conjunction with the Hong Kong International Film Festival, and each year the Hong Kong Film Archive presents two miniretrospective film programs, usually in February and September.

However, the full potential of a living, growing Archive will gain expression when its permanent home opens in 2000. The structure's primary purpose is to serve as a controlled environment for preservation of film prints from the Hong Kong film industry. In many cases, the copies being stored are the only ones in existence. Apart from collecting and restoring prints and other related film materials, the Archive staff will also catalog its materials into data to be stored in its library system for access by scholars and researchers. The new building also houses a 128-seat cinema, an exhibition hall, film laboratories, and a library of film books. The Archive intends to sponsor film shows and exhibitions, hold educational seminars and discussions, and publish study materials, including a complete Hong Kong filmography.

HK Film Archive Mission Statement

The major functions of the Film Archive are to acquire, conserve, catalog, document, research, and exhibit Hong Kong film and related material.

"Hong Kong films" refers to Hong Kong films actually shown or intended to be shown in cinema, including fiction, animation films, and documentaries. "Related material" includes posters, stills, scripts, house biographies, books, and magazines.

The Archive will acquire films and related material mainly by way of donation and voluntary deposit.

Anita Mui and some guy handing out statues at the Hong Kong Film Awards

Starlight Entertainment

For preservation purposes, the Archive will endeavor to acquire original negatives, though positive copies, laser discs, and videotapes will also be welcome.

Hong Kong Film Archive:
Tel: (852) 2739 2139
Fax: (852) 2311 5229
E-mail: awstong@email.usd.gov.hk
http://www.usd.gov.hk/hkfa

the awards

It's all in Cantonese and you won't hear it breathlessly hyped on *Entertainment This Minute*, but Hong Kong has its own version of the Oscars. The Hong Kong Film Awards have been held since 1981, when *Father and Son* and its director Allen Fong won for Best Picture and Best Director.

This is the big event for star-spotters, *paparazzi*, and fans of glitz and glamour. People gather on the giant staircase leading into the hall awaiting the limos disgorging the celebs—hordes of Cantofanatics contained by police barricades, those with precious press credentials trying to dodge the flow of photogs, celebs, and their peers.

Like everything else in the electric-speed capitalist fiefdom of Hong Kong, the market price of celebrities is instantly calculated: those without clout ascend the stairs unencumbered by flashbulbs or greeters,

AVAST YE SWAB

Film piracy is alive and well in the Hong Kong Special Administrative Region (SAR). Despite painstaking efforts from a wide range of governmental bodies to stop the practice, pirated movies are peddled in shopping arcades and on street corners. They're illegal and they're cheap. The medium of delivery is the five-inch CD. Blank media and players have come down in price drastically while popularity has skyrocketed.

Although DVD technology is the new hot setup, the humble VCD is a cheap and effective delivery mechanism (see "Acronym Overload," page 253). Millions of VCD players have been sold throughout the southern China region, making videotapes quaint in Hong Kong. The market for legit VCDs has grown exponentially, and a wide variety of HK and other films are available at reasonable prices. You can buy a legitimate VCD for as little as US$2–$4.

Copies of films are made from pre-release tapes from overseas sources or copied from legitimate laser discs. Then there are the infamous shot-in-the-cinema productions, which feature off-center and/or tilted framing, ringing cell phones, guffawing patrons, and heads obscuring the screen. It's funny . . . *once*. And many of the discs are defective, dissolving into a psychedelic barrage of random pixels and squawks at regular intervals. Guess what, no refunds.

Despite the lamentable quality, pirated products are popular. In an early 1999 survey, more than three-quarters of the Hong Kongers aged 15 to 29 polled admitted to having purchased fake or pirated goods. Three-quarters of the admitted purchasers cited VCDs as the pirated item. Nearly half (46.7 percent) of the total disagreed that it was immoral to buy counterfeit products.

Ironically, the pirates are helping to kill the industry that's supplying their products. But since much of their revenue also comes from booting Hollywood films and Japanese film/television, they may not care.

For fans of HK movies, it's different. Piracy is bleeding profits out of the Hong Kong film industry. It may sound preachy, but responsible patrons should ensure that the filmmakers are compensated by purchasing legitimate products wherever possible. With the proliferation of mail-order outlets on the Net (see Chapter 13), this isn't even close to difficult.

The seriousness of the problem was highlighted on March 17, 1999, when all the SAR's cinemas closed for the day in a protest against piracy. A contingent of HK film people, including Jackie Chan and Tsui Hark, marched in Central to protest the situation.

Needless to say, seeing these films in the cinema is the best of all possible worlds. If this option is available to you, get your butt in there.

regardless of cleavage displayed or cut of suit. Cantogods like Leon Lai or Andy Lau—the objects of obsessive teenyfreak focus—enter to a chorus of shrieks from their faithful, while chief executive Tung Chee-hwa is accompanied by a squadron of security guards in cool gray paramilitary garb. The affable Tung (who, unlike his London-appointed predecessors, has declared his support for the industry) makes it a point to attend the awards, which are broadcast live on local television.

Despite the language barrier, viewers will be familiar with the format: famous glittering presenters handing out statues to winners, interspersed with nominated song performances and commercial breaks. The show is hosted by the beloved Lydia "Fei Fei" Shum (the portly woman with trademark black spectacles) and Nancy Sit, another well-known actress whose prominent and perfectly centered forehead mole is famous throughout Hong Kong.

the HK film freak's perfect Hong Kong day

The Hong Kong Tourist Association (http://www.hkta.org) has many excellent suggestions for tourists visiting the SAR. Ride about on boats, take the funicular railway up to The Peak, groove on Chinese opera, and tuck into a sumptuous spread of dim sum. All big fun and worthwhile.

But what about the HK film fanatic, the type who scrimps all year for a two-week vacation in the Promised Land, arriving at Chek Lap Kok airport with an empty suitcase and a heart full of expectations? For these diehards, riding the sampan out to those floating disco restaurants in Aberdeen just isn't going to cut it. They're on a pilgrimage and they want an overdose of local film culture and they want souvenirs and they want it all before that flight takes them back home. Fair enough.

Our diehard arises in the cramped environs of a Mongkok lodging house prepared to be hammered like an ingot of pig iron in the sweltering forge of Hong Kong's pyretic film culture. The perfect day starts with a typical Cantobreakfast—no twee breakfast buffet here—a bowl of congee with pig innards, a fried doughstick, and a mug of stewed tea murky with condensed milk. Then it's a quick stroll to the Empire Cinema for the 10:15 morning show, whatever it may happen to be. Our hero (or heroine) will attempt to purchase lobby cards and posters from the nonplussed management without success. A quick sampling of the mobile phone ring-tones during the film will show that "Waltzing Matilda" is the most popular, prompting our visitor to reset his or her rented mobile *deenwa* to the Aussie tune. After the flick, a quick trip to a local arcade accessorizes the mobile with a pink "Hello Kitty" case and a light-'em-up Ultraman antenna.

Next stop is the Sino Centre on Nathan Road, where the diehard fan will spend hours purchasing photos/posters/lobby cards/VCDs/keychains/watches and other doodads, arguing for discounts in caveman-Cantonese and otherwise bemusing the staff. After the Sino Centre it's a visit to Allied Plaza where similar bingeing occurs. A new suitcase is purchased out of necessity. Lunch is wonton noodles and a plate of bright green *choi sum* (boiled vegetable dolloped with oyster sauce and clear oil), washed down with iced Horlicks—a malted milk drink of British origin. Greasy fingers punch in "The Yellow Rose of Texas" as the new mobile ring-tone.

The itinerary encompasses the Broadway Cinematheque and the P.O.V. Bookstore in Yau Ma Tei. After a thorough browse of this fabulous bookstore, the suitcase is bulging and there are no HK films on offer at the Cinematheque anyway, so our diehard retires to the lodging house to drop off the case, which has become heavier than an anvil. A quick bowl of bitter medicinal tea at a streetside shop keeps any lingering traces of jet lag at bay while a Bank of China ATM refills the coffers with red and brown banknotes. Rushing off to the Chinachem cinema complex in Tsim Shat Sui East, every local film on offer is watched in quick succession. Our happy and exhausted maniac then scarfs down an assortment of skewered snacks—beef meatballs, *siu mai* dumplings, and gelatinous squares of chewy pigskin— from a street hawker and packs onto a crowded Mongkok bus. Head lolling, completely sated, the HK film fan collapses into bed and drifts into the arms of Morpheus to dream . . . in Cantonese.

get the picture?

Hong Kong is a world-class metropolis buzzing with the energy of 6.8 million

Movies in Mongkok— hand-painted billboards and sprawling residential blocks

Stefan Hammond

souls. Asia does not offer a more engaging or cosmopolitan city. Few world capitals have such a vibrant mix of cultures, or such a heady spirit of no-bullshit entrepreneurism. You can buy newspapers from seven different countries, score a fistful of gold bars at your local bank, attend one of the world's great film festivals, and revel in Asia's most fertile film culture.

A ferry ride to one of the outlying islands, or even the Star Ferry across the harbor, presents a view of that world-class skyline. Great meals await you everywhere, and the humblest noodle shops offer an English-language menu. A late-night tram ride on Hong Kong Island is one of the world's most evocative, memorable travel experiences.

It's a great place to live.

Wu Chien-lien tags a victim and tangles with Lau Ching-wan in Patrick Leung's *Beyond Hypothermia*.

Milkyway Image Productions

the uNexpected

The current HK film industry is composed of small production companies that attempt to create a niche market and fill it with reasonable product, while struggling to stay one step ahead of the VCD pirates. In this Darwinian context, it is not unusual to find production companies replicating their hit products *ad infinitum*—infinity being defined as the point where the box office runs dry.

Thus it's surprising and satisfying to find a production company whose films cleave to a vision unglued to the cash register—films not carbon copies of each other, but crafted with passionate care and worthy of investigation. A company making films reflecting Hong Kong sensibilities yet veering into new directions. Unexpected.

Milkyway Image Productions—Hong Kong's most intriguing production house—was formed in 1996 by producer/director/writer Johnny To Kei-fung and scriptwriter/director Wai Ka-fai. To (pronounced "toe") spent 20 years with TVB, the television arm of the Shaw Brothers empire, where he became close friends with Wai. To directed his first feature film in 1978 and has established himself as one of Hong Kong's most successful directors in a wide variety of styles, directing films as diverse as *The Heroic Trio* (1993) and *Lifeline* (1996). At the Twenty-third Hong Kong International Film Festival in 1999, To was honored with a Director-in-Focus retrospective, while the To-directed Milkyway production *Where a Good Man Goes* made its world premiere as the festival's opening film.

With To serving as managing director and Wai as creative sparkplug, the firm has produced a string of outstanding films consistent in tone and vision yet stubbornly distinct from one other. In an industry whose wheat-to-chaff ratio has declined sharply in recent years, Milkyway's output is all the more remarkable. So too is its in-house leading man: Lau Ching-wan. Lau rocketed to prominence as the lead in Derek Yee's *C'est La Vie Mon Cherie* (1994), which also made a star of colead Anita Yuen. Lau was lauded by Derek Elley in *Variety* as one of the world's 10 best actors in late 1997, and stars in most of Milkyway's films.

The Milkyway interproduction look and feel are ensured by creative personnel like art director Silver Cheung and musical score writer Cacine Wong. The organization operates as a film cooperative, with To selecting directors like Patrick Yau (*The Longest Nite, The Odd One Dies*) and Patrick Leung (*Beyond Hypothermia*) from the ranks of assistants on his various projects. This setup helps the company survive in the current environment. If it is possible to make films this challenging and make enough money to keep doing so, Milkyway has the determination. Says Johnnie To: "I love to shoot films. You give me two people and one camera and I'll shoot!"

Note: Some Milkyway vcds sport teeny-tiny subs and are best experienced in the cinema or on DVD.

beYoNd HypotHermia (1996)

Chilled and paranoid assassin Shu Li (Wu Chien-lien) is calculating and ruthless by default. Her world is cold and blue-lit—surrounded by boobytraps, her need for anonymity making the burning of false passports a habitual ritual. Shu tapes Glock 9mm pistols under her bed, and the black polymer sheen of deadly German-made automatics seems to suit her. She seems most at ease while firmly seating rounds in the magazine of a Heckler and Koch assault rifle. (Wu spent hours at the Hong Kong Gun Club learning how to shoot for the role and proved so adept at handling real firearms that the club offered her a permanent membership.)

Shu is trying to discover her inner child—a difficult task as she was raised to be a killer by supertuff Aunt Mei (Shirley Wong), a middle-aged Cambodian death-pimp who runs a Hong Kong beauty salon. Aunt Mei hires Miss Shu to travel to exotic Southeast Asian locations and liquidate unsavory people. In the film's opening hit, Shu enters an icehouse, breaks the rifle out of an enormous ice block, and waits for her quarry. When the ejected brass casing melts its way into an ice block, its bullet having screwed its full-metal-jacketed path through the head of her victim, the casing is dutifully cooling itself for its mistress' hand—her body temperature is five degrees below normal.

Redemption is warmth in the form of Long Shek (Lau Ching-wan), who has a pivotal though relatively minor role. He's an ex-triad trying to go straight; a lovable heart-o'-gold spud who runs a noodle stall—the kind of guy who treats kids to a meal though he ain't got much himself. Shu spots him while casing the neighborhood for potential enemies. With a child's curiosity, she goes for noodles, wearing a long-hair wig as a disguise. Long calls her "Siu-sin" ("pretty ghost"—a pun on Wu's Cantonese name and identical to Joey Wong's famous ghost character's name in *A Chinese Ghost Story*). Hot broth and plain noodles—she's on fire. He's equally smitten.

Every time she drops by, something's up: hordes of hungry customers demand boiled vegetables, a local food critic offers squid-ball-bounce-criteria tips, local triad Brother Pao demands protection money. When killer and spud do get together, they're like a couple of kids goofing with each other. She flatters the lug by asking if he's got any other women, and he takes this rare opportunity for a little macho hemming and hawing. Shu's response: "No problem, I'll just kill them all." She would.

Romantic conundrum introduced, the film shifts its location to the Korean capital, Seoul (the film was financed by Korean interests). Shu pops Mr. Pok, a local crimelord.

This so enrages Pok's henchman Cheu (Korean actor Han Sang Woo) that he scorches the earth for the terminatrix, executing most of his crime family and his father-in-law-to-be while his fiancee dies in the crossfire. Duran Duran/*manga* hairstyle and psycho snarl intact, he heads for a Korean restaurant in HK where the gangster owners pamper the homemade *kimchi* and hand over a passel of nickel-plated armaments.

No prizes for guessing that this tale of ferocious revenge does not end with the blissfully united couple running Happy Lucky Squid Ball Noodle. Regrettably, the apocalyptic endbattle is played out to the soundtrack of a sappy Korean pop song, which is holed repeatedly by the on-screen intensity.

expect the unexpected (1998)

Even in Milkyway's offbeat catalog, the eccentric angles of *Expect the Unexpected* are unexpected. Main man Lau Ching-wan stars as Sam, a savvy and straight-up flatfoot. He's counterbalanced by Simon Yam as Sam's superior Ken and supporting characters like smooth Ruby Wong and anything-but Joe Cheung. They're a tight-knit group of cops whose fraternalism is caring and playful—more like a bunch of college kids than hard-bitten law enforcers. Ken and

Sam play "who has a crush on whom?" with waitress/star witness Mandy (Yo Yo Mung). The omnipresence of gentle rain and a warm tinkly score by Cacine Wong amplify the fuzz factor.

Complementing this kinder/gentler cop-flick vibe is a bunch of criminals they're after—a gang of bumbling thieves from the Mainland. These potatoheads can't do anything right. They try to rob a jewelry shop but fail to smash the jewel-case glass. The brakes on their getaway car don't work. They neglect to wear masks, leaving the HK cops shaking their heads at the surveillance tape.

More worrisome is a vicious group of local crooks. These deadly creeps thrive on rape, murder, and mayhem, even moving in with their victims to prolong the rape-and-murder fun. And they are particularly fond of shooting at the cops with AK-47s, sawed-off shotguns, and grenade launchers. The police are outgunned severely by this mob, viewing them as a hateful nemesis to be feared and respected yet hunted down and destroyed like the mad dogs they are.

HEX ERRORS 2000

In the 1950s, the seminal American writer William Burroughs developed a technique known as the "Cut-up." He would cut text into phrases with a pair of scissors, then reassemble the strips of verbiage in random order. The Cut-up was hailed as a radical method of ripping chunks of Art-with-a-capital-*A* out of the King's English.

However, Burroughs at his most *outré* could never replicate some of the magnificent manglings of the language perpetrated, unbeknownst, by the unsung heroes who subtitle Hong Kong films. Originally by British law, and now by custom, HK films are routinely subtitled in both Chinese and English, for those who can't understand the spoken language or dialect. Every HK film receives a full slate of subtitles, and some of them are powerfully twisted.

These mutilated subtitles capture the imagination. Hundreds of these spindled chunks of language were printed in *Sex and Zen & a Bullet in the Head* (1996), and lists were reprinted in several periodicals. Once a list of 18 prime hexes hit the Internet, it flashed its way around the world a jillion times—somebody likely forwarded it to your cyber in-box. At one point, some joker hacked off the source listing and added three obviously phony (overly long and unfunny) subtitles. The niche market in cracked HK translations seems viable—in late 1998, a well-known American newspaper printed "Lost, and Gained, in the Translation," a list of purported Chinese translations of Hollywood movie titles. The "translations" came from a Web humor site called "The Top 5 List," and were fake fake fake.

Accept no substitutes! Every hex error in this book appeared in a HK film and is reproduced with its original punctuation and (mis)spellings intact. Genuine hex errors will always have the title of the film attached as a guarantee.

EXPECT
THE UNEXPECTED

非常突然

劉青雲 任達華領銜主演 黃卓菱 許紹雄 黃浩然 蒙嘉慧主演

監製杜琪峯 韋家輝 導演游達志

出品人林小明 王龍緯 行政監製陳志光 製作經理何美儀 何麗媚 策劃陳道好
美術指導蔡國豪 服裝指導歐陽霞 武術指導元彬 原作音樂黃嘉倩(CASH) 剪接陳志偉(HKSE)
攝影指導高照林(HKSC) 編劇司徒錦源 游乃海 周燕嫻

新影城(香港)有限公司出品 銀河影像(香港)有限公司製作

DOLBY
IN SELECTED THEATRES

鳴謝 ACER 卡樂電腦(遠東)有限公司 · KILL HOUSE

©FILM CITY (HONG KONG) LIMITED 1998 ALL RIGHTS RESERVED

Lau Ching-wan
tries to survive
in *Expect the
Unexpected*.

Milkyway Image
Productions

The ongoing soap operatic cop saga and the simmering apocalypse of gangster kill never homogenize in *ETU*, making the film both extremely sophisticated black humor and an enigmatic challenge. Pigeonholing the unpigeonholeable? *ETU*'s subtext is classically Hong Kong: Living for the future is profitless when *now* is all we have. All the giddy crushes-kept-secret are a waste of time—a fruitless void of fantasy when you're a cop in Hong Kong. The ending wraps the entire "whose crush is bigger?" argument in a shock blanket.

The creators envisioned the film taking place entirely in rain, with a sunny interval denoting the climactic endpiece. Alas, the vagaries of HK weather and the pressures of making a feature film for HK$6 million (US$775,000) created an ending framed in rain as well.

A redefinition of supreme villainy: *Intruder*

Milkyway Image Productions

iNtruder (1996)

Retribution is mercurial. Take, for example, former cabdriver Chen Chi-min (Wayne Lai). In a moment of startling lucidity, he blurts out, "I'm useless, I'm not human being, I deserve dying . . . I achieve nothing though I'm 30-something. I know nothing but call prostitute, I'm wasting my life, I'm selfish."

All true. Chen is a dirtbag who spends his time bargaining streetwalkers' fees, having alienated every other woman in his life—his wife, his mother, his cute daughter Yin Yin. Though he's a thorough jerk, the audience has little trouble working up sympathy for him: Chen is the target of a morally bankrupt woman whose predatory instincts devise horrific situations. Don't be fooled by the innocuous slasher-flick packaging; *Intruder* is one long scream of anguish.

Wu Chien-lien is the intruder, Yieh Siu-yan, a mainland Chinese woman who needs new HK identities for herself and her vile mate. She poses as a hooker and coolly garrotes a coworker in a Shenzhen brothel, then strips the corpse of watch, cash, documentation, and hair and adopts her identity. Upon entry into HK, her next task is to find a trick: enter the unlucky ex-cabbie. Despite her gum-chewing streetwise cool, Yieh is not really a hooker. There just isn't much she objects to. She goes home with Chen to case the place.

The next night, she drives a rented car to Streetwalker's Row, spots Chen, runs over his legs, and drives off. His legs in casts,

she talks her way into his house with promises of further sexual adventures, coldcocks him with a metal pipe, kills his dog with a folding stool, and packing-tapes Chen to his wheelchair. After that, it's time for the physical interrogation techniques. When Chen's mom comes looking for him, things get much, much, much, much worse.

The Hitchcock torment edge never lets up in *Intruder*, best experienced in a crumbling cinema on a rainy night. Wu's performance will sink the hook in you, and even if you're not squeamish, you will be by the time this thing is over.

tHe odd oNe dieſ (1997)

Odd as in weird, or odd as in not even? This is a big lovable mutt of a film, lurching at you wanting to be tickled behind the ears.

Go ahead. *The Odd One Dies* Wong Kar-wai winks at you as it reels by, rewarding the viewer with rich visuals, great gags, a dynamite cha-cha score by Wong Yingwah, and a substantive subtext that skewers HK's obsession with big wads of cash. *TOOD* stars Wong Kar-wai bad boy Takeshi Kaneshiro, whose talon-bangs compete with fuming cig smoke to obscure his visage. Mo (Kaneshiro) hires himself out as a hitman to a curry-gorging mystery man

A morphed Takeshi Kaneshiro/ Carman Lee character holds a huge pistol in *The Odd One Dies*.

Milkyway Image Productions

with underworld connections, but then causes a dispute. He gets the gig—and the down payment—anyway, then purchases a funky old car and a 1988 clunker mobile phone (the scenes of image-conscious Kaneshiro striking poses with bulky phone in hand are priceless). Our boy wrestles the curry fiend to the ground until the guy comes up with a subcontractor for the hit.

HEX ERRORS
Dialogues and Micro-Rants

"Dumb-bell, this is a civilized world, better talk, no fighting, man."
"Damn you creeper! You nonsense!"
God of Gamblers 3—The Early Stages

"I despise foreigners with red hair, green eyes
drinking human blood
I won't sell dolls to them."
White Lotus Cult

"Boss, if I can't figure out a vile method to . . .
make them suffer from great loss, then I'll become a small potato."
War of the Underworld

"You tell me, how should I fix your corpse?"

"No!"
"How about frying it? Or make it into sweet and sour pork?"
"I am a vegetarian."
Spike Drink Gang

"Those bastards made me not being promoted.
They made me to remain a small potato.
Go to hell."
Spike Drink Gang

"You know, great women don't have big tits.
Cleopatra, Empress Wu, Margaret Thecher [sic], Queen Elizabeth.
They didn't and don't have big tits."
Top Banana Club

"Nuts!
You fat-headed.

All rascals said they are superiors.
But the greatest one was chopped into 9 pieces."
To Be No. 1

"Nice? you know I've sinned too much so I won't have any latter generations unless I go without sex for 3 lives have to stay a virgin
what's so funny?"
Witch Edited

"Give you an intestine!"
"Damn your intestine!"
Haunted Karaoke

"Grandma, refrain from so much foul language."
"I'm so old, I can speak whatever shit I like."
Trilogy of Lust

The new would-be assassin is played by Carman Lee, an attractive actress who has allowed the makeup artist to beat her with the ugly stick. Resembling death at a slow boil, Lee sports a hair-nest of greasy snakes, the sub-eye darkening of a needle freak, and a street-waif/sewer-rat demeanor. Her nameless character is a bundle of nerves and demands.

Rather than demanding a more competent subcontractor, Mo bonds with his fellow oddball and acquiesces to her increasingly bizarre preconditions. He provides an enormous pistol for her killing work, but she insists on a backup rod, sending him to fetch it from some wastrel named Simon. Sequentially, hilariously, Simon offers marijuana, a used air conditioner, and the sexual services of a topless waitress in lieu of a pistol. Simon has other motives.

So does the ratty one, whose incessant demands cease once Mo finds the gumption to start refusing. She continues to dream of Paradise, depicted on the tourist postcard she carries in her scrapbook alongside glamour shots of people sporting really nice haircuts. When Mo takes his friendly scissors to her snake-do, she is dissatisfied with the result and shears off his signature bangs in retribution. At gunpoint. It's that kind of movie.

the Longest Nite (1998)

> "in a world like this, a war could be exploded from just one gunshot."

Adjectives like *spare* and *mean* limn this dark, tense little film from Milkyway. The rare appearance of sunlight in *The Longest Nite* blasts the characters with vampire-frying intensity and makes them reach for their Ray-Bans. But most of the action takes place during the space of one dark night, hence the title. The first minute or so of the film consists of a rapid-fire salvo of fac-

Real dark, real *noir*: flyer for a Tokyo showing of *The Longest Nite*

Shin-Koiwa Eigakan

toids that set up the plot. Here's what you need to know:

In Macau, a power struggle between a pair of potent triad kingpins is on the verge of detonation. Brother Lung is on his way back to Macau and slated to arrive at midnight. His nemesis Mr. K is determined to join forces with Lung—the ongoing shootout between their respective tribes is an attrition neither can afford. Triad kingpins being practical folk, they seek a resolution to the bad-for-business whackfest. A mysterious elder, Mr. Hung, is returning to Macau to help sort things out as this idiot squabble is hurting his biz as well.

A widely believed rumor has Mr. K offering a five-million-*pataca* bounty for Lung's head. Every gunsel in the Pearl River Delta is making a beeline for Macau, knowing that a few well-placed shots will rake in that five mil. But smashed fingers cannot pull triggers, and tough-guy Sam (Tony Leung Chiu-wai) is determined to shatter those avaricious phalanges with the butt of his gun. Mr. K, anxious to keep Lung alive until a deal can be struck, gave him this duty—loyal Sam has been employed by the powerful gangster for more than a decade. K also warned him especially to restrain Mark, a guy renowned for more gun than brain. Mark, it turns out, is K's son. But Sam is a senior member of the Macau police force.

A mysterious drifter with a shaven, tattooed head (Lau Ching-wan in full glower) comes breezing into town, and things start to happen to Sam. The predicament and its ratcheting tension recall Kurosawa's *Yojimbo* and Hitchcock. The presentation—high-contrast lighting, triad icons—is pure Hong Kong. But the cornered rats trying to avoid the cruel violence that saturates *The Longest Nite* recall the characters of Sergio Leone. Torture and murder are simply tools of the trade, with gunshots so muted they pop like stepped-on Vitasoy boxes. There's nothing in the way of character development here, no human touches—everyone in this film is a goddamn pawn. *The Longest Nite* is *film noir* at its darkest and deepest; once seen, it is not easily forgotten.

too many ways to be no. 1 (1997)

Film people love to talk about films as "texts." Makes sense. Look at the proliferation of pulp in both media: airport racks stuffed with self-help books and lurid novels, the textual equivalent of big-crashing-meteor and weenie-joke films.

Using the written language alone, it is possible to create a voice so distinctive it forms a unique dialect. James Joyce, Thomas Pynchon, Don DeLillo—for writers like these, the language is a sheet of soft metal they hammer into their own shapes. In making such dialects flesh, the power of the written word outstrips the ability of cinema.

一個字頭　成王敗寇
兩種選擇　誰可預測

一個字頭的誕生

TOO MANY WAYS TO BE NO. 1

VIDEO CD

III

Everyone hates
superjinx Lau
Ching-wan in
*Too Many
Ways to Be
No. 1*.

Milkyway Image
Productions

Yet this is what Wai Ka-fai's *Too Many Ways to Be No. 1* accomplishes. The film punches and kicks at the Hong Kong gangster flicks it spoofs like a precocious brat. Shot throughout with wide-angle lenses that transform cramped spaces into reckless expanses, *TMWTBN1* presents its cast in superhuman fashion—looming like skyscrapers or buried as specks amid the scenery somewhere back there.

The distorting camera is in relentless hard-party mode here. It laughs—it *does*. It goes disco during a dance scene. When a pissed-off gangster's wife starts punctuating her sentences with detonations of gunfire, the camera removes itself to a safe distance, and when confronted with a forest of primed-to-go automatics, it hits the floor or clings to the ceiling like a bat. *TMWTBNI* has a look most directors wouldn't envisage, let alone enact.

But film language is never purely visual—without interesting characters and a tightly woven plot, Wai and cinematographer Wong Wing-hang's vision wouldn't work. Wai is primarily a scriptwriter, responsible for many of the other Milkyway/Lau Ching-wan scripts, and *TMWTBNI*'s convoluted high-energy plot is fully loaded. Cacine Wong's Nino Rota-sweats-it-out-in-Taiwan score is sublime, and if you're down with your HK gangster-film referents, you'll be further challenged. But this film will spin you upside-down regardless.

Lau Ching-wan stars as Kau—a triad guy, but really a jinx. Everyone, especially his gang pals Matt (Francis Ng) and Bo (Cheung Tat-ming), knows he's a jinx. When things go wrong, they veer toward Kau, slap him on the back of the head, and tell him he's a jinx. Or, if he's by himself when something goes wrong, yet again, he stares in disbelief at his hands, which bollix up everything they touch.

What goes wrong in his world are not the everyday lost-car-keys and computer-ate-my-homework frustrations. He is a magnet for cataclysmic error, which is frightening as he and his crew are involved in hazardous criminal activities. Kau knows the danger. He just can't laugh about it, so we do his laughing for him.

Us and that camera.

A Hero Never Dies (1998)

Johnnie To directed this stylish, violent tale of a pair of killers who inexplicably bond despite working for rival gangs. Impossibly handsome Leon Lai as Jack essentially reprises his role as suave pretty hitboy from Wong Kar-wai's *Fallen Angels*. Jack's counterpart Martin is played by Lau Ching-wan, recipient of a Wayne Newton makeover. Cowboy hat clamped to his greasy-kid-stuff hair, sideburns, and half-'stache, Lau completes the look with dung-kicking cowboy boots and a cigar the diameter of a cold-water pipe. The boys play "chicken," smash their cars head-on into each other, then go drinking. Their respective dames, Yo Yo Mung and Fiona Leung, know that these lads bond more with each other than with their molls. "One day, either Jack or Martin will die by the other's hand," says Leung, spelling it out.

But an assignment in Thailand explodes into a vicious, stylish shootout, leaving them both injured yet alive. They return to Hong Kong prepared to take revenge on their former crime bosses. The film's hard violence is counterbalanced by its heavy-duty sentimentality—Martin's theme song (heavy-handed out by a bar band or whistled with heavy echo like an Ennio Morricone theme) is the teary ballad "Sukiyaki." As usual in To-directed films, there is love and devotion aplenty, platonic and not. As usual in Milkyway films, there are quirks and gunshots aplenty—at one point in this film, it's raining hitmen. Fiona Leung received a Best Actress nomination for her role.

Happy Together's Yiu-fai (Tony Leung Chiu-wai) is happiest when Po-wing (Leslie Cheung) is asleep.
Jet Tone Films Ltd.

creative chaos: the disorganized world of wong kar-wai

by Jeremy Hansen

Wong Kar-wai was keeping someone waiting. He was hunkered down in an editing room, frenetically cutting the thousands of feet of film that made up *Happy Together*, his sixth movie as director and his entry to the Cannes Film Festival in 1997. In typical Wong Kar-wai fashion, the crucial editing was taking place later than the last minute—an executive from the festival's organizing committee who had come to take the print back to France had already extended his stay. Nobody should have been surprised that it was taking longer than expected. Perpetually laconic, Wong himself had said he didn't know what the film was about until he got into the editing suite. Eventually, a three-hour version of the film was assembled from four months of footage shot in Argentina, before Wong made yet another last-minute decision to cut half the footage out, including some actors' entire appearances. Eventually, he handed over a 90-minute film to the Cannes agent, who immediately jetted back to France to show the Cannes jury the work.

Wong's working style is the directorial equivalent of walking a tightrope, an ad hoc approach that would petrify every test-screening-obsessed Hollywood producer. Making a Wong Kar-wai film requires both cast and crew to battle through a haze of abrupt script changes and aimless days of filming, guided only by the flickering light of Wong's instinct. Wong's longtime cinematographer Chris Doyle, who has collaborated with him on every film since 1990's *Days of Being Wild*, kept a diary of his experience filming *Happy Together* and published it under the title *Don't Try for Me Argentina*. The book beautifully illustrates the seat-of-the-pants nature of Wong's way of working:

1997年 第50回カンヌ国際映画祭 最優秀監督賞受賞

ブエノスアイレス

ウォン・カーウァイ監督

主演:トニー・レオン
レスリー・チョン
チャン・チェン

¿A dónde vamos? Fin del mundo

どこまでいく？
地の果てまで

BLOCK 2 PICTURES INC.
in association with
PRENOM H. CO., LTD. SEOWOO FILM CO., LTD. presents
A JET TONE PRODUCTION
映像・ブレッソン・シャ／テレビ放映 記録・ブレッソン・シャ
ブレノンアッシュ ベストコレクション 9

Japanese
poster for
*Happy
Together*

Katsushika-ku Eigakan

Michelle Reis
in *Fallen
Angels*

Christopher Doyle

Wong as often says "don't change a thing" as "that angle's not interesting enough." Today what he liked most was when my assistant laid the camera on Tony's bed in the break when I went to take a pee. We messed the bed up a bit more, half covered the

lens with a dirty shirt and some underwear and the style for a whole sequence was born! I put the camera in a cupboard, underneath the sofa and bed, on a window ledge, anywhere casual, improbable, or where it hadn't been before.

Sure, this style is a mirror for the discarded feeling Tony has now that he's broken up with Leslie for the umpteenth time. But it wasn't intellectualized into being, or even planned. It just seemed visually more interesting and unexpected, and solved the problem of how to shoot this minuscule space we've been in and out of for 30 days by now! Style is more about choice than concept. It should be organic, not imposed.

TONY'S NEW DIMENSION

Happy Together wasn't an easy shoot. One of the leading men, Tony Leung Chiu-wai, arrived on set in Argentina expecting to play a man searching for his gay father in Buenos Aires. He found the rough script he'd seen when he signed up for the role had changed into what Wong called a sequel to his original proposal, and he was now playing a gay character. This wouldn't necessarily have been a problem, except the revised script called for a blunt, boisterous sex scene between Leung and Leslie Cheung, the other leading man, which later attracted a Category 3 rating from the Hong Kong censors. In his diary, Doyle remembered shooting the scene:

> *It's a beautiful and sensual scene. Tony and Leslie really look great in bed. But Tony is devastated when it's all done. "Wong said all I had to do was kiss," he confides to me, "now look how far he's pushed me." Leslie is in a spirited, bitchy mood. "Now you know how bad I've felt all these years pretending I want to put my thing in that extra hole that women have!"*

Compared to much of Wong's other work, the end result of *Happy Together* is cohesive and straightforward. This is remarkable not only because Wong has a reputation for creating difficult movies, but

because by all accounts the film was verging on the shambolic when Wong started to edit it. It was a production plagued by constant script changes, last-minute cast additions in the hope of reigniting the plot, and an almost overwhelming sense of lethargy and alienation. The plan was to have a six-week shoot; they ended up spending more than three months in Argentina. "Wong is holed up somewhere reworking the script and schedule," says one of Doyle's diary entries, entitled "Director for a Day." "Leslie is leaving very soon. Thursday and Friday there's a general strike. As if boring us to death, delaying us to death and cheating us to death isn't enough . . . We've been here 40 days now, but we've only worked 10. . . . The structure of a Wong Kar-wai film is like a fat man's feet. They more or less get him from place to place, but he can't see them until the end of the day."

"Wong Kar-wai is a very nice guy," actor Leslie Cheung told journalist Frederick Dannen in a rare interview. "But he changes his mind a lot, and it's very hard for an actor or actress to follow him."

Most of *Happy Together* is about how Yiu-fai (Tony Leung Chiu-wai) and Po-wing (Leslie Cheung) make each other miserable. They move to Buenos Aires hoping to start over and resurrect their floundering relationship. Po-wing is flighty, slutty, and selfish—all characteristics that drive serious, sensible, mixed-up Yiu-fai up the wall. Their moments of togetherness are exquisite to watch—when they tango and kiss in the soft light of their apartment building's dingy shared kitchen, for example, or when Po-wing falls asleep like a child on Yiu-fai's shoulder in the backseat of a taxi. But they are fleeting glimpses of happiness in a flood of bitching and bitterness.

In rocky patches in their relationship, Po-wing takes other lovers. These flings usually end with Po-wing being beaten up and running back to Yiu-fai for comfort and a cheap place to stay. Yiu-fai, romantic fool that he is, can't help but take him back.

When they first arrive in Argentina, they buy a car and try to visit the Iguaçú Falls. They get lost on the way there and don't see the falls after all, but still dream of trying again one day. They buy a tacky tourist lamp depicting the falls, which sits beside the bed in their dingy apartment. They mean for it to represent their aspirations, but its twirling lights only mock their failure to reach the falls and, implicitly, their failure to make their relationship work.

Eventually Yiu-fai finds the strength to break free of Po-wing and Argentina. He visits the falls by himself, then returns to Asia. The film ends with the movie's title track booming as he takes a train ride around Taiwan. In a sense, he's been freed from his relationship to embrace the future. But because this is a Wong Kar-wai pro-duction, he'll always be burdened by his past. "We end on a subway ride in the rain," Doyle says of the film's final scene in his diary. "'All that remorse,' is all Wong manages to say."

It's a sad but strangely uplifting movie. When it was complete, both Wong and Doyle thought it was their finest work. The jury at Cannes agreed, granting *Happy Together* the coveted Best Director prize at the festival, the highest award any non-Hollywood director can receive. The only problem was that it was hard to tell if Wong was actually pleased with this triumph. Facing the press after the announcement, whatever delight he might have been feeling seemed to be overwhelmed by his frustration at misplacing his omnipresent sunglasses.

Local boy Makes cool

Wong Kar-wai may not be Hong Kong's most commercially successful filmmaker, but he is one of the city's—and Asia's—most important. A darling of the international art-house film crowd, his baffling, charming, visually stunning films—a thoughtful contrast to the smack-'em-up flicks that normally dominate the Hong Kong box office—are loved and loathed in almost equal measure. Sometimes the adoration can get a bit much. In 1996, for example, *Premiere* magazine embarrassingly anointed Wong as the epitome of hipness. "Ask anyone in today's alt.culture crowd where the coolest movies are made and the answer will be 'Hong Kong,'" the magazine gushed. "But if you ask anyone in Hong Kong who the coolest filmmaker is, the answer is Wong Kar-wai."

Wong's terminal insecurity means such compliments won't go to his head. He seems to see himself as a bit of a geek. "People have said, 'You're the hippest director in the world,'" he says, "and I say, 'I'm not hip.' I think I'm very old-fashioned."

Wong Kar-wai was five when he moved with his mother from Shanghai to Hong Kong. When he arrived in 1963, Hong Kong was regarded as a second-rate shipping port in comparison to the booming, bustling metropolis of Shanghai. Five-year-old Wong was the youngest of three children. He found settling into his new home far from easy. He didn't speak the language, for a start.

"When I got [to Hong Kong]," he says, "I spoke nothing but Shanghainese, whereas Cantonese was, and still is, the local dialect. For some time, I was totally alienated, and it was like the biggest nightmare of my life . . . I did not have a particularly happy childhood."

He was a lonely kid, but he spent his spare time in ways that were to have an enormous influence on his future. His mother loved movies. Every day after school, when his father was still at work, she would take her young son to the cinema, where they would sometimes watch two or three films a day. This experience led to his teenage enthusiasm for the more adventurous filmmaking of Bertolucci, Godard, Bresson, and the Japanese masters Ozu and Kurosawa.

Wong lived in Tsim Sha Tsui, a frenetic jostle of shops and apartment buildings on the southern tip of the Kowloon Peninsula, a 10-minute ride on the old Star Ferries from the center of the city on Hong Kong Island. Today, TST is the tourist and shopping heart of Hong Kong, where glamorous boutiques and hotels battle for space with "Hello Kitty" specialty stores and men hawking copy-watches. (It's also the home of Chungking Mansions, the seedy rabbit warren of brothels, cheap hotels, and Indian restaurants that is the setting for much of Wong's 1994 film *Chungking Express*.) Wong remembers the Tsim Sha Tsui of his childhood being far more down-at-heels than its modern counterpart.

"[It was] an area frequented by girls who were generally known as 'Suzy Wong'—girls who worked in the bars entertaining sailors arriving on those battleships," he told journalist Jimmy Ngai in the book *Wong Kar-wai.* "There were lots of bars and clubs in the area, which was my world at the time, and

I was very much attracted to this sort of sleazy establishment."

Partway through a graphic design course at a local polytechnic, television channel TVB started offering classes in production. Wong quit his studies to join the program, which led to a job as production assistant on some of the channel's regular soap opera and drama series. He soon discovered his pent-up creativity needed an outlet. He started writing screenplays and did well enough at it to be able to leave TVB and take a position as a full-time writer for Cinema City, a Hong Kong company modeling itself on the Hollywood studio system. He worked there for a year without having a single script put into production, and left soon afterward. The next few years he spent on the fringes of the film industry as a freelance scriptwriter, writing comedies, action films, and kung fu and porn scripts—contributing to or writing a total of about 50 screenplays between 1982 and 1987. His most notable (and personal favorite) was *Final Victory*, a tale about second-rate gangsters directed by Patrick Tam.

Wong was making his living as a writer, but he always felt he would eventually direct his own films. He got his chance when his screenwriting talent was noticed by Alan Tang, a well-known 1960s actor who had since turned his hand to producing. Tang liked to give would-be directors a break.

He offered Wong the opportunity to direct *As Tears Go By* in 1988.

gang banging

To a certain extent, Wong's directing debut followed the established Hong Kong formula. *As Tears Go By* included the requisite number of well-choreographed gun battles and epic bloody beatings, but the action took a backseat to an emotional clash of love and loyalty. The film was about the difficulty Wah (Andy Lau), a well-respected gangster, was having keeping face because of the idiotic actions of Fly (Jacky Cheung), his *sai lo* (triad "little brother"). Wah's rough ways are moderated when he falls for the domesticated charm of a second cousin (Maggie Cheung) who comes to visit his flat to recover from an illness. She uncomplainingly washes the bloodstained clothes of his triad mates and buys new glassware to replace the stuff he angrily smashes after a bad night out. But Wah is forever leaping from the bed of his anxious lover to get Fly out of trouble, even though the only reason Fly gets in trouble is because his harebrained schemes to impress Wah usually end up with him lying on the pavement spitting blood.

The film ends miserably. To salvage his irredeemable reputation, Fly goes on a suicidal mission to kill a prominent gang leader. Wah follows him, and when Fly's bullets fail to kill the bad guy he steps in to finish the job and is gunned down himself. The locals loved the sad stuff, and the film scored big at the box office. Wong quickly became one of the territory's directors to watch.

He's lived up to the hype—but in ways nobody could have predicted. Each new Wong Kar-wai film, while retaining some thematic similarities, is a bold step in a new direction, as if Wong feels obliged to reinvent himself every time. Nowhere was this imperative more evident than in his second feature, *Days of Being Wild*, when he all but abandoned traditional narrative structure.

Days of Being Wild begins with a lengthy shot of lush tropical jungle—but a holiday-in-paradise movie it is certainly not. All the elements were in place—a star-studded cast list being the most important one for advance sales—but Wong screwed with them in ways the audience didn't appreciate. The film was set in the 1960s and featured up-and-coming actress Carina Lau, Maggie Cheung, and teen idol and Cantopop star Andy Lau. Leslie Cheung (a Cantopop star himself) played the beautiful, petulant heartbreaker Yuddy, a man with a fondness for whiling away the hours seductively cha-cha-ing in front of his mirror. Women go crazy for him, but he can only break their hearts. Yuddy's vanity conceals a great insecurity—he is an adopted child who doesn't know who his real mother is. The weary aunt who has raised him, dressed in elegant *cheongsam* dresses and entertaining a host of young boy toys, won't reveal his real mother's identity for fear of losing him. It seemed like a perfect recipe for a tale of redemption, but Wong obviously had other things on his mind. He sends Yuddy on a trip to the Philippines, where his real mother lives. Yuddy finds her house, but her servants won't allow him in. He leaves, gets in a fight with some hoods over a forged passport, and is shot and killed.

Mystery tour

Every character is miserable at the start of *Days of Being Wild*, and nobody is any happier at the end. *As Tears Go By* wasn't a happy movie either, but at least it was easy to follow. Wong's fans responded to *Days of Being Wild* with howls of outrage, but Wong didn't seem to care about this or the poor box office receipts. The critics had loved the film and, more importantly, he had made a big discovery.

"My works tend to become 'character films' rather than 'story films,'" Wong says. "[When we made *Days of Being Wild*] I was

"Cuz I'm cooool." Leon Lai does the gangster lean in *Fallen Angels*.

Jet Tone Films Ltd.

cheesy Cantopop records, a Wong Kar-wai movie is a rare opportunity to temporarily cut loose from their slavishly planned careers.

As an actor in a Wong Kar-wai film, you never know what you might end up doing—or where you'll end up doing it. Takeshi Kaneshiro had to massage a pig's carcass in 1995's *Fallen Angels* (Wong says the porcine massage was Kaneshiro's idea), but at least he got to stay in Hong Kong. The actors in the 1994 martial arts epic *Ashes of Time* spent several arduous months filming in the deserts of northwest China. (Asked about the experience on the set of *Ashes of Time*, Leslie Cheung would only say, "I spent too much time on that.") The cast and crew of *Days of Being Wild* spent just as long in the steamy jungles of the Philippines where Wong, in an inadvertent homage to Francis Ford Coppola's erratic behavior during the making of *Apocalypse Now* in the same country, found the tropical heat made him go slightly crazy. ("After [making *Days of Being Wild*]," he says, "I learned to control myself. I would never again forget that I am just making a film.")

Wong's approach sometimes seems as haphazard and random as the lives of the characters he depicts. His disorganization has led some to suggest that other members of his team are the real brains behind his

concerned that a film with some clear characters in it, told in simple narrative form, could be very predictable, thus unappealing. I tried to get around it. One day, I discovered I could chop those happenings into small pieces, and rearrange them with numerous possibilities. It was like I saw the light."

Since Wong cut himself loose from the strictures of linear plot structure, his character experiments have followed an increasingly unplanned path. His unpredictable working style has its fans—not least the Hong Kong superstars who line up to play havoc with their clean-cut teenybopper images. In a town where the leading actors are usually the biggest-selling crooners of

productions. Wong is part of a creative trio that includes Australian-born, Chinese-speaking director of photography Chris Doyle, and art director and editor William Chang. They have worked together ever since making *Days of Being Wild* together in 1991. Doyle started working in film while studying Chinese in Taiwan and got work for Wong after participating in a couple of attention-getting Taiwanese movies. They have been inseparable since their first collaboration, despite Doyle's forays into Hollywood when Wong's unpredictable shooting schedule will allow (notably, to shoot Gus Van Sant's 1998 production of *Psycho*) and his own fledgling career as director (he completed shooting on his first feature, *Away with Words*, in 1998).

In the vacuum created by the absence of linear plot lines in Wong's films, the arresting visuals have become a trademark, an exhilarating mix of techniques that intoxicates some and alienates others. Some say the story should take center stage, but Doyle disagrees.

"The sixties and seventies line was that the best cinematography is seamless, you didn't notice it," Doyle says. "I don't think so anymore. The younger audience is so used to being visually excited by an image. It's a vehicle for emotional impact and the energy of the film. It's much more obvious to the audience, and they think, 'Wow, this looks good!'"

The prominence of his distinctive visuals is what has led some critics to suggest it is Doyle, not Wong, who is the real cinematic genius in their creative partnership. Doyle has obviously become accustomed to fending off such speculation.

"They are visual films, so of course people are going to remark on the visuals," he says. "What you see on the screen is 60 percent [art director] William Chang. I don't think you can separate one from the other. Without being falsely modest, it's very much the collaboration that makes the film, but the idea is Wong's and the way it evolves is his. He usually says things like 'That all you can do, Chris?' which is a very refreshing approach and it pushes you farther. He's so cool and I'm so involved. It's just like a love relationship or a football team—you start to know each other's weaknesses and you work from there."

Very Unhappy, definitely Not together

Most Wong Kar-wai films won't pick you up when you're feeling down—not even the 1994 hit film *Chungking Express*, which is often praised for its lighthearted sense of fun. It is undoubtedly humorous, but the humor is only a weapon the characters use to stave off the great loneliness that surrounds them. The film's slapdash charm is partly a result of the way it was filmed; thrown together during a three-month post-production break in the making of *Ashes of Time* (which by that point had been over two years in the making and was several million HK dollars over budget). Wong produced, directed, and wrote the film himself, scribbling out the script by day and filming at night.

The narrative has two overlapping but separate parts, both focusing on the hard-luck love lives of two policemen named only by their numbers: 223 and 663. Both are pining for ex-lovers who have abandoned them, a lamentation of lost love that is undeniably funny but also terribly sad. They live in one of the world's most crowded cities but are utterly alone. It's as if Hong Kong's bustling, vibrant, neon-slicked streets are conspiring against them, teasing them with chance encounters and fleeting love affairs that are doomed to fail. The city taunts characters in other films in just the same way.

Urban blur: Takeshi Kaneshiro takes off in *Chungking Express*.

Jet Tone Films Ltd.

"We rub shoulders every day," says He Zhiwu (Takeshi Kaneshiro) in *Fallen Angels*. "We may never know each other, but we could become good friends someday." In a Wong Kar-wai film? Not likely. As the cook at the takeaway counter Midnight Express says to 223 in *Chungking Express*, trying to explain that his ex-girlfriend is never coming back: "You wait, time goes. Time goes, heart freezes."

Wong offers no way out of this trap, because any attempt to break out of the tight cocoon of everyday life is an invitation for greater unhappiness. *Happy Together*'s main characters go all the way to Argentina to rekindle their love, only to encounter an even greater sorrow, as bleak and cold as the wintry streets of Buenos Aires. Most of Wong's characters aren't even afforded the dramatic dignity of a downward spiral. Instead, they're on a flat, featureless life trajectory where the infrequent glimmers of hope and inspiration are illusory. People like the hitman Wong Chi-ming (Leon Lai) in *Fallen Angels* have relinquished all hope of shaping their destiny. Wong Chi-ming even pretends he likes it that way. "The best thing about my profession," he says, "is there's no need to make any decision." Considering his profession is the high-risk business of killing people he's never met, the decision-making thing doesn't seem like much of a perk.

Yet it's not as if modern urban living is the problem: the mythic characters who

Beyond the horizon in *Ashes of Time* lies . . . another desert.

Kameido Nezumi Eigakan

populate the vast empty deserts of *Ashes of Time* are also slaves to an apparently eternal melancholy, and worse still, they're unequipped with the wryness their city counterparts use to deflect it. "I don't care how others think of me," Ouyang Feng (Leslie Cheung) says at the beginning of *Ashes of Time*. "I just don't want others to be happier than I." Luckily for him, Wong seems prepared to grant him this wish—the rest of the characters are a laughably unhappy bunch. Huang Yaoshi (Tony Leung Kar-fai) is so miserable he drinks wine of amnesia so he can forget everything. The grief of Murong (Brigitte Lin) is so great she has developed a split personality, becoming not one, but two bitter, off-the-edge characters, Murong Yin and Murong Yang—each of them trying to kill the other. Tony Leung Chiu-wai's character is a swordsman whose sadness is so great it has turned him blind. At one point, Hong Qi (Jacky Cheung) asks Ouyang Feng what could lie beyond the desert in which they live. "Another desert," is Ouyang's grim reply.

Love really hurts

It's not as if the characters in Wong's films don't need love. Rather, they're obsessed with it. In *Chungking Express*, 223 (Takeshi Kaneshiro) munches through 30 cans of just-expired pineapple (his ex-lover's favorite fruit) in a bout of self-flagellation for losing her. Number 663 (Tony Leung Chiu-wai) talks to bars of soap and his dishcloth about his foolishness at letting his ex, a flight attendant, get away. Yet 223 is stricken when he gets a chance to make a romantic connection with the mysterious blonde-wigged assassin (Brigitte Lin) he meets in a bar after vomiting up all the pineapple. He goes back to her hotel room and eats salad and watches TV while she sleeps, leaving early in the morning without establishing a way to contact her later. He hopes the memory of their fleeting encounter, heartbreaking in its insignificance, will last "ten thousand years." (The whole thing would never have worked anyway, since she was a criminal and he a cop.)

Similarly, Ouyang Feng in *Ashes of Time* is crippled with remorse about the woman he let get away, just as she, at the end of the film, is weeping for the love that might have added meaning to her empty life. There's a great big gaping hole in the middle of many of Wong's characters, but most of them are so paralyzed with regret that they're unable to do anything to fill it. The best he'll grant them is another chance at an unspecified future—Ouyang Feng making a move to see what's beyond the desert at the end of *Ashes of Time*, for example. The characters may be allowed to try and make a new start, but Wong will never let them break free of the regrets of their past.

"I guess I find this loss of innocence thing deeply intriguing," Wong says, attempting to explain the misery he puts his characters through. "Time, to me, forever brings a loss of innocence. As you go through time, you are bound to look back with hindsight, you begin to reminisce about things that you dreamed about doing but didn't get to do, you begin to wonder what would have happened on that particular day if you had taken a different turn in the road. You have no answer for sure, but you are distressed by the possible outcome of things you didn't do. You cannot help but regret." And so regret runs like a swollen river through Wong's work.

You could get frustrated at Wong's characters for not trying harder to find a way out, but inertia is actually the best option, because he often punishes the people who try to make a change. Wong's message? Life without love may be lonely, but attempting to take control of your own destiny can have fatal consequences. A historical analogy is irresistible here: that the heart of this sense of powerlessness lies in the tension, the hype, and the frustration that surrounded Hong Kong's handover from Britain to China in 1997. Wong's characters are powerless subjects of the same gusts of circumstance that the people of Hong Kong endured when Britain and China debated the territory's future—neglecting any formal consultation with its people. From the Sino-British Joint Declaration of 1984 to the horrors of the Tiananmen Square massacre in Beijing in 1989 to the handover itself eight years later, Hong Kong's citizens could only do their best to secure a foreign passport or, failing that, adopt a grim sense of resignation as they waited for history to play itself out.

"You know, every time we visit other countries," Wong says, "we people from Hong Kong have been forced to answer the question of 1997 for many, many years. It got pretty boring, repeating your opinion every 10 minutes. One of the reasons I chose Argentina [as the location for *Happy Together*] was that it is on the other side of the world, and I thought by going there, I would be able to stay away from 1997. But then, as you must understand, once you conscientiously try to stay away from something or to forget something, you will never succeed. That something is bound to be hanging in the air, haunting you."

This sense of powerlessness, of suspension, of having no choice but to deal with what fate hands out, is a fundamental part of Wong's movies. Although he has shown signs of mellowing in his later films—in *Happy Together*, Yiu-fai breaks free from his disastrous relationship and returns to Asia, for example—anything other than dull resignation is generally frowned upon in a Wong Kar-wai movie. The punishment for transgressing this code of inactivity is usually death. It's dished out to Wah, the gangster in *As Tears Go By*, who is gunned down just as he's finally falling for the domesticated charm of his cousin and about to break free of his triad life. Yuddy, the heartbreaking drifter in *Days of Being Wild*, is also killed for the transgression of attempting to resolve his rootlessness by finding his real mother. Similarly, Wong Chi-ming, the hitman in *Fallen Angels*, gets shot almost immediately after he decides to throw in his career for the love of the Agent (Michelle Reis). They've spent three years in a business relationship that rarely involves their seeing each other. The Agent arranges his killing missions and faxes him details of where to carry out the shooting. She also cleans his flat when he's out and masturbates on his bed while fantasizing about him. When he finally makes the rather surprising step of deciding to be with her, he's killed off after taking one last job. In the stunningly filmed death sequence, Wong Chi-ming asks, "Who's to die? When? Where?" in a voice-over, as gracefully spinning neon lights herald his slide into oblivion. "It's all been planned by others. I'm a lazy person. I like people to arrange things for me. I've been a bit different lately. I want to change my habit. Be it right or wrong, I must make a decision myself."

defying Malaise

The heart of Wong Kar-wai's films lies in the ways his characters combat this sadness that blocks out the sun from their lives. The only way they can deflect the misery that bears down upon them is with humor,

"Would you like try our chicken vindaloo?" Faye Wong tries out her best line on Tony Leung Chiu-wai in *Chungking Express*.

Jet Tone Films Ltd.

which Wong has grown increasingly comfortable with using. The ultraserious *Ashes of Time* represented rock bottom in his bleak way of looking at the world, but since then he has allowed the smallest hint of devil-may-care defiance to creep into his movies. The hurried production of *Chungking Express* was when Wong first wised up to the power of a laugh, or at least a rueful grin—the perfect antidote to the self-indulgent seriousness of *Ashes of Time*.

Aside from the scripted humor in *Chungking Express*, there's high-wire pleasure to be had in watching Tony Leung Chiu-wai battle to hold back a smile when filming an obviously improvised scene with the real-life owner of takeaway counter Midnight Express, or Takeshi Kaneshiro berating a worker at a late-night convenience store for not considering the feelings of the cans of pineapple he just discarded. Both cops are indulging in a self-aware sort of madness to add some interest to the routine banality of their daily lives, and their unpredictable riffs have an infectious charm.

Wong was obviously exhilarated by the humor injection in *Chungking Express* too; he allowed Takeshi Kaneshiro an almost slapstick performance in 1995's *Fallen Angels*. Kaneshiro plays He Zhiwu, a character so desperate for work that he takes over other people's businesses after hours, forcing passersby to buy things from him.

There's a surreal, farcical scene in which he drives an entire mystified family around in an ice-cream van he's hijacked, forcing them to eat flaming ice cream while he drives nowhere in particular. It's hilarious stuff, but there's still sadness lurking beneath the surface of this escapism. He is mute and lives with his father. His mother was killed after being hit by an ice-cream van. Is he driving away from, or trying to confront something about, his mother's death? We never find out, but the humor of the moment defuses the tragedy, making He Zhiwu's boisterous, brutal optimism into something uplifting.

The best parts of Wong Kar-wai's films are the irresistible moments when the characters are allowed a rest from the daily battle of their lives. In *Fallen Angels* the Agent meets He one day in a noodle shop, some time after his father has died and the hitman has been killed. Before they meet, He gets into a fight with some other diners, trashing the noodle shop in the process. While mayhem reigns just behind her, the Agent sits oblivious, eating noodles and staring vacantly into space. Soon afterward, in the film's last scene, we cut to another shot of the Agent with the same vacant expression on her face, only this time she's sitting on the back of He's motorbike, her head slumped on his shoulder as they speed through a tunnel. The Agent speaks in a voice-over: "When I am about to leave, I ask him to take me home. I haven't ridden on a motorbike for a long time. Actually, I haven't been so close to a man for a while. The road is not that long, and I know I will be getting off soon. But I feel such warmth this very moment."

The misery that Wong heaps on his characters only makes these moments more powerful. When they find comfort despite the tragedy of their lives, they amplify the light from these seductive glimmers of happiness and shine it full-beam back at the audience. It's a poignant, bittersweet onslaught that few can resist.

Home is Where the Heat is

If Wong Kar-wai's ego ever starts to swell, the close-to-home comments would quickly cut him down to size. Local critics have called his work overrated, pretentious, and (a strange insult, this) "European." There is jealousy over the way his films, none of which has been a runaway success, seem to easily attract willing investors.

It often seems that Wong hears these voices of criticism the loudest. In every interview he seems embarrassed by any attempt at flattery and rebuffs it as if it were being directed at someone else. He seems to prefer discussing his mistakes rather than his successes. He even seems to read his

victory at Cannes as the placing of a greater burden of expectation on his subsequent work, rather than something that has opened up new opportunities.

"From day one, it has been like striving to survive," he has said. "I have no idea how I entered into this, but ever since I have been striving to survive. After *Days of Being Wild*, my feeling has always been like a single pair of hands facing an entire army—you don't know when you're going to perish."

Wong has yet to combine praise from the critics with honest-to-goodness financial success, but he keeps finding backers for his films nonetheless. As the output of the Hong Kong film industry continues to shrink and investors spend their money more conservatively, it upsets some filmmakers to see someone they consider to be a self-indulgent risk-taker apparently gliding nonchalantly above the funding fray.

"The whole thing has gone against what our industry collectively believes in," Wong says of the controversy. "Making a film that doesn't sell is already bad enough; a commercially failed filmmaker getting more work is even worse. And on top of that, a whole bunch of people are telling everyone that this filmmaker has made some very, very good films. This is about as controversial as you can get."

Love him or hate him, Wong's profound influence on the Hong Kong film industry

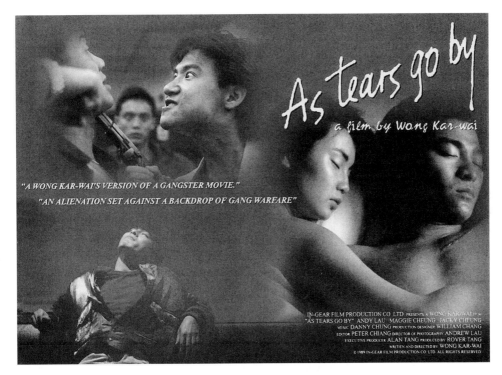

Kowloon squalor abuts the art house in *As Tears Go By*, originally known as *Mongkok Carmen*.

cannot be overstated. In the boom times of the 1980s, producers could make money from a film without worrying about whether it was creative or not. Having big stars on the cast list was enough to guarantee overseas sales, as nobody ever asked to see a script. Conventional wisdom suggested that with the right actors, stuntmen, and action choreographers, a healthy profit was a sure thing.

The production-line method of filmmaking that had served Hong Kong so well

in the previous decade showed a dramatic decline in success in the 1990s, as local audiences and overseas buyers turned away from bloated Hong Kong productions in droves. As producers continue to flail desperately about for an alternative approach, Wong Kar-wai's style—that is, a belief in the quality and input of the cast, in adventurous visuals and a strong directorial vision— may be the best way forward.

As well as the quick assimilation of Wong's filming techniques—so much so that many of them have become visual clichés—it's now possible to sense a greater value being placed on individual creativity in the Hong Kong film industry, and much of this is due to Wong's trailblazing efforts. Established filmmakers such as Stanley Kwan and Ann Hui are still able to obtain funding for their work, as well as a great deal of support from within the industry itself. Actors and crew will work for a lower rate (as they often do in Wong Kar-wai's films), or for no money at all, just to take part in the production of a script they believe in. Some believe that the forces that are bonding this small, supportive, intensely creative group of people together will reignite the Hong Kong film industry. Wong Kar-wai is in many ways the groundbreaker, and therefore carries the hopes of the industry with him in every new project he tackles. Hong Kong informs his work so much that it's difficult to imagine him creating a film within the strictures of the Hollywood system. Wong's maverick tendencies indicate such a mainstream move is anathema to him too.

"Wong's most famous quip about working in Hong Kong rather than Hollywood or elsewhere," remembers Doyle in his diary, "is 'I'd rather work with first-class gangsters than bad accountants.'"

Wong may be one of the leaders of the pack in Hong Kong, but it isn't as if he doesn't owe the industry anything. Its very nature defines much of his cinematic style. If Wong seems compelled to confound people's expectations with each new work, this is partly from necessity. In Hong Kong, where many films are slapped together literally days before they reach the screen, Wong's style constantly has been imitated (and parodied, on occasion: Tony Leung Chiu-wai and Jacky Cheung took the hilariously disrespectful step of playing triad brothers not dissimilar to the pair in *As Tears Go By* in the madcap *Days of Being Dumb*). As jump-cuts, hand-held cameras, and other visual trademarks have been rapidly incorporated into the Hong Kong cinematic lingo, Wong has no choice but to stay one step ahead of the competition.

"If something sells like a hotcake [in Hong Kong]," he says, "everybody tries to make a copy as soon as possible, hoping they are not too late. The situation doesn't allow you to sit and write about something you really want to write about, and then carry it around trying to sell it. Tarantino could have been sitting inside the video shop for many years before he came up with [his] scripts. But the [Hong Kong] industry wouldn't allow that."

Much of Wong's visual brilliance comes from this need to stay ahead of the pack. The results are obvious in every film but particularly so in the unorthodox cinematography of *Fallen Angels*—where the colors are so vivid they threaten to burst the frame—and in the languorous slow motion and artful freeze-frames of *Happy Together*.

"People are always very curious about the visual effects in my works," he says. "The not-so-romantic truth is that lots of those effects are in reality results of circumstantial consideration: if there is not enough space for camera maneuvering, replace the regular lens with a wide-angle lens; when candid camera shooting in the streets does not allow lighting, adjust the speed of the camera according to the amount of light available; if the continuity of different shots does not link up right for a sequence, try jump cuts; to solve the problem of color incontinuity, cover it up by developing the film in black and white . . . tricks like that go on forever.

"Our styles come from the way we work. Like in *Fallen Angels* we started working in a very small teahouse, and the only way we could shoot the scene was with a wide-angle lens. But I thought the wide-angle lens was too normal, so instead I preferred an extreme wide-angle. And the effect is

Happy Together's doomed couple can't even fake a camera smile.

Jet Tone Films Ltd.

stunning because it draws the characters very close to the camera, but twists the perspective of the space so they seem far away. It became a contrast to *Chungking Express*, in which people are very far away from the camera but seem so close. Also, we work with very limited budgets and we don't have permits, so we have to work like CNN, just breaking into some place and taking some shots. We often don't have time for setups, and sometimes when neighbors walk into the frames we have to cut them out, and that becomes a jump cut.

"I think 10 or 15 percent is preconceived," Wong says. "Most of it just happens."

Simon Yam with a dynamite outfit as Big Spender in *Operation Billionaires*, from the Good Fellas Production Company
Universe

cops and rascals

gangsters and motion pictures go together like chilies and squid. Gangster iconography—gunplay, dames, payoffs, rubouts, and smorgasbords of vice—provides natural plot elements, and colorful underworld characters are cinematic perennials. Actors like James Cagney and Edward G. Robinson owe their careers to real-world thugs like Al Capone. Wiseguys on film span the decades from *Scarface* (1932) to *Scarface* (1983) and on into the 1990s and the noughts.

On the Hong Kong variety of gangster flick, a pitfall yawns. The absurd Asian stereotypes proffered by Hollywood, compounded by the cornucopia of cartoony HK wiseguy flicks, may give the impression that organized skullduggery is Asia's *raison d'être*. It should be two-by-four obvious, but let's be ton-of-bricks clear here: the vast majority of Asians are not tattooed thugs

with gold chains, toothsome molls, and murder on their minds. It's just that the tiny minority who are make better camera fodder.

Businessmen at heart, triads (ethnic-Chinese gangster organizations with worldwide tentacles) rarely engage in the wholesale bloodshed that characterizes many wiseguy tribes. Even at their goriest, Chinese turf wars are never as anarchic as the kinetic carnage of Medellin or Mumbai or Moscow or Monrovia or Miami. Hong Kong's cinematic rumbles depicting platoons of chopper-swinging youths may look groovy onscreen but seldom occur in real life. Wiseguy glory makes for a great script, but it plays hell with real-world profits. The term "rascal," which often appears in subtitles to label triad members, helps indicate that Chinese gangsters are not a direct analog to the Western counterparts.

triadſ iN the HoNg koNg fiLM induſtry

In the early nineties, triad interference in the industry was so vexing that, in the summer of 1992, HK film stars—including Jackie Chan—took to the streets in a major protest. But triads are mostly interested in quick profits, and as HK film profits have declined in recent years, so has triad interest.

This is not to suggest that wiseguys have abandoned the Hong Kong film industry— they remain on both sides of the camera. But most HK triads are lower-key than the "rock stars": the bright lights who fade quickly. These baddest-of-the-bad find their luminary careers enhanced by endings featuring imprisonment or (better yet) violent death. And then the cameras roll.

biopicſ aNd boMbſ

Macau is a territory near HK noted for fine food, exquisite architecture, and a successful gaming industry. On a beautiful morning in April 1998, Judicial Police director Antonio Marques Baptista (a Portuguese citizen, as Macau was under Portuguese administration until its 1999 handover to the PRC) was out jogging with his dog. As they approached his automobile, the dog (which had been trained to sniff explosives) suddenly swapped ends and ran the hell away from the

vehicle. Baptista followed suit—a wise move, as the vehicle then exploded, hurling debris in a 10-meter radius.

The dog, a golden retriever, hasn't been seen since.

Baptista refrained from pointless anger or revenge fantasies. Instead, he called in a territory-wide sweep for reputed triad boss Wan Kuok-koi ("Broken Tooth Koi"). That night, the cop nabbed the Hawaiian-shirted alleged kingpin in the restaurant of Macau's most famous hotel, the Lisboa. The arrest— on charges of attempted murder, drug trafficking, employing illegal immigrants, and using phony identity documents—prevented Broken Tooth from attending a film premiere.

Starring Simon Yam, as a gangster. In fact, starring Yam as Broken Tooth, in a HK$14 million production (*Casino*). Financed by the handsome and flamboyant Broken Tooth, who clearly loves the limelight. His arrest costarred the photogenic Baptista—an intense-looking fellow with a bristling, overgrown Van Dyke beard. But Broken Tooth's performance in the police van, nonchalantly masticating a piece of gum as his eyes darted for the cameras and he thrust out his jaw, upstaged the cop for ages. Broken Tooth was born to play a gangster. The weird thing is, he *is* a gangster (allegedly, unproven, verdict pending, as the suits remind us we must so stipulate). As of this writing, most of the charges

against Broken Tooth have been tossed out as witnesses and defendants alike fail to turn up for their court dates—imagine that.

The *Casino* saga received its most ironic twist when, just after its cinematic release, triad members wearing white gloves and armed with metal pipes smashed up three Mongkok shops selling pirated VCD copies of the film.

the big ʃpeNder

Casino was not the only film in which Yam portrayed a triad kingpin. A few months later, he portrayed Cheung Tze-keung, an even more notorious gangster known as Big Spender. Another Cheung epic, *Big Spender*, starring Ray Lui, hit screens in early 1999.

As these films were allegedly bankrolled by the wealthy gangsters they portray, it's not surprising that they flatter the wiseguys' actions to the point of absurdity. In *Operation Billionaires* (1998), from the wonderfully named Good Fellas Production Company, Yam as Big Spender treats his subordinates to lavish meals and hostess-rich karaoke sessions. In an opening scene that shreds credulity like a wet napkin, Big Spender is shown literally helping a little old lady to cross the street. The Spender kidnaps the son of a HK property tycoon, but as he carefully explains to the distraught tycoon, both he and the businessman are just trying to earn a living and are thus not really all that different. He befriends a tough-yet-righteous goon named Cyclone (modeled on real-life Cheung henchman Yip Kai-foon), who is shot in the back by duplicitous minions of the law. The nobility just pours out of the screen.

The real-life Cheung was a hardened criminal with a penchant for stealing from the rich and giving to himself. Cheung and his gang were subsequently arrested on the Mainland, extradition to HK impossible due to a lack of evidence (the wealthy victims

"If I were to ask, 'What's the first thing that comes to your mind when you hear the words Asian or Asian-American?' a lot of folks would probably say Chinese food, kung fu, or fund-raising scandals. The stereotypes of passive, exotic women and inscrutable, untrustworthy men remain strong in our nation's subconscious."

—Dinah Eng, *USA Today*

"[*Lethal Weapon 4*] seems to have gone out of its way to include some offensive Asian stereotyping. Personally, I thought 'flied lice' jokes went out with Mickey Rooney in *Breakfast at Tiffany's*, but obviously I was wrong."

—Fionnuala Halligan, *South China Morning Post*

If you haven't seen the 1998 installment of the buddy-cop *Lethal Weapon* series, yes, there really are shocking, unvarnished "flied lice" and "speakee English?" jokes. The people who scripted and approved LW4 are undoubtedly fine and upstanding folks, but what's up with this? "Flied lice"?!? Try to imagine the outcry if ethnic groups like African Americans or Latinos were subjected to this sort of stereotyping.

Like Fin Halligan, I thought that these jokes had been phased out by the 1960s (Asians considered them offensive in the 1940s), but here they are alive and well, trotted out and presented straight in hopes of a cheap chuckle. Recall the terminology used to describe minorities in the 1940s and 1950s. Is the picture becoming clearer? Let's hope so.

Dog-eating wisecracks and exotic/inscrutable stereotypes are still far too common and accepted. Smoothly rounded stereotypes linger: old guys in kung fu drag clicking solemnly on an abacus, Suzy Wong vamps hung-up crazy on *gwailo* boys, World Wrestling Federation concepts of ass-kicking Orientals—shaven-headed pigtail guys swathed in silk dragon robes and looking for white patoots to kick. Despite the global nature of business and communica-

hushed up the matter). The trial was not a drawn-out affair—Cheung was convicted of firearms smuggling and robbery in a Guangzhou court, fined 662 million yuan (US$80 million, in cash), stripped of his political rights, then taken out and shot. As Hong Kong does not have capital punishment, and Cheung was a HK resident, the case caused some controversy. Still, public sympathy for Cheung on either side of the border was not much in evidence.

Yip Kai-foon was indeed paralyzed by police bullets, but the police did not fire from behind. They were in front of him because he was shooting at them. Yip, who has his own biopic (*King of Robbery* [1996], starring, yes, Simon Yam), had a reputation for enjoying gun battles with the police. Robin Hoods these guys are not.

An interesting sidelight to the Big Spender saga is a popular belief that Cheung bribed the authorities to fake his

tion in our new century, some folks still use the phrase "the Far East" without a trace of irony.

Why is this so? For one thing, education and cultural appreciation of Asia has been sadly lacking. Many Americans, for example, still think of Asia in terms of Japan (see "The Japanese Vector," page 6). But the influx of Hong Kong movies, on video and in cinemas, has helped to change matters. You can't expect a crowd from the Riverside Theater in Minneapolis—a bunch of Midwestern *gwailos* who have just spent a couple of hours cheering for Jet Li or Chow Yun-fat—to guffaw at archaic racial stereotyping. Their paradigm of Asia now rejects the smoothed-out stereotypes and embraces the spiky realities of Asian

life. For these folks, the "Mystic Orient" nonsense retreaded on David Carradine infomercials has become unsaleable.

The West has no monopoly on broad stereotyping. Hong Kong films are overly fond of evil *gwailo* villains—generic foreign devils serving as brigands and killable dogs. Much like Indians in the Westerns of the 1950s, they come rushing out of the metaphysical sagebrush ready to kill or be killed. Neither has the appreciation shown by black fans worldwide been reciprocated in terms of positive role models in HK films. And even the most casual student of twentieth-century Asian history realizes that the Japanese are in for their share of screen malignancy.

But two wrongs don't make a right. Let's hope that Hollywood starts to get it, and gives us more characters who aren't members of the "Fukienese Dragons" or trailed by the detritus of gong sound effects or Rice-A-Roni jokes. Let's have some normal Asian characters doing things like yakking on the phone or worrying about their kids' education and changing their damn engine oil, rather than fleeing oppression or creating same. Let's see Asian characters with all the foibles of actual human beings, like Chow Yun-fat's conflicted NYC cop character in *The Corruptor* (1999). And while we're at it, what the heck, let's see some onscreen romance between an Asian man and a Caucasian woman, rather than the other way around. The sky won't fall.

execution. With the high level of corruption in the PRC and the vast sums of money involved, it has a certain degree of plausibility (Cheung's body was never displayed). If he did survive, he's not heading for the local CNN office to tell the world about it.

With real-life cases like these, it's no wonder that Hong Kong produces such excellent crime films. The interplay between cops and rascals—who both offer incense to the same red deity, Kwan Ti—is

explored for your entertainment in the following films.

9413 (1998)

This string of numbers, when pronounced in Cantonese, sounds like "nine chances to die, one chance to live." Actor Francis Ng makes his directorial debut with *9413*, shot on a budget of HK$3 million. That's about

US$400,000, which wouldn't pay the catering bills on most Hollywood pictures. The excellence of the production is enhanced by moonlighting director Herman Yau, who served as cinematographer on Ng's project. The cooperative effort is laudable, as *9413* is one hell of a film.

Ng plays an eccentric cop named Ko Chin-man, better known as Smash-Head—in Cantonese parlance, a stubborn guy who batters through obstacles unsparing of forehead. Ng's character is a Hong Kong version of the relentless gendarmes portrayed by Japanese actor/director Takeshi Kitano in films like *Violent Cop* (1989). Lucidity is Smash-Head's curse—while most of us pretend that we aren't living on a mountain of garbage, he screams in horror at the stink-ing polyfoam reality of HK's throwaway culture, and he's just as dirty. This loose-cannon cop desperately seeks the smearing caresses of marijuana, alcohol, violence, and sex with drugbunny partygal Mandy (Amanda Lee), who enjoys slipping dope into his mouth with her tongue. The seductive mix fails him—his romantic excursions fall apart when he discovers she's wearing environmentally incorrect plastic slippers, or his bloodstream wins and he passes out. Violence is what he's best at, whether it's smashing up a bar (hurling glasses at a painting of Hong Kong's famed skyline), threatening a witness, or screaming at his superior, Kar (Fredric Mao).

His excesses are tolerated as Kar knows Smash-Head will do dirty work. But when

9413

Mandarin Films

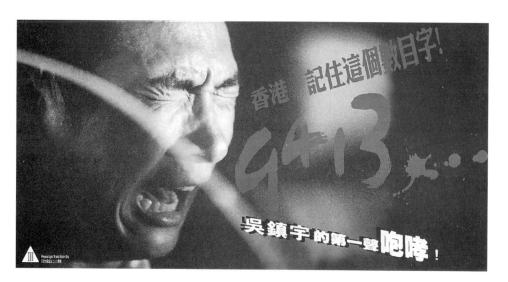

"I am a police, the same with others.
But I am afraid of gangster and bloodshed.
Neither my supervisor nor woman like me."
Haunted Karaoke

"We, cops, have no time for farts."
Twist

"The famous key words of being a police, you know?
A for apple polishing, B for boosting, C for careless, D for dog, E for escaping duties.
If you can do all these, you will be promoted without working hard."
The Log

"Pal, cuff two bastards to the police stations."
Spike Drink Gang

"You went fever with that cop"
Offence Storm

"Finger, finger out the policeman"
The Imp

"Officer, what course is it?"
"It's called: hell-style suicide to transit for 1997.
Pension-guaranteed, dying-for-sure special training course."
Bodyguards of the Last Governor

"Bitch, your kicking is useless, we HK police are competent."
Bodyguards of the Last Governor

"You are paid to be a police, not for the standing comedy."
Haunted Karaoke

"I'm already sick of shooting at the cops."
The Final Option

"I'm not Satan's daughter!
I'm Inspector Chan Shou-ching from the Complaints Against Police Office."
666: Satan Returns

"Officer Pun, you'd be righteous & fair."
Women on the Run

"Officer Cheung, your penis is over."
Women on the Run

Kar hands him a purloined service revolver to pass on to a loathsome Vietnamese gangster for some bad business, he notices the serial number—9413—on the revolver of his ex-partner Fatty Chuen, who was killed by the very same mystically numbered gun. Ko loses his cool and beats the Viet's head against the asphalt until lifeblood flows into Victoria Harbor. Smash . . . Head.

Ko seeks redemption from an angelic therapist, Dr. Carmen Leung (Christine Ng),

who becomes equally enraptured with him. But Kar is not pleased with Smash-Head's duplicity. One chance in nine = slim odds.

Yau's camera crisply grips the urbanscape of Hong Kong as well as the confines of TST's Amoeba Club, where much of the film is set. Rather than sickly Cantopop interludes, edgy industrial synth music mixes with piledrivers on the soundtrack—the perfect complement to this unique *cop noir* drama.

beast cops (1998)

Gordon Chan's *Beast Cops* is a challenging police drama. Chan (who cowrote, produced, and codirected the film) has described it as a comedy.

Which it is. It's a comedy that opens with the up-the-spine screech of a glass-cutter crushing a narrow path through the title, melded with gliding, bleary video of Kowloon neon. It's a comedy that slowly spirals into savage unromanticized violence lubricated by corruption, lust for power, and dope. It's a comedy about the beasts coiled up in men.

Despite the title's plurality, there's only one beast cop in the film: Tung (Anthony Wong), a police officer who knows that cooperation with the powerful triad societies in his Kowloon district is how you get along. Tung, like most of us, spends much of his time bumbling through life. He's not a highly moral person—when we first see him, he is gambling in an illicit casino. Tung's in so deep that he serves as casino dealer when he feels like it.

His fellow cops are easier to decode. Cheung (Michael Wong) is a straight-arrow toughie who's been transferred into the district. Michael Wong reprises his role as no-nonsense cop from *Final Option* (1994) and *First Option* (1996), both also directed by Chan. Cheung drives a Humvee and smokes Churchill-sized cigars, but as Tung

is perennially short of dough, he rents his room to the guy. Another flatmate is goofy-haired Sam (Sam Lee), a skin-and-bones chick magnet whose duties include in-depth interviews of all the local massage parlor girls. He picks up a lot of information but fails to appreciate latex and picks up a few other things as well.

The casino's manager, Alphonse (Roy Cheung), hires a Mainland cut-out to kill a rival mobster. The hit goes well but the getaway goes awry—Alphonse accidentally squishes the hired assassin with his car and has to flee HK. He's in a hurry, and his moll Yo Yo (Kathy Chow), the mama-san at his hostess nightclub, is late. The gangster lets his little head do his big-head thinking, grabs an understudy—a doxy named Suzy—and splits.

Alphonse's sudden "vacation" causes a power shift in his corner of the triad world. The gang boss, Father Tai (Arthur Wong), has his career goals sorted: to eat egg-custard tarts every day and make sure the venerated "Grandpa" gets his monthly stipend. But there's a problem: triad middle manager Marvin has ambitions in this dangerous new vacuum. "Custard" Tai offers promotion to anyone who can solve the problem.

Up steps young turk Ted (Patrick Tam), who deals with Marvin by shooting him repeatedly. Next thing you know, Ted is scarfing those egg tarts with big boss Tai.

But the lad wants more than just Alphonse's business. He wants Alphonse's woman Yo Yo. This causes some friction, as she's now taken up with Cheung. Ted doesn't take rejection well. He starts forcing Yo Yo's girls to push ecstasy in the club, slapping Yo Yo when she argues: "Alphonse never allowed . . ." *SLAP*!

The sharp crack of the young punk's slap outlines the new-school universe of profits-before-everything versus the old-school give-and-take of cops like Tung and triads like Alphonse and Custard Tai. When Alphonse returns from "vacation" to find his business taken over by his protégé and his woman impregnated by the new cop in town, things tangle.

Beast Cops culminates in an extended endbattle. Tung, stoked to the gills on imported beer and imported pills, duels with triad punks in the cagelike under-construction garage-casino with surf music and animal howls as soundtrack. Ted and Tung fire handguns at each other, progress to choppers and sharpened steel pipes and fluorescent tubes, then roll around in smashed soda pop bottles trying to slice each other. The brutality redeems Tung for his moral ambiguity, though whether it restores the old-school structure is debatable.

Beast Cops is unafraid to spin into the details of its characters and paint them in all their frailty. Police stations, uniforms, paperwork don't exist for these guys; they

MEDIA ASIA FILMS (BVI) LTD presents a PEOPLE'S PRODUCTIONS LTD production a GORDON CHAN DANTE LAM film "BEAST COP" producer GORDON CHAN DANTE LAM executive producer TONY CHEUNG screenplay ALFRED TAU music RICHARD HUNG CANDY LEUNG editor CHAN KI-HOP starring MICHAEL FITZGERALD WONG ANTHONY WONG KATHY CHAU ROY CHEUNG director GORDON CHAN JOHN CHONG cinematographer CHAN HING-KAI producer TOMOUS LEUNG MA FUNG-KWOK JOHN CHONG director GORDON CHAN DANTE LAM

Media Asia

Michael Wong and Anthony Wong are a couple of *Beast Cops*.

Photograph courtesy Media Asia. Copyright Star Television Filmed Entertainment.

bond, fight, and die outside the bureaucratic arena. Yet problems in communication and problems with women (often one and the same when it comes to men) lead to the types of conversations men really have with each other. The ad hoc approach (Chan used input from the actors to craft

"Why do you like the Police, they are
so boring.
We gangsters are much more
interesting."
Haunted Karaoke

"I know you, Tony is the nasty bad egg
of Japanese triad society!"
Once upon a Time in Triad Society

"If a rascal is trustable, even a pig will
climb up a tree!"
Sexy and Dangerous

"They are living in the black spots of
juvenile delinquency."
Suicide

"We are progressive rascals. We are
making an art film."
Mahjong Dragon

"Is this your territory?"
"Yes, this is called Street of Copyright
Infringement."
Suicide

"And, you bastard, a triad society is a
triad society."
Once upon a Time in Triad Society

realistic dialogue) helps add depth to this unusual and worthwhile film. *Beast Cops* was the opening film at the Twenty-second Hong Kong Film Festival and won a slew of awards at the HK Film Awards. Note: the characters' names listed here are from the DVD version; the original print listed Ted as "Pushy-pin," etc.

big bullet (1996)

What a title! Eschewing the customary HK title slate, *Big Bullet* barges straight in, presenting central character Bill Li (Lau Ching-wan) in mid-shootout during a hostage drama gone awry. His testimony before an investigatory tribunal fingers his scummy superior Inspector Guan as the culprit. Li's

an obvious hothead, as pointed out by Inspector Yang (Francis Ng), who suggests transfer from the Serious Crimes Unit to the less-edgy Emergency Unit. Yang and Bill Li are obviously close. As Li exits their chat, he shares an elevator ride with a cuffed-and-escorted badass named Professor (Yu Rong-guang). The two hotheads glare at each other. No words are exchanged, but suddenly the perp starts singing a delicate and traditional Peking opera refrain: "Now I'm locked up/But still I'm tough . . . it's Mandarin, you should learn it," taunting the Hongkie cop. Li spits the lines back in Cantonese then slugs the handcuffed crook in the belly. The stares get better.

Out on the street, Professor is released from custody by his confederate Bird (Anthony Wong), who punches out his escorts with a 12-gauge pump. Professor was busted by Interpol, who took his nine million in cash and locked it up as evidence. Now he wants it back. He sends Bird into a cafe to interview Richard (William Tuen), an Interpol cop, about the matter. Yang and Li are on the scene and slowly wise up to the situation. Tension clicks up as the principals circle 'round. Richard's girl Sandra, a pleasant sort, isn't taking to this too well. She starts to whimper.

So Bird shoots her through the head with a .44 Magnum Desert Eagle automatic pistol. Warfare ensues. Principals are tracked throughout the fury, and most survive. When the smoke dissipates, Li is left with his crew in the EU van, led by rigid officer-candidate Jeff (Jordan Chan), who can't adapt to Li's flexible policing style. The crew learns to get along so they can foil the heinous plans revolving around Richard's gun hand, which was blown clean off yet somehow went missing. . . .

Big Bullet is a swaggering and satisfying crowd pleaser. The slick production, with its destructive car chases and apocalyptic gunfight sequences replete with tracking camera, will impress action fans. Yet at its heart, this is a police procedural: the plot twists won't surprise anyone, but the attention to detail will. Supervisors advise on avoiding news photographers during tea breaks. Li responds to queries about on-the-job stress by declaring that since he won't hang out

Big Bullet—'nuff said

singing karaoke with his superiors and kiss their collective ass: "That's stress, I guess." These insightful bits of business intersperse with hard action, creating a fertile and virulent mulch. *Big Bullet*'s excellent villains are potentiated by eccentricity: Bird spouts off in Italian for no discernible reason while piloting the getaway car, and Professor's detachment while capping furiously at his foes is remarkable. *Big Bullet* did not go unnoticed at the 1997 Hong Kong Film Awards, garnering nominations for Best Picture, Best Director, and Best Actor (Lau).

Lau Ching-wan metaphysically bonds with Ringo Lam in the superb *Full Alert*.

Brilliant Idea Group

full alert (1997)

Director Ringo Lam's crime dramas—like 1992's *Full Contact* and 1987's *City on Fire*, both with Chow Yun-fat—have become well known in HK film circles. Delving further into the Lam lexicon yields nuggets like 1988's *School on Fire*. In 1996, Lam shot *Maximum Risk* with Jean-Claude Van Damme and Natasha Henstridge but was forced to reshoot a "happy ending," which didn't make him happy. Lam then returned to Hong Kong to make *Full Alert*. The film stars two of HK's finest actors—Lau Ching-wan and Francis Ng—at their very best and is a must-see for fans of HK crime films.

FA is highly autobiographical—Inspector Pao (Lau) is a perfectionist workaholic cop-in-charge whose impatient rages mirror those of Lam himself—known as the "dark-faced god" for his intensity on the film set. In one scene, Pao can barely contain his fury at officials of a hidebound Hong Kong institution, whose intransigence impedes vital details of his job—symbolic of Lam's rage against Hong Kong officials who refused to issue permits to allow filming on HK streets. "They treat me like a criminal," fumed Lam, who went to the Philippines for his next film (where the authorities let filmmakers shoot real guns and/or rockets, depending on the script).

Although Pao is Ringo Lam's antacid-gobbling, stress-fueled *doppelganger*, he's also Lau Ching-wan's most fully developed police character. Vulnerable yet Kevlar-tough Pao is up against Mak Kwan (Ng), a focused criminal. Mak was a civil engineer jailed for peddling explosives intended for construction. Though he served his time, no contractor will hire him now, and he intends to use his engineering skills to pull a serious job and leave HK with his much-adored girlfriend, Chung Lai-hung (Amanda Lee).

Plot puzzle pieces float in like the muted choral touches of Peter Kam's evocative score. Pao realizes that he and Mak are more alike than different, and begins to doubt his verve for command. "My gun is getting heavier and heavier," he tells his loving, long-suffering wife.

The poster makes it look like another bang-bang big-fun flick, and *Full Alert* delivers on the action front—a car chase woven around HK's famous double-decker trams puts your heart in your throat. As the cops pursue a speeding Benz full of armed baddies, Bill (Chin Kar-lok at his best) observes: "They are all nuts." Ringo Lam said much the same of his stunt crew in filming the scene—nobody warned the tram drivers in advance. As for the film's explosion, which rains flaming debris on Kowloon's crowded Nathan Road, well . . .

People do get perforated in *Full Alert*, but the real violence lurks in the emotions of the people doing the killing. This is the big taboo for action filmmakers, one that few are willing to tackle (Clint Eastwood in *The Unforgiven* is a notable exception). Many action films feature an orgy of high-velocity slaughter followed by wisecracks from the victorious shooters—FA explores the destruction to the shooter's soul. Even with Ringo Lam's impressive resume, *Full Alert* is a standout.

to live and die in tsimshatsui (1994)

"Sometimes, I don't know who am I. A human or a ghost. If I am a human, how can I betray my friend? Or if I am a ghost. But I am a policeman," muses Jacky Cheung in *To Live and Die in Tsimshatsui*, directed by Andrew Lau. Cheung, better known for his role in John Woo's *Bullet in the Head* and his Cantopop singing career, stars as Crazy Lik, an undercover gone so deep that his humanity is threatened more than his life. He endures the duplicitous moral hell of living as a triad because he craves promotion from his superior, Officer Suen (Kwong Wah). But as his triad sponsor Brother Tai (Roy Cheung) reminds him: "Money is easy to get, but lives are easy to lose." Lik is never rewarded with triad wads of orange HK$1,000 banknotes, but the lives of his cohorts are easily lost.

Crazy Lik is starting to crack, and when his gal pal Moon (Gigi Lai) invites him to her mom's birthday banquet, things start to crank unpleasant. As an undercover masquerading as a gangster, he can't exactly brag about his job, so the praise goes to upstanding Officer Suen. He challenges Suen to a drinking game which descends into hurled insults, drunken fisticuffs, and the bum's rush for pariah Lik. He consoles himself by hanging out with triad buddies Ah Bong (Chan Ka-bong) and Ah Fai (Tony Leung Kar-fai). Moon ditches him for Suen, but he eventually succumbs to the girlish crush of Brother Tai's sister, tough triad babe Ah Bo (Wu Chien-lien).

All this camaraderie is spoiled by the brutality of crime chieftain Father Man (Ng Chi-hung). The gaggle of cough-syrup-chugging teeny punks trailing Father Man like a string of ducklings is much like an actual bunch of Mongkok triad kiddies. A pair of these kids is summarily executed after a botched hit, and as their blood splashes on spooled-out flypaper hanging from the ceiling of their Mongkok squat, it's clear that Father Man doesn't read the same comic books they did.

Suen forms an alliance with Tai, and Crazy Lik's pals start going down. The stage is set for a big gun battle with a bunch of really dangerous guys. In this regard, *TLADIT* is no different from a hundred other gangster gunplay films, but Cheung's agonized performance makes this a worthy addition to the portfolio of HK copper/rascal operettas.

tHe Log (1996)

Police work has been described as years of boredom interspersed with seconds of sheer terror. In recent years, cop flicks on both sides of the Pacific have given us more perspective into the lives of the people involved. The result in many cases has been more complete characters and thus better films.

The Chinese title of director Derek Chiu's *The Log*—"Three Unlucky Policemen"— gives a better indication of its contents. The film employs heavy-handed symbolism at times—it spans December 31, 1996, to New Year's Day of you-know-when (framed pictures of Queen Liz go smashing to the ground, that sort of thing). Otherwise, it's delicate and complex.

The three cops are a diverse lot. Dixon (Michael Wong) is a hardass inspector who feels more comfortable speaking English than Cantonese. He's a hothead, yet his troops respect him as tough but fair. Jerry (Jerry Lamb) is a young street cop who identifies more with triad punks than with his fellow officers. The central character is

Gump (Kent Cheng), a balding shlump of a guy who has been around forever and knows he'll never get promoted. Cheng, who shaved part of his head for the role, won Best Actor at the Hong Kong Film Awards for his masterful performance in *The Log.*

The three unlucky cops find their fates written in lead. Dixon goes heatedly into a hostage situation, kills both kidnapper and kidnappee, and is thrown in jail. Jerry confronts some rascals making trouble in a teashop and accidentally blows one's brains out. The punky cop is forced to visit the morgue and confront the deceased's family, who seem less upset than he is; they knew that this guy would come to a bad end. Jerry is saddened by the pain of death and seems to mature overnight, his streetwise glamor tarnished by remorse.

As for Gump, he is the nonaligned, the negotiator, the guy who brings warring factions together and makes everyone get along. It never occurred to him that his workaholic tendencies would drive his wife to seek comfort from another (his supervisor, Koo). The horns of the cuckold bore holes in his brain and he is flayed by jealousy. Something has snapped, and he invades the senior officers' traditional New Year's Eve celebration—the rear-echelon types decked out in ice-cream suits and performing silly duck-kissing rites—with red thoughts and a .38 snub in his pudgy hand. Though his wife still loves him, though his

Three unlucky cops in *The Log*

Entertainment Power Ltd.

son wants to be a cop, though he's played by the book all through his undistinguished/unblemished career, Gump is the unluckiest policeman of all.

TEN BEST MOMENTS OF *GOO WAT JAI*

Goo *what*?! Translating this term from Cantonese is inappropriate, as this phenomenon is an only-in-HK thing. You could call them "triad kids," but that's just not descriptive enough.

The *goo wat jai* genre originated in a series of comic books heavily influenced by Japanese *manga*: stylized dramas in which steroid-muscled tattooed opponents violently vie for (1) power and (2) impossibly cantilevered molls. These comic fantasies play well among the disaffected urban bumpkins who shake down street vendors and peddle bootleg software in Hong Kong's densely populated environs. The Cantonese phrase *goo wat jai* is best compared to a Japanese term for their *yakuza* equivalents: *chimpira* (little pricks).

Why are these films popular? Blame it on Cantopop—the bland pop tones so prevalent throughout southern China. With no defined musical alternatives, GWJ films have become the louder/harder/faster anthem for Hong Kong's disaffected youth. Not coincidentally, their soundtracks bristle with hard-edged tunes.

The seminal GWJ film is Andrew Lau's *Young and Dangerous* (1995).

Comic-book meatboys with tats and cigs

Fei Leung Comics

Mister Y&D himself is a pop singer originally known as Noodle Cheng, now known as Ekin Cheng (he was Dior Cheng for a while). Cheng sports a big fake dragon tattoo and plays a teen triad leader whose adventures form the core of each Y&D film.

The GWJ shenanigans have raised concern from sociologists about the glorification of gangster lifestyles presented to Hong Kong's impressionable youth. Things came to a monstrous head in early 1999 when a group of youths received lengthy prison sentences for the execution of a fellow teen. The vic-

tim had been first tortured, then dispatched, in a manner depicted in the GWJ comic *Teddy Boy*. It was not a nice way to go. Such incidents are rare, but the comics are popular.

GWJ protocol dictates lots of melodramatic double-crossing and perilous romance. Macho posturing, scowls, and disdain for social norms prevail. The male-bonding quotient is that of a sports bar. The look-and-feel is pop-metal: hair worn long or cropped and colored, black leather or skimpy minis, cigarettes, and preening. A staple of these films is the cleaver melee, where combatants flail furiously en masse, chopping their opponents with the machete-like cleavers known as choppers or beef knives. The myriad Y&D sequels and spin-offs have exploited these elements to the extreme.

One of the more interesting sidelights to these films is the inventive use of curses and insults—alas, few survive the translation from the original Cantonese. The context of these films also fails to travel well; just as viewers in Asia are confused by the urban Americanisms of gangsta films like *Boyz N the Hood*, so too are Western viewers puzzled by the patchwork quilt of HK concrete squalor, bad education, and triad tra-

ditions displayed in the *GWJ* films. As spectacle, these films have their adherents, though few over the age of 15 are going to glean any heroic vibes.

Here's a series of *GWJ* moments to cherish:

10. Billy Tang's *Sexy and Dangerous* (1996) refreshingly transposes *goo wat jai* to *goo wat lui* (triad girls). The gang is led by tuff chick Marble (Loletta Lee) and butane-snorting butt-kicking moppet Van (Karen Mok), stylin' from her pixie haircut to her big goofy Doc Martens, as first lieutenant. Marble has eyes for long-

haired pretty-boy Brother One (Michael Tong), but is also desired by loser George (Francis Ng at his dopiest), who advertises his low triad rank of "49 Boy" by wearing a T-shirt with the number emblazoned on it. Marble's smooth and glamorous underworld life is complicated by the homicidal Lurcher (Ben Ng) and his partner in hatred and revenge, Aids (Lily Chung—yes, the name of the character is Aids). Lurcher and Aids don't like . . . anybody.

A furious girlie fight erupts when Aids and a bunch of her murderous followers invade a sauna. Van, nursing a hangover, is marinating her spiraling snake tattoo in a gigantic hot tub as towel-wrapped cuties display their tats for the camera. Choppers unpeel. Van comes whirling out of the tub and assaults them with the blade she'd been hiding under the water. She kicks a bar of soap under the foot of one, slices the others, and goes off to help Marble struggle with Aids.

9. Roy Cheung's edgy performance as Brother Crow in *Young and Dangerous 3*. He's just weird

The girls take the reins in *Sexy and Dangerous*.

Mei Ah

enough to remind you of people you know, but let's hope you don't know anybody quite this homicidal. Cheung has been at this a long time—check him as Brother Smart in Ringo Lam's 1988 *School on Fire.*

8. *Street of Fury* is a violent *GWJ* drama made, like most of 'em, in 1996. Hot-head Hu (Michael Tse), the teen terror of Kowloon's grimy Kam Tin district, is on the outs with his cutie-pie girlfriend Yi (Gigi Lai). She gives him the air and takes up with less-pleasant triad dude Brother Beast (Ben Lam). In one scene, Hu and Yi both visit separate fortune-tellers in Temple Street, spinning their tales of romantic woe. Then they start shouting at each other over the heads of the startled soothsayers. Hu comes over so he can shout at Yi more effectively. Then, obviously still caring for one another, Yi offers Hu the timeless advice every pouty gangster-toy moppet gives to every young punk hell-bent on wiseguy apocalypse: "Hu, forget it, even if I part with Beast, we can't get on together again." Awwww.

7. The first *Y&D* introduced Spenser Lam, a fiftyish ex-soccer announcer, as a priest. As the gang hangs out in a local coffee shop, he tries to convince them that Jesus' biblical actions prove he's the ultimate "big brother" and they should follow him rather than earthly mobsters. Chicken (Jordan Chan), whose hair color changes from scene to scene, is contemptuous. The attempted conversion is interrupted by the arrival of Chicken's father-in-law, an imposing triad boss played by Wang Lung-wei, and Chicken goes chicken. Bull-necked and gold-chained, the veteran Shaw Brothers actor looks better than ever: Wang Lung-wei, the Harvey Keitel of Hong Kong. Why all the SAR's Tarantino-and-Ferrara equivalents don't use him more is a mystery.

6. Shuk Fan (Karen Mok) gets a teaching job in *Y&D 4*—she's not really a triad, just kind of triad-friendly and fond of Chicken (Jordan Chan). But she gets thrown straight into Band 5, the lowest-ranked students in the HK school system and thus the best candidates for triad recruitment. As one of Shuk Fan's students points out: "We are the sacrificed ones under the HK existing education system. We are the trash, rubbish, dirts." Much as in real life, they are also big fans of *GWJ.*

5. Jordan Chan's tribal neck tattoo in Herman Yau's *War of the Underworld* (1996). Any Mongkok kid wild enough to sport something like this would likely be kicked out of the gang.

4. A couple of interesting *GWJ* films are *Once upon a Time in Triad Society* (*OUATITS*, pronounce it as you like) and its sort-of sequel: *OUATITS 2.* The films star Francis Ng and have an odd appealing quality—Ng's triad middle manager is the polar opposite of sexy pop star Ekin Cheng.

OUATITS 2 features a big gang showdown, which is set up to allow the youths to breathe hard and go home talking tough, but gets touched off by accident and turns into sad and scary carnage. One furious moment is triumphant—Roy Cheung as Dinosaur, chopper in hand, spin-kicks his way into the *lobby* of the Newport cinema on Jordan Road. The spacious and open lobby of the cinema serves briefly as cinematic triad-punk-warfare arena as Dinosaur chops at his enemies under a poster from fellow *GWJ* film *War of the Underworld*. Art imitates life, and life chops art.

3. 1997's *Y&D 4* took advantage of the "democracy debates" of the handover year by staging an absurd debate between the two candidates for the branch leader of Tuen Mun. With all members of the Hung Hing triad seated in Tuen Mun Town Hall listening attentively, Chicken and Barbarian (each with his own microphone and podium) start dissing each other's credentials. "Barbarian, since the death of your boss Dinosaur, Tuen Mun has become a mess," accuses Chicken. This gangster-sponsored exercise in democracy is terminated by a big gang fight.

2. Denied Ekin Cheng, director Billy Tang populates his *GWJ* films with interesting characters and a paucity of metal/cleaver "rhetoric." *Street Angels* (1996) revolves around Tung Yen (Chingmy Yau), a street-tough lady bound to wiseguy beau Walkie Pi (Simon Yam).

Supporting characters include ravishing Valerie Chow as Tung's nemesis Karen—Canadian-born Chow became a Revlon covergirl under the name Rachel Shane. Elvis Tsui chews some scenery as lustful Brother Moro and Maria Cordero (HK's best female singer: a powerful Filipina diva) belts out a Cantotune live.

But *SA*'s most intriguing character is Ming Ming—Shu Qi, in one of her earlier film roles. Shu plays a cheerful teenage hooker Tung recruited from a sleazy Mongkok brothel. Her performance is delightful—in her inaugural scene, she greets a morbidly obese patron with a cheery "Hey Fatty, can you see your dick while pissing?" and complains of repetitive-stress-injury symptoms from giving too many handjobs.

Walkie Pi betrays Tung, so good-hearted Ming Ming duplicitously dolls up in a *kimono* to serve him dinner in a private room at a Japanese restaurant. She flatters his male ego and drops the *kimono*. Walkie strips off his gaudy gangster garb, showing marvelous fake dragon/tiger tattoos. "Don't you fear I'll melt you?" he asks, and sniffs at her

neck like an animal.

The resultant scene is a skillful blend of passion and danger, and when Walkie has Ming Ming up against the wall all sweaty and pink, she whips out the killing spike hidden in the hairpin. He nonchalantly pinions her homicidal hand, finishes, grins triumphantly, tosses her around not very nicely, then grabs a delicate Japanese pottery bowl filled with super-hot green *wasabi* paste. Walkie Pi is not a nice guy.

1. *Y&D 3* introduces Karen Mok's character Shuk Fan by having her slide under Chicken's car while she's rollerblading in Causeway Bay. He steps out to see if she's OK, and she pops up spewing blasphemous curses in a spotless, dead-sexy British accent (that's Mok's real voice, by the way). Then, in mid-curse, she switches to Cantonese, delighting the boys. Chicken draws himself up and gets in her face with a vile Cantorhyme as Pou Pee (Jerry Lamb) gesticulates in mime behind him. Shuk Fan retorts not. She knees him in the crotch, then head-butts him. He goes down and she blades off blasé as his cohorts let rip a hearty cheer.

神腿鐵扇功
SNUFF-BOTTLE CONNECTION

Peking opera flexibility assists greatly when attempting the Tonsil Thunder Kick.
Seasonal Films

SO. YOU THINK YOUR KUNG FU'S . . . PRETTY GOOD. BUT STILL. YOU'RE GOING TO DIE TODAY. AH HA HA HA. AH HA HA HA HA HA.

Shaolin masters of savage, violent death. Flying pigtails, acrobatic fighting, punches and kicks that sound like bashed rotten cabbages. Badly . . . dubbed dialogue with odd pauses. These cinematic images of Chinese martial arts and kung fu Iron Fisted their way into 1970s' pop culture.

These films are electric versions of martial arts tales that have been told and retold for centuries. Scholar John Minford, in the foreword to his translation of Louis Cha's *The Deer and the Cauldron*, summed things up:

> Bruce and Jackie are just the tip of the iceberg. Their films are only a tiny fraction of the vast kung fu film industry, and that industry itself is only one of the most recent growths of a much older tradition of Chinese storytelling that goes back well over a thousand years. Since at least the tenth century crowds have gathered in Chinese teahouses, marketplaces, and parks, to hear stories told of the great heroes of their past, often to the accompaniment of a drum and a musical instrument.

Louis Cha (also known as Jin Yong) is a modern-day novelist who writes epic martial arts novels. His books have served as blueprints for many Hong Kong films, including *Swordsman II* (1992) and Jeff Lau's *The Eagle Shooting Heroes* and Wong Kar-wai's *Ashes of Time* (both 1994), among others. Cha's popularity attests to the staying power of martial arts as a creative force. It is no less important as a film genre—before HK films came into vogue in the 1990s, most nonnative fans of the movies were martial arts students attracted by the stances on display.

But still . . .

Photograph courtesy
Media Asia. Copyright
Star Television Filmed
Entertainment.

Some of the earliest films from HK or Shanghai were simple dramas with martial interludes, and the first HK film star was Kwan Tak-hing, a martial artist whose portrayal of legendary *sifu* Wong Fei-hong spanned 99 films from 1949 to 1970 (yes, that's 99 feature films). The exploits of Wong, a Chinese hero comparable to Western legends like Wyatt Earp, continued in the 1980s with Lau Kar-leung and in the 1990s with Tsui Hark's *Once upon a Time in China* films (see Chapter 9).

But what of kung fu flicks in the Western film markets of the 1970s? Kung fu punched its way into American pop consciousness with a film from HK's Shaw Brothers studio (more about them later) called *King Boxer*, but retitled *Five Fingers of Death* for the Led-Zep-on-the-8-track drive-in-movie crowd of 1973. The plot of FFOD was none too taxing—nerd gets oppressed by bad guys, learns deadly kung fu skills, comes back and puts them in the hurt locker—but the fanciful fisticuffs, killer kicks, and jumping-to-the-rafters thrilled and impressed audiences. A hilarious sidelight was the dub-

Martial arts is a broad category that encompasses traditional Chinese performing arts as well as the pugilistic stuff. Singing, dancing, punching—all revolve around timing. It's no coincidence that many of HK's action heroines like Michelle Yeoh, Cynthia Khan, and Moon Lee were ballet-trained prior to stepping in front of the camera, and many action heroes had Peking opera or acrobatic training.

bing: inane dialogue, ridiculous music, and thwack-a-sonic sound effects. "How could anything so coolly violent have such a doofus soundtrack?" thought the guys lounging in their hood-scoop funny cars and Buick Electra 225s with their dates, slugging down Boone's Farm wine, and honking their horns at every skewering and butt-kicking.

FFOD ignited the kung fu craze in America, predating the usual landmarks: *Kung Fu* the TV series, Carl Douglas's Top 40 hit "Kung Fu Fighting," and everybody's main man: Bruce Lee (see "Little Dragon," page 89). An enormous amount of wild kung fu product continues to be popular in with-it video shops and in the collections of people who like to stay up all night watching *The Clones of Bruce Lee* or *Wolf Devil Woman*.

The grindhouses of urban America— faded movie palaces found in districts like New York's 42nd Street ("The Deuce") and San Francisco's Market Street—pumped out triple-bills of badly dubbed chopsocky to mobs of urban denizens. As far as the grindhouse faithful (an audience raised on ghoulies, roughies, and kinkies) was concerned, the over-the-top hyperaction and maniacal bloodletting of the kung fu flicks were sheer delight. Their concern was not the flawless execution of a Wing Chun form but the number of wings broken and legs splintered.

Kung fu films were notorious for killing people in particularly hideous and novel ways. This was part of the thrill, of course, and made them a natural inclusion on a grindhouse triple-bill—sandwiched between a head-busting Italian zombie film and a blaxploitation wonder where *wicka-wicka* guitar punctuated shootouts between leather-clad urban warriors topped by beachball-sized afros.

The grindhouses featured sticky rivers of spilled soda pop embedded with flattened nuggets of popcorn, the noise of cassette-blasters mingled with the shouts of patrons threatening death for the blaster-owners, the aroma of noxious weeds consecrated by fire to the god of stupefaction, drunken patrons yelling wisecracks at the screen or muttering or snoring, aisles filled with salesmen murmuring "Smoke, smoke, smoke" and guys in wheelchairs rolling up and down and yelling: "Tony! *Tony!* Where the hell you at, Tony?" It was a glorious time.

Urban audiences appreciated kung fu in their own (frequently quite vocal) way. In London, kung fu films would show at the Scala, a notorious rockin' funhouse near King's Cross Station. When the combatants squared off in their fighting stances, shouts of "Shapes! Shapes!" would come from the crowd, expressing appreciation for the geometric patterns of robed bodies. An absurd leap or wire effect would be greeted with

鉅鑽風雲

演員：陳星、占基利、譚道良
導演：李作楠

GOLDEN FLARE VIDEO LTD.

Fly to the bone—Jim Kelly funks out in *The Tattoo Connection*.

Yaumatei Video

Many U.S. cities supported a thriving kung fu moviegoing population. A few cinemas on The Deuce specialized in it, dodging other grindhouse staples like mondo documentaries, soft-core porn, and zombie massacres. Actor Wesley Snipes has spoken of growing up in the Bronx and seeing guys walking around his neighborhood decked out head to foot in kung fu garb, from the black slippers to the Mandarin collars. What an image!

Nowhere in America was kung fu more warmly embraced than in the urban black moviegoing community. Black action films—popularly known as blaxploitation—often featured kung fu as a thematic element or plot spine. Black martial arts stars like Jim Kelly and Fred "The Hammer" Williamson emerged, and black-oriented action films like *Black Belt Jones*, *Way of the Black Dragon*, and TNT *Jackson* were chock a block with mythic kicks and monosyllabic yodeling. Some went so far as to include location shooting in Hong Kong; Jim Kelly brought his afro and polyester flares to the then-Crown Colony for *The Tattoo Connection* (1974). Rudy Ray Moore (America's greatest black comedian) performed a side-splitting parody of Bruce Lee's kick-yo'-ass stances and vocal excesses in *The Human Tornado* (1976).

"Lies!" but a well-executed maneuver would draw the accolade "*Wicked* lies!" Black fans would take the tube up from Brixton to join in the fun, feeling more of a kinship with the Chinese guys fighting onscreen than they might with their fellow Brits at opening day at Ascot.

Many of these films remain beloved by people nourished in the sickly blue glow of late-night television ("Kung Fu Theater presents . . .") or in the grindhouses. Jimmy Wang Yu's one-armed swordsman was a limb-challenged death machine who spawned many a sequel. The flying guillotine was also popular (this was a sort of Frisbee attached to a chain, which would transform into a head-slicing cakebox when thrown at a hapless victim). The differing styles of martial arts were the subject of much serious banter among the martial arts students. Those Bronx badasses were more interested in working Shaolin-Buick-Reverb moves into their streetfighting routines.

temple of ∫haw

Even today, decades after establishing themselves as the generation engine for the Hong Kong film industry, Shaw Brothers (SB) remains very much a closed shop. Their revered library, 800 films strong with at least a couple hundred put-ya-on-the-floor super-action disco kung fu somersaulting-wizards martial-arts-masters features, was walled

"Check it out, hurled like a sack, Jack!" scream the grindhouse faithful at scenes like this.

Photograph courtesy Media Asia. Copyright Star Television Filmed Entertainment.

CHICK FLICKS
Shaw Brothers' Kung Fu Films
BY KAREN TARAPATA

Long before Calvin Klein uncovered the marketing muscle of underdressed men, movie moguls Run Run and Runme Shaw uncovered an interesting fact: bare chests sell seats. The shirtless stars of Shaw Brothers' kung fu epics filled movie palaces around the world. Men may have come for the mayhem, but the ladies came to see the boys.

These Hong Kong chopsockies of the late 1970s and early 1980s delivered some of the most eye-blistering male beauty ever tossed on screen. Month after month, year after year, the Shaws sold prime-quality beefcake in a kaleidoscopic selection of sizes, shapes, and personalities. The boys were buff; the look was lush, colorful, and sensuous; the stories were simple

Veganza! El sangre de Alexander Fu Sheng.

Cinereal Mexico DF

variations of the classic heroes' tale of feuds, revenge, and redemption.

No other movie company got it so right. The Shaws knew how to pick them, how to dress them, and how to film them. The effect was devastating. The Shaw Studios movie machine brought female fans whole coveys of stars possessing physical beauty, martial precision, and animal energy.

Picture one of these kung fu heroes. A finely muscled torso rises from soft white harem pants. His waist is wrapped with a broad silk sash. From the waist up he's exposed iron, from the waist down . . . concealed silk.

Subtle androgyny was the key to their red-hot appeal. Chinese clothes look oddly feminine to the Western eye. An open vest cinched over a hairless

away in the mid-1980s. Most of these films have never even been transferred to video.

The vitality and longevity of the classic Shaw films far outpace most other HK output. Many fans discovered John Woo and Jackie Chan before beginning their appreciation of old masters like Chang Cheh and Lau Kar-leung. Some of these films achieved a special patina through the unique English-language dubbing they enjoyed/were subjected to (see "Ya Bastard, You Must Be Tired of Living!," page 86). The production values soared far above their meager budgets and assembly-line construction.

chest. A gold-wrapped topknot or pony-tail. A long gown flicked aside before a fight. What made these stars so enticing were the boundaries they crossed. It's light-years from the Hollywood aesthetic of more brawn and bigger guns.

The effect is pure fantasy. A death-blow delivered with a little black slipper in a fresh white sock. These boys have total animal presence, but they're clean; they don't smell. They have virtually no body hair, just impossibly thick, shiny braids to swing around their necks before they begin the carnage.

And the fights. Those unending, unrealistic fight scenes were the foreplay, main event, and afterglow of these films. Extended kung fu fights let us see these magnificent boys kicking, leaping, and rolling on the floor. Every fight leading to the final showdown leaves the hero with fewer clothes. Those fighting heroes climbed the walls, and so did the women watching.

The combination of beauty and sensual violence was sexy without sex, violent yet unthreatening. Here are a few tips:

Ten Top Shaw Throbs

1. Ti Lung
2. Alexander Fu Sheng
3. Chan Kwan-tai
4. Chi Kwan-chun
5. Lo Meng
6. Sun Chien
7. Chiang Sheng
8. Lu Feng
9. David Chiang
10. Kuo Chui

Ten to Make Your Socks Roll up and Down

1. *Five Deadly Venoms*: Five foxy fighters. The Snake's demise is worth the whole trip.
2. *Crippled Avengers*: The showdown with the rings is the one to watch.
3. *Avenging Eagle*: Ti Lung and Alexander Fu Sheng, well dressed. 'Nuff said.
4. *Heroes Two*: Fu Sheng fights for righteousness while removing his clothes.
5. *36th Chamber of Shaolin (Master Killer)*: The debut of Gordon Liu's bald head.
6. *Dirty Ho*: Long gowns flicked aside before fights.
7. *Opium and the Kung-fu Master*: Ti Lung tragic and appealing.
8. *Martial Club*: Wang Lung-wei gets to be a good guy.
9. *Five Shaolin Masters (Five Masters of Death)*: Exotic weapons and all.
10. *Water Margin (Seven Blows of the Dragon)*: Ti Lung and the boys in some of the best long-form fights.

Although Shaw Brothers is most famous for its kung fu and martial arts films, the flying-pigtail pugilism represents only a small part of its total output. Shaw Brothers was the *ne plus ultra* Hong Kong production studio for many years, and it made gambling movies and soft-core porn and big-head/dumb-ass comedies and psycho slasher films and anything that might draw in the crowds on a weekend or two and help put the rice in the bowl. More than a few of these flicks are yawners: nobody's going to bust down the doors to pick up a DVD of *Disco Bumpkins* (1979), for example.

Although the kung fu stuff was primo, the supernatural films—which combined wild acrobatic martial action and swordfights with blastin' colored lights, witches, wizards, monsters, and righteous heroes; cheeseball-synthesizer sound effects; and scratched-on visual effects—should never be overlooked.

A proper history of Shaw Brothers' hundreds of films would run several volumes. It is hoped that with the current interest in cataloging and preserving HK's movie past, the full story can someday be told.

the Master of disaster

Though the urban audience was mostly unaware of his very existence, their favorite martial arts director is the Shaw Brothers' Chang Cheh. Chang understood the dramatic potency of screen violence and employed it with abandon. As a Shaws employee, Chang directed in a variety of styles, including the odd musical. A Chang Cheh musical (like *The Singing Thief*, 1969) would start out with opulent, choreographed songs, sure, but sooner or later a bunch of guys would start battling with each other—gouging, piercing, slashing, burning, and kung fuing the poo out of one another.

Chang didn't direct many musicals. His first big-deal movie starred Jimmy Wang Yu as the *One-Armed Swordsman* (1967), a guy who got his arm chopped off and came back to chop everything off of the guys who chopped him. Then Chang and Wang made *The Golden Swallow* (1967), which is also known as *Girl with the Thunderbolt Kick*. Neither about birds nor mystic-kicking females, it's a film about blood and death and sticking sharp objects into one's opponents. But the film that stands as his best known (and, many say, his best) is 1978's *Five Deadly Venoms* (aka *Five Venoms*).

Five Deadly Venoms' intriguing characters and banging kung fu fight sequences chisel the film into the kung fu pantheon. The plot's simple: some *sifu* taught five "venom" kung fu styles to five guys. They all wore masks while training so they don't know each other—really bitchin' masks to reflect their badass kung fu names: the Snake, the Scorpion, the Centipede, the Lizard, the Toad. Each venomous fighter has a distinct fighting style—every one creepy-crawly and deadly. This seminal work established the five main characters as the "Venoms Team," and they continued to make films together until the early 1980s.

To catch a glimpse of the master, get ahold of *The Angry Guest* (1971), a kung fu thriller featuring Ti Lung and David Chiang

Five voices
shout: "Toxins
rule!"

Made in Hong Kong

killing people with bulldozers. In one scene, they go to Tokyo and are confronted with the big-cheese Japanese arch-criminal—a scary guy who pulls a Robert Burns Black Watch cigar out of its white tube, fires it up, then watches his erring flunky commit *hara-kiri*.

"Mister Yamaguchi." Chang Cheh.

"the pops"

Call him "Hong Kong's neglected master," as Brad Roberts and Karen Tarapata did in a 1985 retrospective at Minneapolis' Walker Arts Center. Call him "The Pops," as did author Bey Logan in his book *Hong Kong Action Cinema*. His real name is Lau Kar-leung, sometimes spelled Liu Chia-liang, and his work at Shaw Brothers in the 1970s and 1980s took the martial arts film in new directions.

Lau and his films are worthy of a volume of their own. Lau made films with spirit, heart, and humor. His *Shaolin Challenges Ninja* (1979) explored the dynamic love/hate relationship of China and Japan through a marriage between martial arts masters of the respective cultures. *Shaolin Challenges Ninja* (also known as *Challenge of the Ninja*) is utterly different from a Chang Cheh bloodsoaker—no one even dies in this film!

Another transcendent number is 1983's *The Lady Is the Boss*, starring Lau-discovered ingenue Hui Ying-hung (sometimes known as Kara Hui, Wai Ying-hung, or Claire Wong). As the film opens, Lau himself (who often took a starring or supporting role in his films) is brandishing a bamboo pole in front of his kung fu school as the Wong Fei-hong theme song (if you've seen the *OUATIC* films, you're humming it now) plays. He's the master of a moribund old-fashioned kung fu school that has its silk-bound dogma split open by the arrival of the founding *sifu*'s granddaughter, Miss Hui, who comes bounding into Kai Tak Airport with a Mickey Mouse T-shirt and a big plastic guitar. Before you can say "Blast of the Iron Palm," she's teaching aerobics to the bemused kung fu students and offering special promotional lessons to the hostesses at a local karaoke joint. The PR girls learn how to do the kung fu. Next thing you know, the girls are giving hard elbows to the groping customers at the nightclub, infuriating the gangster owner. Mayhem ensues.

KUNG FU OF DAMMOH STYLES

Renting kung fu videos can be tricky. Don't stagger into your local video rental shop late at night and slur, "Gimme that . . . damn kung fu," or you might end up with *Kung Fu of Dammoh Styles*.

Tung Hop Kee Films

This delightful film shows that Lau was not only capable of evolution (fight sequences incorporate nontraditional weapons like BMX bicycles, and the endfight takes place in a gymnasium where the trampolines are visible, for a change) but capable of poking fun at himself. His grumpy *sifu* character learns that he must change to survive, a lesson Lau was teaching himself at the same time. The lightness of Lau's

HEX ERRORS
A Pox on Thee!

"I promise to punch you less than before."
Give and Take . . . Oh! Shit!

"You mis-shaped my busts, beat it!"
Street Angels

"Don't think you Rats are powerful!"
Run and Kill

"Listen. Don't shit with my Big Brother.
Otherwise, I crash you penis to pieces."
To Live and Die in Tsimshatsui

"Damn you Fatty.
You are in deep shit now."
Run and Kill

"Don't snap my pork!"
A Chinese Odyssey Part 1: Pandora's Box

"I wanna kill you bastards to death!"
Walk In

"Threatening me? I'm scared to pissing!"
Vengeance Is Mine

"Try my cotton bomb."
Dragon from Shaolin

"Sharks are not breast feeding!"
Aces Go Places V: The Terracotta Hit

"Yankee pancake! Disgusting!"
An Autumn's Tale

"Fat-head, you neet your Waterloo!"
The Odd One Dies

"Slighter, you asshole."
Kidnap of Wong Chak Fai

"Your boss is quite trash!"
Final Justice

"Don't wet my gun by your urine."
Hero

"Don't hit! Don't smash!"
Big Circle Blues

"Go and snap your mother!"
Offence Storm

"You won't tell? I must beat your pubic parts."
Bodyguards of the Last Governor

"Shut your poisoned lips!"
Troublesome Night 4

"But you, you're stink."
Ghost Story "Godmother of Mongkok"

"Let him be the food of earthworms."
The Beasts

"How come there's man like you, lazy and slacken
You know nothing but ask me for money, aren't you ashamed?"
OCTB—The Floating Body

"What a coincidence! You wanted to shit & there was traffic jam!"
Legendary Couple

"Just take him as pork and chop!"
To Be No. 1

"You make a hill out of mold."
Nightmare Zone

"If I don't blow your head off, I wouldn't have a sound sleep tonight."
Casino

"Pal, both your chickens and you are illegal immigrants."
Untold Story 2

humanity was the leavening agent that made his whopping doses of straight kung fu digestible. Lau took his own lessons to heart and emerged as a survivor, codirecting what may be the last great kung fu film ever made, Jackie Chan's *Drunken Master 2* (1994). Lau, The Pops, a living legend, is the General who Jackie fights under the train in the opening reel. That guy with the fur hat and the spear and the triangular nose and that big honkin' mole. That's him.

Ironically, Lau's most remarkable film stands in sharp contrast to the levity and messages of hope embedded in so many of his films. It is 1983's *8-Diagram Pole Fighter*—retitled *Invincible Pole Fighters* for those audiences who might be confused by the need for eight diagrams in a pole-fighting technique.

The film's opening scene kills off most of the Yang family, deadly pole fighters all. One who survives (Alexander Fu Sheng as Brother Six) goes insane and returns home to scream in madness, clutching a tasseled spear as he recounts the death of his brothers. In real life, Fu was killed in an auto wreck during the filming of *8DPF*. Although the surviving cast members completed the film, Fu was a much respected longtime friend, and his death put everyone in a wretched mood.

The other surviving pole fighter, Brother Five (Gordon Liu), walks the earth in torment before arriving at a monastery. He wants to learn the monks' powerful pole-fighting techniques, but they want none of him—he's more like a mad dog than a potential Buddhist. These monks use big weird wooden wolf models for pole practice—their goal is to rip out the metal teeth of the hideous wolf dummies, which spin around as the monks whack them with their poles.

8DPF's central themes of revenge and sacrifice are explored through exuberant martial performance interspersed with unbridled cruelty. Fu was never elevated to martyr status like Bruce Lee, but he was a talented martial artist with animal-magnet charisma and a wonderful screen presence. Fu's ghost is said to haunt the Shaw Brothers studio to this day.

Little dragon

> "Live fast, die young, and leave a good-looking corpse."
> Apocryphal Hell's Angels motto

Bruce Lee's slice of the HK movie pie is wildly out of proportion to his brief career span. His death in 1973, coupled with his successes in both Hollywood and HK, elevated him to the mythic stratosphere. His popularity remains undiminished.

Is it deserved? Certainly. Lee, a supremely talented martial artist, was screen dynamite and knew it. His ascendance shifted the focus of martial arts films from the fight to the fighter.

For many fans, Lee's buff-yet-emaciated physique (sunken cheeks, veins throbbin' along his cord-tight biceps and delts) was the thriller. For others, the exhilaration of Bruce's lightning moves as he mopped the room with bad-guy sweat was the kung fu zenith. Then there were the duck calls Lee let loose as he did his thing—somewhere between a turkey gobble and a war whoop.

His signature behavior was that of reluctant hero: righteous and loathe to fight, but always kicking every ass in sight when left with no other path to justice. The scene in *Fist of Fury* (1974) where he kicks apart a signboard that reads "No Dogs or Chinese" is a classic.

Lee's athletic grace and ripped physique belie the curious fact that he was never overtly sensuous in his films. He treated each of his female costars like one of the guys—there to be rescued, not wooed. But the Bruce sex appeal boiled beneath the surface as—topless—he showed a gaggle of villains just who was alpha male. As longtime martial arts film fan Karen Tarapata put it: "In a time of talky films and sensitive heroes, Bruce was a shot of pure animal energy, rebellion with something to back it up."

Although Bruce was a star in Hong Kong movies and a guest star on TV shows from *Green Hornet* to *Ironside*, his Hollywood success came only in his last film—*Enter the Dragon*. As an expert from the Shaolin Temple, Bruce infiltrates the fortress island of the evil Han (Shek Kin), a drug dealer and babe-enslaver. In this, his last film (discounting the cobbled-together *Game of Death*), Lee transforms himself into some sort of wild Christ figure: dripping stigmata inflicted by his opponent's *Dr. No* death-claws as the camera zooms repeatedly into his contorted face, the trademark battle whoops cranked to the max. His *shtick* became so well jelled that every imitator from Bruce Lie (spelled Li/Le, etc.) to Jason Scott Lee (Hollywood biopic) knows exactly what to do.

But there was a lot more to Lee Siu-lung ("Small Dragon Lee," Bruce's Chinese name) than painted-on blood stripes in the hall of mirrors. Lee was obsessed with self-improvement and physical mastery, and the energy he put on film raised the expectations of action movie fans worldwide. According to Bey Logan's book *Hong Kong Action Cinema*, Lee's lifelong interests in Chinese heroes and fantastic weapons—rooted in his martial philosophy of *jeet kune do*—might have spurred him in the direction of more traditional kung fu films, films that were eventually made by his contemporaries in the 1970s and 1980s. The screaming face and sinewy fist icons have passed into the pop culture lexicon, and premature extinction brought him that first-

The spirit of Bruce incarnate. Half-man and half-dragon, multiarmed like a Hindu deity, he emerges from cataclysm clutching precious icons—a 1970s smiley-face, a flailing *numb-chuck*, a *feng shui* mirror, a fistful of dollars, and the severed head of his *gwailo* nemesis.

Illustration by Ross Sit

class ticket to the souvenir shop, just as it did to celeb death-mask icons like Marilyn, Elvis, James Dean, and Jimi Hendrix.

Through his fame, Bruce Lee represents the Hong Kong movie industry for many fans. But as talented as he was, as deserving of his myth as he is, Bruce Lee is not the be-all and end-all of Hong Kong's martial arts genre. There are filmmakers every bit as vital among his contemporaries and many have yet to receive their due. Directors and stars like Sammo Hung, Lau Kar-leung, the late Lam Ching-ying, the late Alexander Fu Sheng—all these guys have resumes of hard-made world-class martial arts films that will light up the viewer like a pinball machine. And the sum of their tribute should surpass the trivial pursuits of collectors bidding for Bruce Lee's credit card receipts.

As Bey Logan puts it: "I'm a Bruce Lee fan, and I carry that creative energy into other areas of my life, things like writing and producing, and express my admiration that way, which I think is true to his spirit. Creative-crazy, that's good. Fanatic-crazy, maybe not so good." Well said. Perhaps a few of the faithful need to be reminded that the original purpose of *Green Hornet* lunchboxes was not to deplete coffers, but to carry lunch. As for the Little Dragon, his wired, win-at-any-cost attitude assures that he's still trashing legions of the unrighteous. Hope those angel wings don't cramp his style.

TEN GREAT KUNG FU
MOVIES (FOR THOSE
WHO DON'T LIKE
KUNG FU)

BY BEY "TRY MY IRON HEAD"
LOGAN

Call them "period Chinese martial arts movies," "chopsockies," or "kung fu movies," reactions to this subgenre of Hong Kong action cinema run the full gamut from devotion to derision. Awareness of the films can range from a few moments of channel-surfed *Black Belt Theater* to a fond remembrance of midnight shows in the kung fu–crazy 1970s. Casual video renters might pick up the occasional Hong Kong fight flick to go with their Friday night beer and pizza, to be amused and amazed by the inept dubbing, the outrageous use of pan-and-scan, the wacky haircuts, and the over-the-over-the-top performances, while the *cognoscenti* will only accept their kung fu cinema straight—in Cantonese or Mandarin, subtitled, letter-boxed, and uncut. What was once a bona fide cult phenomenon has now entered the mainstream, with companies like U.S.-based Tai Seng and Britain's Made In Hong Kong spearheading a video campaign to bring pugilism to the people.

Despite the breadth and longevity of its appeal, the kung fu flick has enjoyed relatively little in the way of serious critical examination. Whatever the relative merits of Chinese martial arts movies as examples of world cinema, they are part of an underresearched sociological phenomenon—a genuine example of transculturalism. Where hip-hop, sneakers, and baggy-to-the-max basketball shorts are *de rigueur* for Hong Kong youth, Stateside black youth culture has adopted the Tao of the wow. Check out the huge success of the Wu Tang Clan, a group steeped as much in the politics of Ching dynasty China as they are in the lore of the ghetto.

The different martial arts styles performed in the films are now, ironically, practiced with greater accuracy and zeal by "foreigners" in Europe and the United States than they are in their native land. While Hollywood blockbusters have made serious inroads into the Asian movie market, Hong Kong martial arts action cinema is a hot item on the American cinema agenda. Many of the stars and directors featured in the following top-ten list are currently forging fresh fame for themselves in Tinseltown.

Any top-10 list will cause dissent. The list that follows effects a balance between my own tastes and those films that have had the most profound effect on the industry. None of these films should be ignored in an overview of the genre.

10. *The Magnificent Butcher.* Director Yuen Woo-ping and actor/fight choreographer Sammo Hung film the legend of Lam Sai-wing. Lam, a martial arts master depicted in many early black-and-white Wong Fei-hong films, brought WFH's Hung Kuen style to Hong Kong. For *The Magnificent Butcher*, Yuen Woo-ping retained Kwan Tak-hing as the Cantonese folk hero Wong Fei-hong. Sammo's performance as Lam Sai-wing is definitive, and *TMB* also presents several stalwarts of 1980s kung fu cinema, including Yuen Biao as one of Lam's fellow students and Lee Hon-san as Master Ko—the misguided (rather than malevolent) villain of the piece. Burly character actor Fan Mei-sheng is great fun as the film's Falstaffian drunken beggar. The script (by a young screenwriter named Wong Jing) offers little more than an excuse for the protracted training and combat

scenes, which reminds me of the pitch John Ford once gave for one of his Westerns: "No story, just characters."

9. *36th Chamber of Shaolin*. The film that demystified martial arts yet created a new myth in the process. Most earlier Hong Kong kung fu films had presented the audience with heroes who had already mastered their martial skills. In *36COS*, Gordon Liu's character is an everyman figure— a callow youth living under a brutal foreign regime. A member of the oppressed Han majority, Lau travels to the Shaolin Temple to develop the skills he needs to use might for right.

The film follows his painstaking (and painful) odyssey through the 35 existing chambers of the temple. He excels to such a degree that he is given the name San-te ("Three Virtues") and allowed to create his own thirty-sixth chamber to teach Shaolin martial arts to lay-men. Director Lau Kar-leung, the star's adoptive older brother, demonstrates genuine kung fu (the phrase translates as "skill developed after long practice") with *36COS*. The film was an urban cinema hit in the United States, where it was released as *Master Killer*. It launched the entire Shaolin cycle of movies and TV series, which continues to the present day.

6. *Warriors Two*. This may well be the first movie in history that kills off its title character halfway through. Director Sammo Hung packs the film with memorable characters, especially Leung Kar-yan ("Beardy") as Leung Jan, a *sifu* expert in Wing Chun style. Wall-to-wall martial arts action is sparked by one of Sammo's many high-kicking protégés, the wonderfully named tae kwon do exponent Casanova Wong. Leung's death scene is a power-ful last bow, and *Warriors Two* features one of the genre's most protracted—and imaginative— final-reel combat sequences.

7. *Martial Club*. A classic Shaw Brothers title, this early kung fu comedy influenced both *Drunken Master* and *Once upon a Time in China*. Gordon Liu (director Lau Kar-leung's cinematic alter ego) stars as Wong Fei-hong. During the course of the film, Wong makes the journey from a naive youth, led astray by his mischie-vous best buddy, to the noble kung fu fighter of legend. *Martial Club* features a classic one-on-one empty-hands kung fu duel between WFH and a Northern-style master played by Shaws great Wang Lung-wei. The pair fight their way down an ever-narrowing alleyway, adapting their techniques to suit the changing environment. Killer!

6. *Iron Monkey*. Donnie Yen's finest hour sees him incarnate Wong Kay-ying, father of the better-known Wong Fei-hong, in this Yuen Woo-ping–directed film. WFH is played by young Tse Man, who is (in tradition started by the black-and-white Fong Sai Yuk film series) a girl playing a boy's role. Father and "son" travel to a small and impoverished town where the corrupt local officials are being robbed of their ill-gotten gains by a Robin Hood–like Iron Monkey (Yu Rong-guang). The standout fight sequence is one in which Yen takes on a quartet of corrupt monks, before going foot to flying foot with a wicked *wushu* witch woman. The film is memorable for having as much heart as it has martial art.

5. *Dreadnaught*. Another Yuen Woo-ping/Wong Fei-hong classic that witnesses a real-life changing of the guard. *Dreadnaught* bids adieu to the great grandpappy of the genre—Kwan Tak-hing—and delivers pugilistic pup Yuen Biao. Yuen Shun-yee (the director's brother) plays a bizarre serial killer stalking a small town. An inept lawman calls in wFH for help, following a comedy of errors involving Wong's student Leung Foon (Leung Kar-yan) and a cowardly laundry boy (Yuen Biao). After tragedy strikes, Yuen Biao finds that he has both the courage and the martial arts moves to save the day.

4. *Drunken Master*. Jackie Chan's career took off with his first effort for Ng See-yuen's Seasonal Films: *Snake in the Eagle's Shadow* (1977). *SITES* was the prototype, but *Drunken Master* is the finished vehicle. This is the first *bona fide* kung fu comedy, and it remains the best. Chan stars as the young and boisterous wFH, Yuen Siu-tin (father of the film's director) as drunken master Beggar So, and Korean superkicker Wang Jang Lee as the villain. These characters participate in a blistering series of fighting sequences tied together by a tight plot structure. Huge fun from start to finish and a good introductory film for newcomers to the genre.

3. *Fist of Fury*. No salutary list of martial arts films (or combat movies of any kind) would be complete without a Bruce Lee film. *Fist of Fury* is the finest of Lee's Hong Kong productions, and the only period martial arts movie he ever made. Lee plays Chen Jun, a young martial arts master who returns to postwar Shanghai to find that his *sifu* has been murdered. Worse yet, his school—Cheng Mo Mun ("The Doorway to Excellence in Martial Arts")—is oppressed by a bullying rival Japanese karate school. Chen does something rarely seen in a kung fu film—he sets out on a bloody trail of vengeance.

Lee's on-screen persona was never more manic as in *Fist of Fury*. The Little Dragon tapped into a bitter wellspring of resentment that the Hong Kong Chinese still harbored for the foreign powers—both the nineteenth-century Brits and the twentieth-century Japanese. This was a *Braveheart* for the 1970s; it established Lee as the greatest martial arts movie star of all time.

2. *Once upon a Time in China*. Tsui Hark's masterwork was the first martial arts art-house movie—a kung fu flick that highbrow audiences could enjoy. It made a star—belatedly—out of Jet Li: patriotic hero Wong Fei-hong turned out to be the role Li was born to play. Director Tsui Hark understood that Li was as luminous while standing still as he was fluid while in motion. For

the first time, martial arts in cinema became a metaphor for the political turmoil in the world beyond. The film introduced a whole new style of fight choreography and reinvigorated the WFH legend for a whole new coterie of fans (*OUATIC 2* deserves honorable mention as the best of the sequels).

I. *The Prodigal Son*. Plot, performances, production values, and, of course, masterful movie martial artistry: director Sammo Hung brings it all back home in the world's best kung fu flick. Yuen Biao plays a young version of Leung Jan, the Wing Chun master depicted by Leung Kar-yan in *Warriors Two*. He's a spoiled rich brat who thinks he's a kung fu stud, but his father is secretly paying his opponents to lose.

An encounter with real kung fu maestro and Peking opera performer Leung Yee-tai (Lam Ching-ying at his best) forces Leung Jan to wise up. After

"Iron Head" Logan swears that *The Prodigal Son* is the single best kung fu movie ever made.

Photograph courtesy Media Asia. Copyright Star Television Filmed Entertainment

Leung Yee-tai fights a challenge match with another spoiled-rotten fist-punchin' brat named Ngai (Frankie Chan), both his life and that of Leung Jan are endangered. The unlikely pair retreat to a remote farmhouse, where Leung Jan receives hard-knock lessons from both the elegant Leung Yee-tai and his rough-and-tumble kung fu brother Wong Wah-bo (Sammo Hung).

Prodigal Son is the "traditional" kung fu movie *in excelsis*.

It contains the finest stylized one-on-one, hand-to-hand duel ever filmed: a Lam Ching-ying/Frankie Chan fight set in and around a floating restaurant. The film is packed with memorable sequences, including Ngai's spaghetti western–style showdown with the one-armed opponent he crippled in an earlier encounter, and Hung's comic calligraphy lesson. No Jackie, no Bruce, no Shaw Brothers shield, just the single best kung fu film ever made.

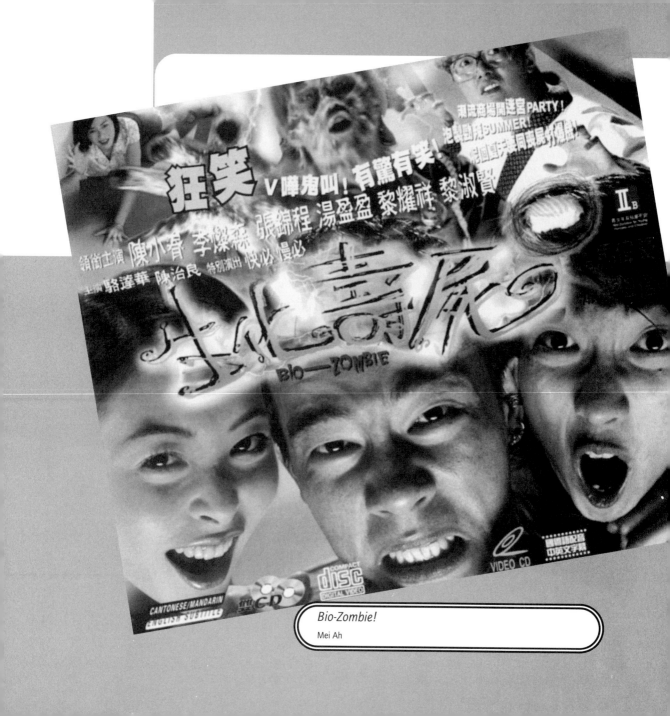

Bio-Zombie!

Mei Ah

dodge that flying witch's head

Scaring the bejabbers out of the audience has been *a priori* since the invention of the sprocket hole. Hong Kong-style spooking and howling takes full advantage of the breadth and depth of Asian ghostlore—a slithering caveful of ghoulies, gangrenous witches, and blood slurpers.

Certain horror film conventions are universal: the snarling visage lit from beneath; the malfunctioning flashlight that precedes the lightning-quick charge of the imp; the rotting monster plucking vengefully at your flesh. Other scary jolts are unique to HK: the scrumptious strumpet who morphs into a cackling buck-naked crone; the vampire in Ming dynasty silk hopping with outstretched talons, stiff as a board from *rigor mortis*, sniffing frantically for your breath as he (or she) craves a bite; the valiant yellow-robed Taoist master with an altar of idiosyncratic demon-repellers, setting paper charms afire and cutting chicken necks in the never-ending struggle against bad stinky ghosts. To jump into the ocean of HK spookflicks means battening on ghoul plankton, blood guppies, and horrorhead sharks.

What fuels this shuddering engine of oozing, green-lit goblins and succubi? Often, the selfsame fears and angst that plague fans of Western ghoulie flicks. Hong Kong horror manipulates old, familiar fears and presents some new and very different ones.

beware . . . the Chooper!

All scary stories service one basic reptilian emotion: fear of the Chooper. What the hell is a Chooper? Maverick American director Ray Dennis Steckler invented it for his film *Blood Shack*. This 1966 tale of terror, made on a budget of several hundred dollars, featured characters mortally terrified of a shadowy figure known cryptically as "The Chooper."

When the fearsome monster was revealed in the final reel, it was a skinny guy wearing a black stretch leotard with a painted-on mustache and a plastic sword. Steckler had no budget to make a monster, but he understood that the *idea* of a Chooper was what generated the fear: For any audience, the object of terror that can be conjured in their heads is far more potent than anything you can show on the screen.

Across all time, across all cultures, humankind's ghostly fears boil down to one potent goblin: the Chooper, your personalized nightmare, what you see lurking in your closet when you turn off the light, be it bogeyman, wraith, or satanic manifestation. Ancient Choopers were Verdelaks, incubi, and trolls; modern Choopers are international terrorist organizations and deadly new viruses.

beLittLiNg gHouLſ Leadſ to big troubLe

With Hong Kong's pedal-to-the-metal mix of spiritual beliefs—a brew of Confucianism,

Buddhism, Taoism, animism, and what-not—HK supernatural danger is diverse and fascinating. One thing that must constantly be averted is bad luck. Divining one's luck is a never-ending pastime in HK, where *feng shui* experts, geomancers, and shamans enjoy primal prestige and command hefty fees for their services.

Respecting the dead helps ensure good luck, which is why Hongkies burn huge amounts of ghost paper and incense for their ancestors in the afterlife. Stock market gone south? Mother-in-law besotted with avarice? Boyfriend astray? Setting fire to incense or setting out food is sure to provide insurance against such calamities, or act as a salve *ex post facto*. In the case of the food (cooked chickens, steamed buns, oranges, and pieces of roasted pork are preferred), the ghosts consume the essence and what remains can be taken from the altar and enjoyed in an earthly fashion—HK spirituality may be arcane but it is not impractical.

The troubles start when young cosmopolitan Hongkies start wisecracking and disrespecting the ancient forces of witchin' nature. Whether blockheaded vampirology students or lust-frustrated sex tourists, they invariably get the stern warning from Those Who Believe: Don't diss the dark side. They laugh it off, with predictably ballistic consequences. This is analogous to the Hollywood slasher films of the 1980s, where drinking/huffing/shagging teens were offed by an implacable maniac in direct proportion to their sinful activity.

ghost stories— three at a time

Oral traditions are strong in Hong Kong and take many forms. There's the tall tale, the dirty joke, and, of course, the ghost story. The latter form is still popular in the West; witness the "urban legend" phenomenon that has spawned books, Web pages, and a recent horror movie, *Urban Legend*. In Hong Kong, ghost-story films often take the form of triptychs, with a narrator introducing the three terrible tales.

A stern warning for uppity HK youth is an ongoing theme of the *Troublesome Night* series from director Herman Yau. The first *Troublesome Night* opens with an arching overhead shot of Simon Lui in a graveyard—Master of Ceremonies for the screaming teen faithful: "Well, do you believe in ghosts?"

TN 3 revolves around a group of people who work at a mortuary. They are an insular group, due to the traditional fear of

Another *Troublesome Night* for those who disbelieve

Mandarin Films

anything associated with death in most Chinese societies. Fennie Yuen plays the head mortician who has tremendous problems getting a date due to her profession. She meets a studly young guy named Daviv (Michael Tse) at a bar, they fall in love, and he offers to marry her. Next thing ya know, he's not returning her calls, he's being a creep, finally he blurts out that he can't stand the thought of her touching those corpses—despite his earlier protestations to the contrary. What a cad! Cliffs being in short supply in urban Hong Kong, she hurls herself off a concrete building. But if you think that's the end of this tale, you haven't seen enough HK ghost flicks: just wait until he brings a hot date over a week later, anxious to play his new "Japanese VCDs" . . . spooked outta his socks, as you may have guessed, by the green-lit ghost of the dead mortician. Ghosts *always* collect their debts.

TN 4 ratchets up the stakes by plunging a bunch of lust-crazed HK stooges into the wilds of the Philippines. Nudity is added to the mix, as Filipino audiences won't bite the ticket bullet without a bit of salacious skin. Yau twists the knife by transforming the yummy disrobing Filipinas into cackling topless, toothless grannies at random, terrifying the rest of the characters. The fifth installment in the *Troublesome Night* series premiered in the first few weeks of 1999, 20 months or so after the first *TN* film. If the

popular *Terminator* series had kept pace, we'd be seeing *Part 63: L'il Baby Terminator—The Prequel* in cinemas now.

pint-sized Nosferatu

European vampire traditions descend from a single parent: Bram Stoker's *Dracula*, a late nineteenth-century novel that introduced a character of gothic menace who still transfixes imaginations. The creature was part dashing nobleman, part blood-draining ghoul, and was inspired by a fifteenth-century Wallachian despot—Vlad Tepes—with a penchant for impaling people on not especially sharp wooden stakes. Western vampire dress, customs, and antidotes are known to all, mostly from the dozens of films featuring such blood swallowers.

The origins of Chinese vampire legends are murkier. One useful cinematic convention is the "*sifu*'s explanation": early on in most of these films, the wise one will explain, for the audience's benefit, just why the sticky rice and inked string are so important in dealing with hopping corpses.

Mr. Vampire III (1987)
Vampire films ruled Hong Kong in the mid-1980s, and the *Mr. Vampire* series was the most beloved of them all. The MV films featured Lam Ching-ying as the wise, white-

eyebrowed *sifu* and various actors as his oafish assistants. *Mv 3* is the best of the sequels, but once this film had exhausted its cinematic run, the only way to see it was on unsubtitled pan-and-scan videotape, a sorry state of affairs. But now the film is available on letterboxed, subtitled VCD—and, soon, DVD as well. As mentioned elsewhere, one of the delights of being a current Hong Kong movie fan is rediscovering previous efforts in new and pristine form. And out of the dozens of Chinese vampire films cranked out in the mid- to late 1980s, this particular one proves exemplary.

In the Ricky Lau–directed *MV 3*, Sammo Hung produces and stays behind the camera except for a brief cameo. Lam Ching-ying reprises his role as the *sifu*, an omnipotent and wise wizard who uses his Taoist techniques to vanquish evil and to help his fellow humans tread the righteous path. The film begins with a freelance Taoist named Ming (Richard Ng) trying to earn a few *taels* by ridding a rich man's house of some noxious poltergeists. Ming is a charlatan, employing

a pair of friendly vampires as subcontractors: adult Ta Pao and his kid brother Hsi Pao. The ghouls are sucked up into umbrellas (a typical stunt) and Ming is paid, but then the *real* poltergeists show up on a carpet of blue-lit dry-ice fog. The idiot rich guy built his house above their family grave, and its weight is pressing on the ghosts. A pitched battle ensues, and Ta Pao saves the day by extending his arms out several

Lam Ching-ying (center)— forever on our side

Photograph courtesy Media Asia. Copyright Star Television Filmed Entertainment.

TOP 10 LOBBY-CARD INDICATORS OF A RIPPING-GOOD HK SUPERNATURAL FILM

This lobby card indicates that it's time to grab a bag of pork buns and scoot into the cinema.

Kwong Yuen Shing Films

10. Ghost mahjong. If you are invited to play mahjong and all your fellow players are dead blue ghosts, resolve to burn more incense next chance you get.

9. Green-lit actors. This is your green light to scoot into the cinema.

8. English titles with "Curse," "Witch," or "Demon." Oddly, "Ghost" is not the best indicator, even if potentiated with "Erotic."

7. Lam Ching-ying. This actor, usually with bushy eyebrows and a mustache, and dressed in yellow Taoist robes, was Ghostbuster Numero Uno in HK films. Often paired with bumbling assistants who would do stuff like steal his urine to fight ghouls, Lam always knew exactly what to do: when to trap the fiend in an umbrella, how to hurl the sticky rice, which Chinese character to scrawl in chicken blood, etc., etc. Sadly, the past tense applies to Lam, who shuffled off this mortal coil in 1997, to battle his nemeses on their home turf. RIP.

6. Weird eyebrows. Big bushy ones at weird angles indicate serious witchery.

5. Helena Lo. Better known by her Cantonese name—Lo Lan—this wonderful actress has experienced a renaissance in the ghost films of the 1990s. She may look like someone's kindly auntie, but this 60-something actress can wield a French blade with the best of 'em. Green-lit from beneath, she'd spook Casper himself.

4. Titles in green. And they drip too.

3. Disembodied witch heads in flight. Don't worry; they're completely harmless.

2. Stuff exploding. Better yet, monsters exploding.

1. Comely female ghostresses. We're not talking sappy Demi Moore with a bowl haircut here.

Helena Lo in attack mode

Mei Ah

VAMPIRE BUSTER

Looks like it's time to call the *Vampire Buster*.

Shun Loong (HK) Co. Ltd.

meters (*Nightmare on Elm Street*–style) to throttle the bad ghosts. The grateful Ming burns a pair of baby-blue shiny-vinyl robes for his pet vamps to replace their standard Ming dynasty vampdrag. The relationship between these dead-yet-cute ghouls and their human master is a tender one.

But then Ming is grabbed by a group of brigands led by Captain Chiang (Billy Lau) who are convinced he is one of a band of horse thieves. Chiang is about to cleave Ming's skull when *Sifu* (Lam Ching Ying, the ultimate ghostbuster, the guy who was duking it out with headless witches when you were in diapers) shows up and saves Ming's Taoist ass.

The horse thieves appear, and they are far worse than *Sifu* and his Chiang-led gang had imagined. Not only are they unkillable save by miraculous Taoist sword techniques, but they are led by a shrieking demon girl whose dizzying array of black magic attacks includes burping up magical maggots that can heal gaping neck wounds. Most combatants survive, but Chiang is perplexed by the cabalistic nature of the horse rustlers. *Sifu*: "They sleep outdoors and drink blood/They eat venom and drink dew." Chiang: "They are no ordinary people." There you have it.

Ming is irked by Chiang and commands his blue-clad vampires to humiliatingly possess the captain and make him do stunts in a restaurant. *Sifu* figures out the game and sucks Ta Pao into a large clay pot, seal-ing it with a yellow-and-red Taoist charm. He then folds the child vampire over his knee like a tent and stuffs the ghoulish tyke into the pot. The dual-ghoul pot is stored in *Sifu*'s storehouse of bottled-up demons, but Ming sneaks in and absconds with it, only to be confronted by *Sifu* and Chiang.

Sifu wants to know if Ming's manipulation of these vampires has made his life easier or harder; Ming admits that his chicanery has made everything tougher. The clay pot is returned: "You decide yourself." *Sifu* knows that Ming is deep-down righteous and will do the right thing: smash the pot and set the ghouls free. Of course, this *sifu*-bonding moment leads to just that.

But the zealous Captain Chiang has discovered that coating himself with tar renders him invisible to ghosts. He adds a barrel-like coat and conical hat, which makes him look like surrealist Alfred Jarry's Ubu character, and tries to capture Ta Pao with a magic lasso fired from a hollow gourd (Chiang's love for ghostbusting technology makes him a sort of pre-electric techno geek).

All hell breaks loose when the demon girl suddenly appears and steals the larger vampire as well as Ming's Taoist robe. She rips the head off an iguana and guzzles the blood, then bewitches both purloined garment and ghoul. Busting her way into *Sifu*'s stronghold (a classic arrangement of traditional Chinese buildings around an open courtyard), the banshee assaults with swarms of cockroaches and bats. They counter with Taoist technique and bamboo tubes filled with *Sifu*'s urine. She's pierced with a coin-sword and thrown into a well but returns. Her followers are hanged and thrown on a funeral pyre but return. They are resubdued, given the ol' Five Elements technique, then deep-fried in a gargantuan wok, but *still* return ("Bad, only medium rare!" shouts the distraught Ming). Finally, the unified Taoists and the helpful vampires combine to knock this awful demon girl into hell where she belongs. Some ghouls are pitiable and useful, and some are just pure evil. Some vampire flicks are silly fun, and some give you everything you'd want in a supernatural film. *Mv 3*, from Sammo and his late colleague Lam Ching-ying, is one of the latter.

the living dead are back, and they're ready to party

Zombies are beasts of the West, having originated in Haiti. But HK is not averse to importing the concept, as evinced in this topical juve flick, which takes place in a shopping arcade modeled on Wanchai's 298 Hennessy Road (see page 6).

Bio-Zombie (1998)
Bam! *Bio-Zombie*'s opening credits assault the viewer from frame 1. Cruddy woodcut-looking things, reminiscent of a cheaper-than-dirt Filipino zombie classic from the 1960s. Whap! Right into the glassed-in aisles of one of Hong Kong's shopping arcades, where the fluorescent-tube lighting makes everyone look bluish and pasty even if they're not a zombie. A couple of punks—Woody Invincible (Jordan Chan) and Crazy Bee (Sam Lee)—strut the arcade. They are pirate VCD peddlers and petty thieves but have ambitions to become higher-level criminals someday. When some pencil-neck nerdo comes in to complain about the lousy quality of their pirated product, they yell at him ("If you want to see clearly, go to the theater!"), threaten him with a plastic computer-game pistol, donate a couple of porno discs, and send him packing. These guys are smooth.

Woody Invincible and Crazy Bee, a pair of tweaked twerps nurtured in the glow of videogames, children of the electric-speed McLuhan generation, spineless tough-talking goobers, find themselves the Alpha and Omega of the known universe through a series of bizarre and horrific circumstances. While driving their triad boss's car back to the arcade, they run over a passerby. They pour some Lucozade (a soft drink) down his throat. But the innocent-looking bottle actually contains a secret Iraqi serum that turns people into hideous rotting flesh-eating bio-zombies. Thus the title.

"My wife is human, how come she's a rabbit?"

Erotic Ghost Story—Perfect Match

"Do you think you can become fairies? Damn you demons!"

The Demon's Baby

"You're splitting, doesn't it hurt?"

666: Satan Returns

"Does it suck blood, like the foreign ones?"

The Musical Vampire

"I don't know whether I can beat Against-nature Boy hollow."

The Tantana

"I've lost every cent gambling here in the underworld!"

The Occupant

"I must let you try heaven tortures."

Erotic Ghost Story—Perfect Match

"Now, I'd like to open your mysterious 8 sinus."

Top Bet

"Don't be afraid. Tie up that monster and it'll be allright."

The Imp

"This is called 'Fairy carrying sword,' it's appetite."

The Log

"Don't panic, invite Monk Mo-chunk here."

The Demon's Baby

"Is there telephone in hell?"
"No, they transmit with frequency wave."

Haunted Mansion

"You bastard, you want to have fun, don't you?
You said you saw a girl in nude, and you said you saw ghost. . . .
Well, tonight, I'm sure a group of female ghosts will chain rape you."

Troublesome Night

"Crazy, this is corpse!"

The Beasts

"Crazy Corpse, kill them for me!"

Ten Brothers

They dump the guy in the trunk and drive to the mall. Needless to say, he busts out and starts biting people. And when you're bitten by a zombie, what happens? And to neutralize a zombie, you shoot them where? *You* know, because you've seen living-dead flicks in grindhouses where all the kids yell "in the *head*!" Crazy Bee doesn't know what a grindhouse is, but he's played the appropriate video game. He tells the cops where to shoot. But the zombies rip teethfirst into the spurtin' cops anyway. You can see where this is heading.

The grafting of the zombie film onto a triad-punk drama is aided by the use of inexpensively blurred and processed "zombie vision." Incidents of sloppy sentimentality produce lapses between attacks of the undead and gory live-action videogame fun. But a stream of zombie-film staples—the tough bastard who goes jelly-nellie, the emotional torment of waiting for bitten pals to turn zomb, the crucial handcuff keys falling into the insensible ghoul's mouth— ensure that the stream of entertainment continues to flow in great red gouts throughout *Bio-Zombie*.

ʃhamanʃ and ʃex

Southeast Asia—especially Thailand, Indonesia, and the Philippines—has a close relationship with Hong Kong. Close by, cheap, and spacious, these countries are natural destinations for business or pleasure. Every Southeast Asian capital has its Chinatown and Chinese restaurants, and Hong Kong movies are usually on offer as well.

But of course, Southeast Asia is wild and unruly—filled with odd superstitions, bag-shanties, opium dens, and people not from Hong Kong. As a result, the entire region is a great source of filmic tension, and Hong Kong characters visiting Southeast Asia can expect trouble.

The Eternal Evil of Asia (1995)
Bon (Chan Ka-bong) is passionately attached to his lovely fiancee May (Ellen Chan), but when his three buddies crave a laddish odyssey . . . what are ya gonna do? The quartet of Hongkies set off for Thailand primed for (what else?) illicit sex with perky nubiles. They pile into a taxi headed for a mythical neon-lit sex bar located somewhere in the middle of Thai nowhere, making condom jokes along the way.

The joint is writhing with friendly working gals, but suddenly one comes lurching at them from a back room screaming, "I have AIDS!" The idiots panic and rush out toward the taxi driver, who is of course not their friend but rather allied with the stream of chopper-wielding goons pouring out of the bar in hot pursuit. Our heroes run into the forest to escape and take shelter in a nearby hut, the residence of a sorcerer named Laimi (Ben Ng).

The wizard is not pleased, as he's busy preparing for a duel with a rival sorcerer couple. Besides, his uninvited guests are smartin' off. He warns them ("In Thailand, a wizard won't use enchantment as a joke"), and when Kong (Elvis Tsui) calls him a "dickhead," the exasperated shaman transforms the frustrated sex-tourist into a literal dickhead. His pals split their sides at Kong's new "German helmet," but there's no time for frivolity, as sorcerer couple Barran and Chusie show up and immediately square off. Green explosions fill the darkened skies of rural Thailand as the witchy couple supernaturally flies through the air gettin' after it doggy-style to prime the ju ju, then wrap Laimi in a monstrous green-and-gooey witch-born placenta.

Bon saves the day by impulsively dousing Laimi's opponents with enchanted powder. The grateful wizard introduces his minxotic kid sister Shui-Mei. She develops a girlish crush on Bon and persuades big brother to cook up a love hex. But the preternatural love-bomb misfires and bewitches his three stoogelike comrades instead. When Shui-Mei emerges from her daze to realize the naked unpleasantness of the results, she goes ballistic and falls on a 10-inch fruit knife. Dadgum it.

The numbskulls return to HK to escape the wrath of the Thai shaman, a ploy which fails miserably. Nam is possessed, annihilates his family and the nosy neighbors with a cleaver, then hurls himself out the window and is impaled on fluorescent light tubes. He returns, *American Werewolf in London*–style, to dispense advice and scare the hell out of his surviving chums, while the jagged tubes protruding from his bloody torso blink on and off. Kent is afflicted with hideous voracity while noshing at a restaurant with his girlfriend, eats his spaghetti, eats his girlfriend's spaghetti, orders Mediterranean fried rice with vegetables, chews off portions of his fellow patrons, then devours his own left arm.

Kong seeks the help of a local Taoist but is tricked by the wizard and given a "pin hex" which transforms him into the HK version of Pinhead from Clive Barker's *Hellraiser* films. The shaman holds Bon in spiritual bondage and demands that May satisfy his revenge-inspired lust. Laimi

"Once you are enchanted, you will suffer much!" Hong Kong's answer to *Hellraiser*'s Pinhead (Elvis Tsui) looks for a sweet spot to grab on unsuspecting May (Ellen Chan).

Mei Ah

pours the blood of seven people over his naked body and astrally projects into May's boudoir, setting up a scenario of mythic over-the-top sex between them—with only one visible at a time. Sleazed-out sax music puffs the soundtrack as May wraps her pouting lips around . . . nothing, succulently serenading a rigid shaft of air and expanding the boundaries of thespian credulity in the process. Moral: If you're a native Hong Konger, stay the hell out of Southeast Asia.

The man
Starlight Entertainment

7

the chan canon

When it comes to the subject of Jackie Chan, exactly what more needs be said? The guy is no longer the biggest-star-in-Asia/unknown-in-the-West anomaly he once was. Jackie Chan is now On The Map, and few are more deserving.

Jackie's dedication to the craft and the hard, hard work that he has put in constructing his resume are justifiably legendary. This is an entertainer who has spent two decades literally putting his neck on the line for our entertainment. He is precise yet fortunate, and his fortune seems to lie in the few centimeters that have consistently separated him from injury or death (on *Armour of God* [1986], Chan almost bought the farm when he fell during a jump and was brained by a rock).

Jackie Chan is the most famous living Chinese person in the world. He has torn an attention-getting hole in the box-office fabric of Hollywood. He spearheads the entertainment wave coming out of Hong Kong, and he does it all with grace and goodwill.

His recent Hollywood success has injected Jackie into the mainstream layer of the PopCult Mediasphere. But he hasn't abandoned Hong Kong. Despite the success of films like *Rush Hour* (1998), Jackie continues to contribute his annual Chinese New Year film for Asian audiences, including 1998's *Who Am I?* and 1999's *Gorgeous*. Chan is very active in HK, assisting other filmmakers and his stuntman association.

Certain facets of the Chan Canon have assumed mythological proportions on the order of Zeus's ascension to Mount Olympus. The Jackie mantras ("He does all his own stunts/*om mani padme hum*/ Bruce kicked high, Jackie kicked low/*om mani padme hum*") have been repeated in

THE SEVEN LITTLE FORTUNES

Peking opera–style acrobatics and choreography formed the basis of training at HK's Peking Opera Research Institute, run by *Sifu* Yuen. A performing troupe of seven cute tumbling and flipping kids from the school became known as the Seven Little Fortunes. They would later become some of Hong Kong cinema's key figures: Yuen Biao, Yuen Wah, Sammo Hung, and Jackie Chan. Behind-the-camera Yuens include Corey Yuen and Yuen Woo-ping (see "The Afterburner," page 149).

The prevalence of the name Yuen throughout the ranks of Hong Kong directors and action directors stems from a Peking Opera Research Institute tradition by which students would adopt the name of Master Yuen as their own. Their subsequent film industry success can roughly be compared to that of former vaudevillians like Jimmy Durante, Bob Hope, and Buster Keaton who transported their stagecraft to early American silent films and talkies.

The world *loves* this guy.

Ikebukuro Bungei-za

every sheaf of verbiage, every press kit, every Pay-Per-View teaser. You know now. And you know about the Mountain Dew commercials, the MTV Lifetime Achievement Award in 1995, all that stuff. These salient facts have been repeated so often that one would think they define Jackie. But they do not.

Here's part of what you need to know about Jackie: This guy came from a back-

Jackie lends a vein to the Hong Kong Red Cross.

ground of stuntmen performing martial arts and Peking opera–styled acrobatics (see "The Seven Little Fortunes," page 110). After achieving Asian fame through straightforward kung fu movies, he went to Hollywood in the early 1980s and cranked out some forgettable stuff before returning to Hong Kong. Chan's *Police Story* (1985) is one of the seminal Hong Kong films, redefining him and the industry at one go. In the mid- to late 1980s, Jackie Chan produced, directed, and starred in a multitude of films that remain transcendent masterpieces of stunts, physical comedy, and derring-do, often costarring his Peking opera schoolmates Yuen Biao, Yuen Wah, and Sammo Hung. Inspirations include silent-film-era greats like Harold Lloyd, Buster Keaton, and Charlie Chaplin.

Here's what else you need to know about Jackie: There is nothing like being a single cell in the sprawling organism that is the audience at a Jackie Chan cinema offering. Hallucinatory epiphanies come rolling to the front of the brain as the audience groans, screams, laughs, cheers. And 100 years from now, when cinemas will have been knocked into dust to make room for mile-high shopping malls and people's five-second attention spans will be wired directly into the bazillion-channel cyber-TV-universe, Jackie will be more than a footnote to the twentieth-century chop-socky craze. What the man has done onscreen has never been equaled, *can* never be equaled. Viewing these films as first runs in Chinatown theaters was a huge part of my own awakening to the power of HK film. Jackie Chan is a passionate filmmaker, and his globeful of admirers return that passion, which is as it should be.

And one more thing you should know: Jackie Chan is one of the few Hong Kong celebs who promotes worthy causes, and he picks good ones. Jackie's public service announcement for the World Wildlife Fund's Year of the Tiger campaign urged his fellow Hong Kongers to stop buying endangered tiger products. Shown on Hong Kong television at the start of the Year of the Tiger

(1998), these PSAs featured the world's most famous Chinese guy, speaking in Cantonese to other Chinese guys, humbly asking them please not to buy endangered tiger products. Cooler than *any* stunt. Even gutsier was his public personal blood donation for the Hong Kong Red Cross. Jackie may gleefully slide down a 70-foot banner, but like many of us, he doesn't much care for needles.

Jackie's career stretches long enough that it is time for retrospection, introductions having been made. The authors presented here have all written about Chan's films for a decade or more. Naturally, it's bittersweet to see Jackie, at the turn of the century, being packaged for sale to an American audience. All of us are delighted to see Jackie succeed, but we can't forget the strife of trying to proselytize in the 1980s, trying to drag y'all down to Chinatown and all that.

Here is a series of essays on the best: a core sample drilled straight through the magnificent pyramid of the Chan Canon. Many of his best efforts are now available—letterboxed and subtitled—on VCD and DVD formats. You can't go wrong with these recommendations, so invite 20 of your friends, break out the shredded squid and the Mountain Dew, pop on the DVD of *Police Story* or *Dragons Forever*, and watch them turn rigid and go mental in your living room. Chan can. Always could.

Police Story (1985)

In everyone's lifetime, there are specific instances of stimuli imprinting themselves upon the brain with napalm certainty, burrowing into conscious and subconscious simultaneously. Sometimes these are instantaneous flashbulb memories. Sometimes they are sensory-interwoven slow-burn wonders: sweat and tears commingling at the birth of a child; diesel fumes and the ping of shrapnel as the helicopter plummets; the Ramones stuffing "I Don't Wanna Walk Around with You" into your earhole, live, in 1977. Things like that.

For the first-time viewer, Hong Kong films often operate in this instant-tattoo manner. Selected films are famed as one-shot conversion experiences—flicks that render the victim rigid and activate the Hong Kong Movie region of the brain, a pea-sized gland which then begins to throb, vascularize, and demand regular feeding. Jackie Chan's *Police Story* (1985) is such a film. It doesn't matter how many action films you've seen—the last 10 minutes of this film will *put you on the damn floor*.

This ability to body-slam the audience is *Police Story*'s trademark, but the film has much else to recommend it. This was Jackie Chan's break with his kung fu and Hollywood flirtations of the 1970s and 1980s. The "police procedural," which became a mainstay of HK films around this time, owes stylistic debts to *Police Story*.

Chan's extensive involvement with the film included roles as director, star, and stunt coordinator.

The stunt where Jackie slides down a light pole crashing through glass canopies is an invariable inclusion in his Ten Stunt Commandments. Although it's a hell of a note (the lights on the pole were plugged into the wall socket and Jackie required burn treatment), and it's repeated three times in succession, it's one of several world-class stunts in *Police Story*. Early on, a pair of automobiles chase one another *through* a purpose-built squatter village, ripping corrugated tin shacks asunder and setting off explosions as they battle their way down a hillside so steep and bump-strewn that the cars frequently appear on the verge of flipping front-first. Then there's the scene where JC goes asphalt-skiing from a hijacked double-decker bus careening through traffic—the stunt ends when the bus stops abruptly in front of stock-still Jackie and two stuntmen erupt through the upper-deck windows, only to crash onto the road below. They were *supposed* to land on the specially padded car directly behind Jackie, but the bus didn't impart quite enough inertia. And then there's the phenomenal endbattle, which takes place in a shopping mall, a nonstop bacchanal of destruction and revenge that shatters so much display glazing that Jackie's stunt-people called the production "Glass Story."

Chan plays Ka Kui, a righteous cop highly desirous of busting rich pig scumbag gangster Chu-tu (Chua Lam). In the opening scene, Ka Kui and his compatriots are setting up the bust. There's no corning or mugging—these guys are professionals under pressure and things are tense and tight. As all hell breaks loose, one pisses his pants from bullet terror. The scumbag escapes, but Jackie collars his bus single-handedly and brings him in. However, the scumbag is sprung by his slick and amoral lawyer. Injustice sets up the mechanism of

Jackie finally collars the villain in *Police Story*.

Photograph courtesy Media Asia. Copyright Star Television Filmed Entertainment.

revenge, which winds Ka Kui up like a watchspring.

This film, true to its mid-1980s milieu, contains several comedic sequences—Jackie has a series of cakes jammed in his face, Jackie scrapes poop off his shoes, Jackie literally juggles four phone conversations while rolling around in a chair. But its central theme of revenge against the corrupt forces of HK society is as raw today as it was 15 years ago. When Jackie finally detonates in the last reel, your fists will clench too.

Dragons Forever (1987)

by Chuck Stephens

The name of that saber-toothed sage of yore escapes me just now, but his message, simple and profound, is seared forever upon my brain: "Sometimes," the master explains, fiddling with his stogie, "a cigar is just a cigar."

His words hover and waft, gray and ethereal, before thinning into wisps. Darkness returns.

Then, striking a safety match across the forehead of a waiter who looks suspiciously like Sammo Hung, the master—grinning Cheshire—reappears. Gazing out across the flotsam-dotted slosh of Victoria Bay, he touches the fragile flame to the tip of the wand in question and continues to billow and puff: "Sometimes, however, it's a well-gobbed truncheon; a hand-wound tobacco sap; the lonely *numb-chuck*—slick and gnawed at one end, sizzly and smoldering at the other—with which men of action batter and bash their affection for one another into bruised valentines and bloody pretzels."

The grin again dazzles, again fades, and memory's clouds regather.

Drat, Mnemosyne: who was that sage? Was it the potheaded "Popeye" Doyle of Francis Ng's *9413*? The mighty Moe Howard, mysteriously materialized on the mean streets of Mongkok, furiously huffing a mescaline Macanudo? Ringo Lam, Tiparillo ablaze, on location somewhere deep within the darkened furrows of his sharp and surly mind?

No. No . . . wait; it was—I remember now—that guy, Yuen Wah.

Yuen Wah, deceptively slight but dapper indeed; a shoo-in, if ever the opportunity arises, for the lead role in Stanley Kwan's Cantopop bio-pic of Sigmund Freud. And not just any Yuen Wah—sure, he once stunt-doubled for Bruce Lee, and he's done plenty since—but specifically the Yuen Wah of *Dragons Forever*. The Yuen Wah whose Fred Astaire physique stands in caustic counterpoint to his Al "Scarface" Pacino film-opening paraphrase: having his flunkies finish off a sniveling crime boss, then offering the corpse's freshly unemployed gunsel a new job with the winning team. Yuen Wah: the Don Knotts of death.

Michelle Yeoh

Michelle Yeoh's career parallels the ascendance of modern Hong Kong films. Malaysian-born and London-trained as a ballerina, she was cast in a lead role in *Yes! Madam*, in 1984, a film that paired her with Cynthia Rothrock, a martial arts champion from Pennsylvania nicknamed "The Blonde Fury." The film was a hit, and Yeoh went on to make *Magnificent Warriors* and then *Royal Warriors* before retiring.

Her triumphant comeback was in *Supercop* in 1992, where she costarred with Jackie Chan in one of his best films ever. Yeoh's Hong Kong career was resparked, and her early 1990s roles in films like *The Heroic Trio* (with Maggie Cheung and Anita Mui) became popular with Western audiences. After the semiautobiographical *Ah Kam*, which featured a stunt that put Yeoh in the hospital for a while, she relocated to Hollywood and emerged as a "Bond Girl" in *Tomorrow Never Dies* (1997). But rather than a googly-eyed help-less type, Yeoh's character in *TND* is a competent warrior woman, actively helping Bond subdue the forces of evil. Reviewers raved and movie fans in her native Malaysia so loved *TND* that the Malaysian grosses actually exceeded those of that ship-versus-iceberg movie.

Keith Hamshere

SELECTED FILMOGRAPHY

Supercop (1992), *Butterfly and Sword* (1993), *Holy Weapon* (1993), *Once a Cop* (1993), *Tai Chi Master* (1993), *Wing Chun* (1994), *Wonder Seven* (1994), *The Soong Sisters* (1997).

Yeoh combines a ballerina's grace with an athlete's power and intense charisma. International diplomats should carry themselves with the poise of this remarkable woman.

Shu Qi

Christopher Doyle

SELECTED FILMOGRAPHY
Viva Erotica (1996),
Love Is Not a Game, But a Joke (1998),
Extreme Crisis (1998),
Gorgeous (1999).

Face it, Shu Qi gives you the horn. She gives everyone—men, women, aliens—the horn. But besides being a total brain-crushing babe, she has a *joie de vivre* that infuses her film appearances. Mischievous and girlie is her vibe, and it works. I'd rather watch a three-minute film of Shu Qi eating pizza, lips eclipsing mushrooms and olives and dripping double doses of mozzarella (soundtrack: "Soulfinger" by the Bar-Kays), than *Raise the Red Lantern*. Wouldn't you?

Shu Qi (sometimes spelled Hsu Chi but pronounced "Shoo kay," and not to be confused with Hong Kong filmmaker Shu Kei) is Taiwanese. The trophies she scooped up at the 1997 Hong Kong Film Awards, for both Best Newcomer and Best Supporting Actress in *Viva Erotica*, gave her career a rocket boost, and she has since appeared in a myriad of films and television shows, and on magazine covers. Shu Qi has chiseled her smoky-gorgeous self into dreams worldwide. Much like early silent star Clara Bow (the "It" Girl), Shu Qi is IT.

Karen Mok

You can scrutinize a thousand photos of Karen Mok, marvel at her various guises from ragamuffin cutie to pixie-punk to power starlet, her astounding photogenuity, and her cute "corn teeth," and fall into any state of rapture you might like. You can study her film appearances in slow-mo until your eyes drop out of your skull. But nothing yet invented can capture the inner electric glow of Karen Mok in person, like a buried floodlight illuminating marzipan. Mokzipan!

Part of this generous luminescence can be chalked up to the graciousness with which Mok handles public appearances. Intuitively, flawlessly, she donates large portions of her public time to both the media and her fans.

Lately, Mok has been concentrating on her singing career, which keeps her busy recording in Taiwan. But in early 1999 she returned to HK to make *The King of Comedy* with Stephen Chiau and the Sylvia Chang–directed *Tempting Heart* with Takeshi Kaneshiro and Gigi Leung.

Keenie Ho

SELECTED FILMOGRAPHY

Fallen Angels (1995),
Sexy and Dangerous (1996),
God of Cookery (1996),
First Love: The Litter on the Breeze (1997).

Michael Wong

Fitto Movie Co. Ltd.

SELECTED FILMOGRAPHY

Legacy of Rage (1986),
First Option (1996),
The Wedding Days (1997),
Beast Cops (1998).

Raised in New York and Los Angeles, Michael Wong has been making movies in Hong Kong for more than a decade. His 1980s costars included Michelle Yeoh and the late Brandon Lee, and he was nominated for Best Actor at the 1996 Hong Kong Film Awards for *First Option*, in which he played an SDU (Special Defense Unit) officer. In between, he found time to have a singing career in Thailand (where his Thai-language hit "Chan Ma Klai" went to No. 1 on the local pop charts), raise a family with his fashion-model wife Janet Ma, and obtain a helicopter-flying license.

Wong's good looks are the product of a Chinese father and an American mother. Of his four brothers, two have also appeared onscreen. Russell Wong is Hollywood-based and has appeared in *The Last Emperor* and *Tai-Pan* and starred in the *Vanishing Son* series on U.S. television. Professional magician Declan Wong had a memorable role in John Woo's *Once a Thief* (1991), performing a spectacular end-duel with Chow Yun-fat where he assaults Chow with razor-edged playing cards and bursts of fire.

Aaron Kwok

Aaron Kwok is better known as one of the "Four Kings" of Cantopop, and is an extremely popular singer throughout the Pearl River Delta. In 1998, Kwok signed with Pepsi-Cola and his "Generation Next" song was used as the Pepsi theme song for a while. In 1999, Kwok did a Pepsi TV commercial with Janet Jackson.

Kwok's film career is more interesting than most Cantocrooners'. Check him out as the villainous Fox in *Saviour of the Soul*, or as a kung fu whiz in Johnnie To's *The Bare-Footed Kid*. Kwok pumped a lot of iron so he could get semi-naked, bruised, and sweaty in the boxing drama *Somebody up There Likes Me*. And he rips around on a big motorbike with Wu Chien-lien on the back in *A Moment of Romance 2*.

Starlight Entertainment

SELECTED FILMOGRAPHY
Saviour of the Soul (1991),
Millionaire Cop (1993),
Anna Magdelena (1998),
Storm Riders (1998).

Pinky Cheung

Universe

"In real life Pinky is a whimsy lady," say the liner notes for the *Raped by an Angel 3: Sexual Fantasy of the Chief Executive* DVD.

That's all fine, whatever it means. Pinky is terrifically prolific—the Hong Kong film fan might come home after catching her latest shot-in-a-week feature film, flip on the TV, and be eye-blasted by a closeup of her bloody fanged mouth—within the context of a vampire soap opera. Her erotic appeal is potentiated by her rumbling, husky voice, which rolls out thick chunks of piquant Cantonese dialogue. Ms. Cheung habitually transcends the films she appears in and the more you see of her (slow-whirling, angular, sexy, and scary in *RBAA3: SFOTCE* or flipping out as a long-haired spectre in *Horoscope 1: The Voice from Hell*) the more you appreciate the lass. Think Pink.

SELECTED FILMOGRAPHY

Chinese Midnight Express (1997),
Young and Dangerous 4 (1997),
Raped by an Angel 3: Sexual Fantasy of the Chief Executive (1998), *Body Weapon* (1999),
Horoscope 1: The Voice from Hell (1999).

AIMEn WonG

Almen Wong is well known for the poster of *Her Name Is Cat* (1998). She says that the blue bikini she wore was made of plastic—not especially comfortable or durable—but her career as a model, she says, has made her used to wearing odd garments. The resulting photo (tough, sexy, complex, and alluring) has proven popular—see the cover of this book!

Wong's first film role was in Alfred Cheung's little-seen *My Mistress, My Wife* (1992). Her role in the Leslie/Andy vehicle *Shanghai Grand* (1996) involved tormenting Leslie with an enormous serpent. Wong's striking good looks have led to her being cast as an object of temptation in films like Derek Chiu's *Final Justice* and Julian Lee's *The Accident*.

A Los Angeles toymaker was so taken by *Her Name Is Cat* that he created an Almen Wong plastic action figure based on the movie. It's fitting, as Wong is toned and athletic and has been featured as one of the models in ads for HK buff-pit California Fitness. "I'd like to be the female *Terminator*," says she, and that's a movie that really should be made.

Almen Wong

SELECTED FILMOGRAPHY
Shanghai Grand (1996),
The Group (1998),
The Accident (1999).

Athena Chu

Starlight Entertainment

SELECTED FILMOGRAPHY
Tom, Dick, and Hairy (1993),
Vampire Family (1993), *Ah Fai the Dumb* (1997),
Love and Sex of the Eastern Hollywood (1998),
Raped by an Angel 2: The Uniform Fan (1998).

A goddess, but of what? Athena Chu's career was characterized by cute-yet-vapid roles in films like the comedic *Chinese Odyssey Part 2: Cinderella* (1995). Until . . .

In 1998, Chu traded in her scrubbed image by starring in *Raped by an Angel 2: The Uniform Fan*, in which she played a voluptuous-yet-hard-boiled policewoman opposing a homicidal dentist with a thing for women in uniforms. The Hong Kong Police Department objected to their uniforms being portrayed as erotic, providing delicious publicity for the press piranhas. Chu promptly appeared in five more movies during the year.

After *RBAA2:TUF*, Epson Computers sacked Chu as their spokesperson, claiming that the move had nothing to do with her career tweaking. But though she may have added a few salacious roles to her resume, Chu is still super-scrubbed and squeaky-cute.

According to several of the rabid fans posting Athena Web pages, Chu's most disliked creature is the mosquito.

Christy ChunG

Christy Chung is from Montreal, of mixed Chinese-Vietnamese parentage. After winning a local beauty contest in 1993, she decided to relocate to Hong Kong and try her luck in the movie industry. She then triumphed in a variety of roles, including an action-oriented role in *Aces Go Places 97*, where she performed a variety of stunts.

Chung, though, is not noted for her stunts, but for her exalted status as rave-babe extraordinaire, starring in the dreams of Hong Kong movie fans from Nova Scotia to Sarawak. In 1998 Chung was pregnant and off the screens, but she has since reemerged mighty trimmed and toned.

Starlight Entertainment

SELECTED FILMOGRAPHY
The Bodyguard from Beijing (1994),
Troublesome Night (1997).

Takeshi Kaneshiro

Christopher Doyle

Raised in Taiwan, half-Japanese and half-Taiwanese, Takeshi Kaneshiro is known as Gum Sing-mo in Cantonese. But he's famous all over the world. In the past few years, he's made Hong Kong movies, Japanese television commercials, Japanese movies, and Japanese TV drama, even finding time to star in *Too Tired to Die* (1998), costarring Mira Sorvino.

Kaneshiro is best known for his work with Wong Kar-wai in *Chungking Express* and *Fallen Angels*. But be sure to check his performance as a loopy hitman in The *Odd One Dies*.

SELECTED FILMOGRAPHY

Executioners (1993),
Chungking Express (1994), *Fallen Angels* (1995),
First Love: The Litter on the Breeze (1997),
Hero (1997), *The Odd One Dies* (1997).

Kelly Chen

Someone once remarked that Kelly Chen and Ekin "Young & Dangerous" Cheng look so much alike that they must be the same person. For some time, it was impossible to find photos of them together, and it did make you wonder . . .

Then, in 1998, Kelly and Ekin made *Hot War*—a cyberthriller from director Jingle Ma—together, putting those nagging rumors to rest. Like many actresses, Kelly Chen's singing career is paramount. In an article in the *South China Morning Post*, Chen gave the following tips for vocal maintenance: drinking lots of water, avoiding drinks that are sweet and sour, avoiding junk food, and drinking a lot of soup "mostly prepared by my mother." Aspiring *chanteuses* take note!

Starlight Entertainment

SELECTED FILMOGRAPHY
Whatever Will Be, Will Be (1995),
The Age of Miracles (1996),
Lost and Found (1996),
Anna Magdalena (1998),
Hot War (1998).

GiGi Lai

Starlight Entertainment

SELECTED FILMOGRAPHY

Dragon in Jail (1990),
Queen of the Underworld (1991),
Kung Fu Cult Master (1993),
Street of Fury (1996), *24 Hrs Ghost Story* (1997),
Super Energetic Man (1998), *The Accident* (1999).

Sweet-faced Gigi Lai (not to be confused with sweet-faced Gigi Leung) achieved fame as Ekin Cheng's stuttering girlfriend Smartie in the first three installments of the *Young & Dangerous* series. Lai is vehemently photogenic. Her appearances at movie premieres cause phalanxes of press photogs to surround her eagerly, each and every one calling "Gigi! Gigi!" simultaneously to draw her soft brown eyes into their lenses—a surreal symphony.

One of Lai's better roles is as a separated girlfriend in Julian Lee's *The Accident* (1999). But her role as Lychee (a pun on her Chinese name, Lai Chi) in 1998's bizarre *Super Energetic Man* is the one viewed by Gigi-freaks as legendary. Burnish your brain with this: *SEM* is a simultaneous parody of Popeye the Sailor Man and Rowan Atkinson's Mister Bean, featuring Lai as Olive Oyl. With a Chinese title that roughly translates as "Dorky Bean-Bean Chasing Girls," and a director who calls himself "East Island Long Eyebrow" to avoid trouble from the unamused Popeye franchise, things don't get much weirder.

Sam Lee

Sam Lee was discovered by director Fruit Chan, who cast him as the lead in 1997's shoestring-budget *Made in Hong Kong*. Not only did MIHK take Best Film and Best Director awards at the HK Film Awards, but Lee picked up the Best Newcomer award as well. Despite his relatively short resume, big-eyed, ultraskinny Lee is one of the bright lights of the industry.

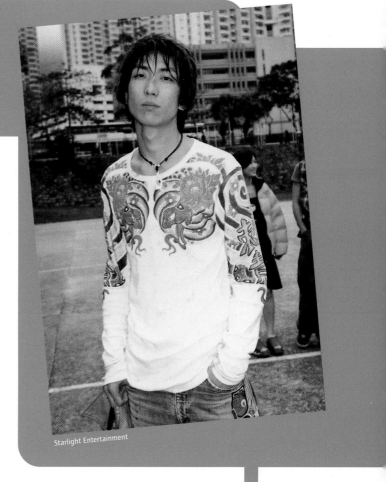

Starlight Entertainment

SELECTED FILMOGRAPHY
Made in Hong Kong (1997),
Nude Fear (1997),
Beast Cops (1998),
Bio-Zombie (1998), *Gen-X Cops* (1999).

Wu Chien-lien

Right Stone

SELECTED FILMOGRAPHY

A Moment of Romance (1990),

The Returning (1994),

To Live and Die in Tsimshatsui (1994),

Beyond Hypothermia (1996), *Intruder* (1996).

"Don't call me Jackie," says Wu Chien-lien, a reaction to her erroneous appellation as "Jacqueline" on various Net sources. "I have no English name. Call me 'Ah Lien.'"

Taiwanese-born Wu got her break in HK movies when Milkyway boss Johnnie To produced the Benny Chan–directed *A Moment of Romance* (1990), starring Andy Lau. Director Sylvia Chang showed To a picture of a fresh-faced Taiwanese starlet named Wu Chien-lien, and he flew to Taiwan to meet her, but the meeting fell through. Back in HK with two days until shooting commenced, he still hadn't cast the lead actress. In a bit of panic, he sent for Wu. She flew into Hong Kong and started shooting the next day.

Wu has since costarred opposite most of HK's leading men and received a Best Actress nomination for *The Returning* in 1994. She usually plays a willowy romantic figure, which makes her role in *Intruder* (1996) all the more shocking (Wu herself said she enjoyed the role). Like many HK personalities, Wu has singing careers in both Cantonese and Mandarin. She also does TV in Taiwan and the PRC. But it's her Hong Kong work that impresses—see Chapter 2.

Michelle Reis

Michelle Reis is also known by her Chinese name, Lee Kar-yan. The tall Portuguese-Shanghainese lovely was raised in Macau, but became Miss Hong Kong in 1988. She made her film debut in *A Chinese Ghost Story 2* in 1990, but is perhaps best known for her role in *The Wicked City*, an adaptation of a Japanese *manga* comic by producer Tsui Hark. Another side of Reis was showcased in Wong Kar-wai's *Fallen Angels*, as she knots her fishnet stockings in unrequited lust for doomed killer Leon Lai. And *Young & Dangerous 4* finds her cozying up to triad superpuppy Ekin Cheng.

Christopher Doyle

SELECTED FILMOGRAPHY

Dragon from Russia (1990),
A Kid from Tibet (1991), *Royal Tramp II* (1992),
Sword of Many Loves (1992), *Swordsman II* (1992),
Zen of Sword (1992), *Fallen Angels* (1995).

GiGi LEuNG

Starlight Entertainment

If you're a diehard Gigi Leung fan, you'll want her *Gigi in Africa* VCD as well as all her Cantopop albums. You'll want photos of yourself standing in front of huge billboards featuring her hawking cosmetics. And you'll definitely want to see *Full Throttle*, where director Derek Yee gave Leung her big break by casting her as the girlfriend of heartthrob Andy Lau.

But if you ever bump into Gigi Leung, be sure to wear your big-boy boots, 'cuz Leung (not to be confused with Gigi Lai) is 177 centimeters tall.

SELECTED FILMOGRAPHY
Feel 100% (1996),
First Option (1996),
Hitman (1998).

Lord, they don't make 'em like Yuen Wah anymore. A god among gods, he is . . . and God knows they don't make 'em like *Dragons Forever* anymore.

A comic jewel within the cosmic lotus formed by Jackie and his "brothers"— Sammo Hung, who also directed; Yuen Wah, slurping his cheroot; and Yuen Biao, who mugs and bugs and, as usual, steals the show—*Dragons Forever* is the finest straight comedy in the Chan filmography. How "straight" this gnarled frenzy of wormy sexual politics, furtive fisticuffs, and far-out eyeshadow is, though, is up to you.

Ostensibly detailing the intrigue surrounding a civil suit between the Hua Chemical Works and the Yeh Fish Hatchery, *Dragons Forever*'s plot is but a harebrained cover for all manner of abstruse meditation. Among its musings: the relation of fish to communism and birds to capitalism; the vagaries of sanity and psychoanalysis; and the delicate bonds that are forged between men who seem only to be caught up to the simplest sorts of skirt-chasing. That much in the way of the film's verbalized substance comes from the mouth of the apparently unhinged Yuen Biao—substance emitted largely during a succession of psyche-scourings, à la "How can a nice man like me, so loyal to his friends and a social element dedicated to the community, meet with frustrations and mental ravages?"—suggests

that, in this case, every cigar should be given the closest examination possible.

Or, as Jackie puts it to Pauline Yeung, early in the course of a courtship built largely on deceit, obfuscation, and prematurely curtailed dating games: "A dog has run down a lamp."

Dragons Forever—just read the review.

Arch-*sifu* David Chute suggests that *Dragons Forever* has been poured in a would-be Three Musketeers mold, though perhaps the Three Stooges might evoke a closer parallel, what with the various and sundry exaggerated preenings, eye-gouging, and gravity-defeating ostentations undertaken by our heroes. Forever on the make, Sammo's opera-able gun runner, Biao's messianic misfit (a hair-trigger Pee-Wee Herman), and Jackie's hormonally emboldened barrister spend much of the film contorted within one another's arms. The script, meanwhile, doubletimes 'round these *follies amour* with a succession of "romance" montages involving walks in the park, moonlit beaches, and motor-scooter rides. Polluted fish farms, fish swimming through Lucite tubes, fishing as avenue to "peace of mind" . . . there's something spoiled at this sushi bar, and before it's over, someone needs to fish or cut bait.

I'll bite: *Dragons Forever* is nothing less than a resurrection of the glory days of the Buena Vista comedies—those sappy-go-lucky programmers Disney used to churn out, back when Kurt Russell was a teenager and Fred MacMurray was not only alive but still getting laid. One can, in fact, align the archetypes. Imagine the following transpositions: When you see the spry and befuddled Yuen Biao, think of the young Dean Jones, boyishly handsome, but with a certain serial-killer *savoir faire*. When Yuen Wah pops his eyes, paddles his foot, and puffs his stogie, bring quickly, if you will, the bone-clattering Don Knotts to mind. And when Sammo Hung pitches woo all over Deanie Yip with the aid of a megaphone, imagine in his stead an eye-blackened, collar-torn Tim Conway.

As for Jackie, well, the Kurt Russell paradigm should apply, were it not for—or is it perhaps because of—the film's climactic appearance of the fleetingly Russell-esque Benny "The Jet" Urquidez, Jackie's kickboxing nemesis from *Wheels on Meals*. Overdressed in an undersized hand-me-down from some washed-up power-popper's steamer trunk, his eyes ringed in tarantula-legs of heavy mascara, Urquidez strides about the film's showdown set—an industrial-sized, Antonioni-toned drug barn—flexing his skull and crunching his neck like a crack-brained refugee from *The Rocky Horror Picture Show*. Does Jackie kick his ass anyway? Is Wong Kar-wai a moody guy?

When you get Buena Vista on the line to talk about remake rights, please pass me the phone. I've already taken out a copyright on *The Kickass Wore Tennis Shoes*, and I'm ready to negotiate.

Project A Part 2 (1987)
by David Chute

Everybody's favorite Jackie Chan movie tends to be the one they saw first. The qualities that make him irreplaceable, his earnest good humor and his unique brand of acrobatic slapstick kung fu, are present to some degree in all his films. The quality, if not the quantity, of the delight is fairly uniform. Even less successful efforts like *City Hunter* and *First Strike* have occasional eye-popping sequences.

Project A Part 2 was my introductory dose, caught first-run at the late lamented Kim Sing Theater in L.A.'s Chinatown. I had never seen anything like it, or like him, and became an instant fan. Experience has since confirmed that *Project A Part 2* is one of Chan's strongest self-crafted vehicles, with the action and comedy elements just about perfectly balanced. The first *Project A* (1985) may be lighter on its feet, and the handsome Kirk Wong-directed *Crime Story* (1993) is probably still the best-made Jackie Chan movie. But as a showcase for Chan at the top of his game, as both filmmaker and performer, *Project A Part 2* is unbeatable.

The period setting is an asset. It's the early 1900s in the flourishing British colony of Hong Kong, and the horse-drawn carriages, the crisp sailor suits, and the pretty girls (including a dazzling young Maggie Cheung) in their flowery floor-length ball gowns contribute to a nostalgic Gilbert and Sullivan comic-opera atmosphere.

The plot recalls *The Untouchables*: The last honest cop in Hong Kong is transferred to dry land from the harbor patrol and

Jackie with a couple of his leading ladies, Joey Wong and Rosamund Kwan

Starlight Entertainment

assigned to clean up the city's most corrupt precinct. The first half-hour is a little sluggish, as a dozen opposing factions are wheeled into position. These include a pack of leering mobsters (led by David Lam), some Sun Yat-sen–aligned revolutionaries (led by Rosamund Kwan), a gang of haughty imperialist spies, and a wonderful eccentric band of comic-opera Chinese pirates, imported from *Project A* with their silly wigs and ill-fitting "civilian clothes" intact, who slink around en masse, brandishing matching hatchets.

Once the action starts, and the machinery begins humming along smoothly, the film becomes buoyantly airborne and remains there. Lovely set pieces include a hand-to-hand tussle inside a revolving wire drum full of drifting feathers, and an elaborate hide-and-seek sequence in an apartment crowded with grimacing spies, concealed behind curtains and sofas and closet doors—a near-perfect piece of fancy-farce footwork. These scenes offer proof positive that Chan is a magnetic screen presence even when he isn't falling from a great height or kicking somebody in the head.

There's less of the latter, here, than some hard-action fans would like, and the major set-piece mega-stunt is an all-too-direct lift from Jackie's idol Buster Keaton. But Mr. Chan is not, finally, a hard-action icon. In fact, that's the whole point. That's exactly *why* he's irreplaceable.

Project A Part 2 is a perfect embodiment of the lessons Jackie Chan absorbed from the great American silent comedians, when he studied them in his formative years, looking for ways to set himself apart, desperate to get out from under the shadow of Bruce Lee. He learned from Keaton and Lloyd that he could show off his skills in limb-stretching acrobatic displays while seemingly straining every nerve to avoid conflict. Like an American musical performer who seems most prodigiously gifted when he pretends to dance badly (Ray Bolger and Donald O'Connor are obvious examples), Chan is never more impressive than when he makes his triumphs appear accidental, when he ducks and dodges and winces after every blow and still manages to lay out a dozen thugs.

Chan rarely plays vigilantes or avengers. His characters are usually earnest functionaries struggling to do the right thing, to fit in, and to serve the establishment. The archetypal Chan character is a reluctant master of mayhem, a well-meaning straight arrow who doesn't know his own strength—although as a crafty performer and self-promoter, he makes damn sure that *we* know.

Mr. Canton and Lady Rose (1990)
by Dave Kehr

Many longtime Jackie fans are disappointed by his most recent films. Instead of accepting the physical limitations of his 40-plus years, Chan seems more determined than ever to punish himself for his fans. The stunts grow more painful and the trademark assembly of botched stunts and breakdowns at the end of his films grows longer, grislier, and harder to watch.

A grace has gone out of Chan's physical presentation; instead of the smoothly whirring windmill of gestures he used to present, he seems bent, off-center, distracted. He shows effort and grim determination where there once was nonchalance and joy. The stunts in films like *Supercop* (dangling from a helicopter flying over downtown Kuala Lumpur) or *Rumble in the Bronx* (being repeatedly rammed by a hovercraft) look more like tests of endurance than displays of skill. It's as if, in sensing the diminished agility and slowed reactions of middle age coming on, Chan had decided that what he had to offer was the spectacle of his own suffering. The end-credit shots of Jackie being hustled off in ambulances are the final proof that he's willing to do anything to keep his audience's attention and preserve the loyalty of his fans.

This may mark a turn in Chan's career, but it is a logical extension of his screen character. Jackie is the great conformist among comic heroes. He's not a willed outsider like Chaplin or Keaton—who created characters poetically out of sync with their worlds—but a young man eager to fit in, to make good in a foreign environment (hence the frequent theme of Jackie as a country bumpkin freshly arrived in the big city, be it Hong Kong, New York, or the Old West). He'll do whatever he can to be accepted, and it turns out that the talent most valued in his new environment is his gift for violence—a gift that, almost magically, he possesses in spite of his fundamentally gentle, boyish nature. Chan's comedy is a result of the wide gap that exists between his preternatural prowess as a martial artist and his unassuming, innocent demeanor. He's a bunny rabbit who bites like a Doberman.

As that skill diminishes—even Jackie can't defeat the ravages of time—his character is left with little but the dark underside of his talent: his ability to withstand pain. To win the hearts of the supporting characters in his films—the sweet young girls, the adoring little boys, the avuncular old men, and, by extension, his huge international audience—Chan feels compelled to greater and greater risks, to absorb greater falls and more furious blows. Like Kafka's hunger artist, he's become the impresario of his own agony.

That it didn't have to be this way is the lesson of *Mr. Canton and Lady Rose*, a 1990 film that has had even more export titles than usual for a Chan film, including *Miracles*, *Black Dragon*, *The Canton Godfather*, and *Oiji*. MCALR reveals Chan as a director, actor, and writer (he coauthored the script with Edward Tang) of fully integrated abilities. Basically a remake of Frank Capra's 1961 *Pocketful of Miracles* (itself a remake of Capra's 1933 *Lady for a Day*), it's a film that has received little distribution outside Asia. But in retrospect it seems the last great film of Chan's greatest period, the extraordinary 1980s run that began with *Project A* and ended with *Operation Condor*.

Following the archetype, MCALR begins with Chan's character Dragon arriving in the Hong Kong of 1930 from somewhere deep in the hinterlands, rope-bound suitcase in hand. He impulsively buys a flower from an old lady, an act that sets off a chain of lucky events. Jackie's streak begins when he narrowly misses being run over by a speeding car, and ends when a dying gang leader appoints Jackie, a stranger who protected him, to be his replacement at the head of his syndicate. In a moment, Dragon's life is transformed.

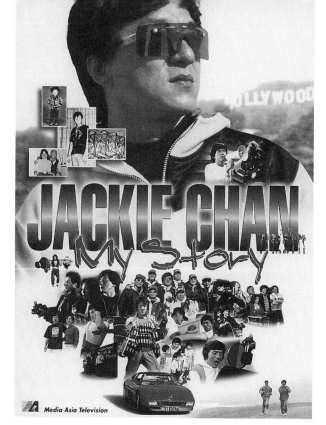

nightclub and hires singer Anita Mui to front a Busby Berkeley–style floor show.

It's Dragon's second transformation—from gangster to producer—that seems most to intrigue Chan as director. MCALR is itself a sumptuous, beautifully staged film that uses the widescreen format to create a distinctive sense of space, constructed around vast interior sets. Using cranes and the Panaglide camera (one of the outtakes at the end of the film shows Chan operating the Panaglide rig himself), Chan creates a number of highly complex shot sequences—Wellesian flourishes that express nothing so much as an unbridled pleasure in the filmmaking process.

Dragon gets his second chance to create a theatrical spectacle when the aged flower seller, whose nickname is Lady Rose, learns that her long-unseen daughter is coming for a visit. Rose has led the girl to believe

This kind of miraculous, sudden success seems to have its parallel in Chan's own career: the discovery of his comic abilities in 1979's *Drunken Master* instantly turned him into a star. As MCALR moves along, the parallel expands: following the advice of an older mentor, Dragon learns to play the part of the tough-guy crime chief, and is quickly accepted as boss by the gang members, but his real interests seem to lie in show business. He turns the gang's tumbledown tearoom into a plush Art Deco

that she is a rich widow (while actually sending every penny she earns to pay for the girl's education abroad), and doesn't want to shame her. Jackie and Anita come to the rescue, digging up a fabulous wardrobe for the old woman and installing her in a huge suite in Hong Kong's finest hotel. It's Dragon's finest act of *mise-en-scene*, even if the players feel obliged to drop their masks in the end.

MCALR is one of the few Chan films in which the action sequences are organically integrated into the plot. They actually advance the narrative (instead of suspending it for a martial arts interlude) by marking the stages of Dragon's development from naive outsider to assured leader. The final fight scene is an anthology piece in itself—a battle in a rope factory that turns into an aerial ballet, with the combatants flying, swinging, and catapulting through the cavernous set—but it also brings the plot to its moral climax. Instead of pummeling the rival gang chieftain who's caused all the trouble, Jackie gives him a symbolic pat on the cheek. He's put violence behind him and is ready to move on to something new.

That "something new" is precisely the character comedy that MCALR explores in its nonaction moments. As a comedian, Chan acts just as he fights, using his whole body. His lines are accompanied by a flurry of rapid hand gestures that make subtitles superfluous; every limb is in expressive movement, in a way that suggests the vigorous physical acting style of early film. There's no longer a discontinuity between the action scenes and the connective tissue that surrounds them. Rather, there is a smooth relay of rhythm and sense. MCALR suggests that even if the fighting were gradually to fade out, there would still be much Jackie Chan to take its place.

Twin Dragons (1992)
by Wade Major

Ever since Alexandre Dumas's *The Man in the Iron Mask* and Charles Dickens's *The Prince and the Pauper*, fictional forms have been glutted with variations on the "twins separated at birth" and "trading places" scenarios. Motion pictures, however, have largely ditched any serious exploitation of these themes for their broader comedic potential. From Bob Hope's *My Favorite Spy* (1951) to Roberto Benigni's *Johnny Stecchino* (1991), human splittists have emerged as one of the cinematic farceur's most popular devices. One need look no farther than the Baby Boom generation's reverence for Walt Disney's *The Parent Trap* (1961, remade in 1998) to appreciate the depth of the saturation.

Jean-Claude Van Damme's separated-at-birth twin brothers entry into the genre, 1991's *Double Impact*, was not warmly received. Tossing martial arts into the mix seemed to further trivialize what was already a woefully tired routine. At the time, some critic (me) wrote that "there's hardly a shared frame between the two Van Dammes that won't elicit a moan from audiences."

Given *Double Impact*'s universal dissing, it's hard to imagine any actor in his right mind wanting to revisit the idea—particularly a martial artist—if only to elude any comparisons to Van Damme. Fortunately for us all, Jackie Chan has never really been in his right mind.

A decade's worth of masterpieces notwithstanding, it seemed inconceivable that even the formidable talents of Jackie Chan could wring anything new out of this weathered old farcical rag. Jackie may have been a genius, but he was no alchemist. Or so we thought. It took me two years to even sit down and watch the thing—fortunately, with an audience.

By the time it concluded, I was hopelessly in love with what I still consider one of the funniest films ever made, a comic masterpiece worthy of the silent greats that Jackie cites as his inspirations. With time my appreciation has only increased, for in the broader context of Jackie's body of work, *Twin Dragons* is both an obvious and a not-so-obvious anomaly, an unusually multi-layered work that impresses as much for what it doesn't say as for what it does.

The twins are separated when an escaped convict (*Crime Story* director Kirk

Wong) barges in on the celebrating parents (actress/director Sylvia Chang and composer James Wong) and steals one fresh baby for use as a hostage. When the smoke clears, the convict is recaptured but the baby has vanished, rescued elsewhere by an alcoholic hooker (*Soong Sisters* director Mabel Cheung). Grief-stricken over the loss of their child, the parents flee to the USA where the one brother—Ma Yau—develops into a renowned concert pianist and conductor. His twin, meanwhile, grows up in Hong Kong under the name Bok Min, an able-bodied auto mechanic and streetwise brawler.

Twenty-eight years later, when Ma Yau (Jackie 1) returns to Hong Kong for a concert appearance, a psychic connection develops between him and Bok Min (Jackie 2), making each increasingly sensitive to the physical sensations of the other. As the connection intensifies, the long-lost brothers find themselves on a direct collision course with one another. The resulting confusion wreaks havoc with their respective girlfriends—lounge singer Barbara (Maggie Cheung) and socialite Tong Sum (Nina Li). The gangsters blackmailing Bok Min for the release of his tiny troublesome buddy Tarzan (Teddy Robin Kwan) are equally perplexed.

An all-star collaboration to raise money for the Hong Kong Film Directors Guild, *Twin Dragons* is a potpourri of giddy insider gags featuring dozens of cameos by celebrity directors (John Woo as a priest, Lau Kar-leung and Wong Jing as a feuding doctor and supernatural healer, respectively), two of whom—Tsui Hark and Ringo Lam—are credited with codirecting the film. Whatever the real nature of this alleged collaboration (imagine a co-directing venture between Steven Spielberg and Abel Ferrara, starring Sly Stallone), it is Jackie's signature that comes through most visibly—his sense of humor, irony, slapstick, and impeccable action choreography indelibly engraved on every scene.

But the film also marks a courageous departure from the action film conventions that had characterized most of Jackie's prior work. Despite the blackmail subplot, *Twin Dragons* is irresistibly fluffy and buoyant, devoid of any real sense of danger or jeopardy. If not for the rousing fights that bookend the film, it would be hard to categorize *Twin Dragons* as a martial arts or action movie. Its broad physical comedy, the self-conscious cleverness of its situations, and the whimsy with which Jackie breezes through his double role belong more to the tradition of Ernst Lubitsch, whose classic comedies found their greatest joy in the creative escalation of confusion, rather than in its resolution.

Far from the hackneyed device of Van Damme's doppelgangers, the psychic connection between the Jackies is a fiendishly inventive contrivance that enables Chan to entertain the most difficult kind of physical comedy—the imposition of the mechanical upon the human. Rivaling such masters as Danny Kaye, Donald O'Connor, and Peter Sellers—whose *Dr. Strangelove* remains the definitive example—Jackie so completely masters the deceit that the otherwise impressive action scenes pale. A nail-biting motorboat chase where Bok Min and Tarzan flee an attacking armada of gun-toting mobsters is a means to a more entertaining end as Ma Yau—seated in a restaurant miles away—frazzles and bedazzles restaurant patrons, the pulchritudinous Tong Sum, and himself by inexplicably swaying, bobbing, and wobbling in sync with the boat's motions. By the end of the chase, Bok Min and Tarzan are safe, but Ma Yau has left the restaurant in tatters and Tong Sum drenched in drinks. A scene in a hot tub, where Bok Min and Ma Yau must somehow convince Tong Sum that she is in the bath with only one of them, will make you spit shredded squid out of your nose. The finale, set at the wondrous Automobile Testing Facility, astonishes with Jackie's feats of agility in dodging and running over moving vehicles. But the magical moment when Bok Min—trapped in an adjacent testing chamber—saves Ma Yau from an attacker by miming the necessary moves, psychically puppeteering his twin to victory, emerges supreme.

When Bok Min and Ma Yau finally meet (at adjacent restroom urinals), the timing is so crisp, the interaction so lifelike, that you can't imagine a real pair of actors topping it. Elsewhere, the film manifests an almost Chaplinesque pathos, as when Maggie Cheung's downtrodden lounge singer Barbara finds herself falling head over heels for Ma Yau, their shared love of music bonding them spiritually to each other and to the audience. Still other scenes, like Bok Min's spur-of-the-moment conducting of Ma Yau's orchestra, evoke the manic spontaneity of the Marx Brothers, eruptions of unpredictable zaniness with no narrative function, just showing the audience a good time.

And what a good time it is. For those fortunate enough to have seen the film with a roaring audience, the experience is both magical and transformational—proof positive that no genre is more universal or better served by the social dimension of filmgoing than comedy—especially when in the hands of such an able master.

Like Bok Min, Jackie was separated from his parents at a young age, raised by a surrogate, and thrust into the world with little formal education. But like Ma Yau, he went on to become a world-renowned artist, beloved in every corner of the world. In a very real sense, the two characters address the insecurities to which Jackie himself has repeatedly confessed. If his talents had gone unnoticed, if good fortune had failed to smile upon him, would he

have continued to live in meager obscurity like Bok Min? Conversely, if he had never been separated from his parents, if he had been raised without training in the martial arts, would he still have been able to succeed like Ma Yau? Whatever the confusion between the two characters in the film, it would seem but a shadow of Jackie's own confusion with respect to his fame. By his own admission, he still grapples with the price of success—the harsh, parentless upbringing—and whether or not, in the end, it was all worth it.

The romantic entanglements in *Twin Dragons* provide a resolution of sorts. After falling in love with men they believe to be from their own social classes, Barbara and Tong Sum discover that they have actually fallen for kindred spirits from opposing classes, men whom they might never have met under normal circumstances. The greater truth, however, is that they have both fallen in love with Jackie, a realization crystallized in the film's final shot when the two brides-to-be jokingly remark that it no longer matters which brother is which.

Indeed, to his fans, it has never mattered which Jackie is which. We have always and will forever love them all.

Supercop (1992)
by Andy Klein

Most Jackie films in the early 1990s represented changes of pace. On the outs with

The colonial architecture of Kuala Lumpur forms the backdrop for copter stunts in *Supercop*.

Photograph courtesy Media Asia. Copyright Star Television Filmed Entertainment.

Sammo and clearly concerned about the new box-office threats of Wong Jing and Stephen Chiau, Jackie abandoned directing and worked with a series of different directors. The result is a strange grab bag of flawed projects and experiments that ranged from the manic *City Hunter* (1992) to the somber *Crime Story* (1993).

Supercop (also known as *Police Story 3*) was Chan's first collaboration with director Stanley Tong. Their subsequent efforts— *Rumble in the Bronx* (1995) and *First Strike*

(1996)—were clearly made with an increasing eye to the American market. For many Chan devotees, this represents a turning away from what made them love the star's work in the first place, and few would count either among his very best. But *Supercop*— the third of Jackie's *Police Story* series about Hong Kong cop Chan Ka Kui—deserves a place on any Jackie top-10 list.

Supercop was a change of pace from the extraordinary string of Chan films directed by either Sammo Hung or Jackie himself, from *Project A* (1983) through *Armour of God 2: Operation Condor* (1991).

While Jackie had years earlier given up on the American market, it's easy to imagine that Tong, getting his first huge break on *Supercop*, already had his eye on Hollywood. He would later fulfill that ambition with *Rumble* and, eventually, the Sammo Hung TV series *Martial Law*. But when one revisits the film itself the only arguable "Americanization" is the reliance on explosions and big action at the expense of the more contained, tightly choreographed fight scenes that grace Jackie's greatest films, and the shift seems more a natural extension of the earlier *Police Story* and *Armour of God* movies than a break with tradition.

What made the film fresh was the casting of Michelle Yeoh. It is axiomatic that (in contrast to a Hong Kong industry where women are often active, ass-kicking protagonists) a female lead in a Jackie Chan film is always "the girl"—that is, someone for Jackie to rescue. Even when "the girl" is not a shrieking ninny, she is still not physically competent to survive without Jackie's intervention.

Yeoh, coming back from a career hiatus, managed to match Jackie in all areas. If she didn't actually upstage him, she came mighty close, and this is probably why Jackie hasn't had a similar female lead since. Because Yeoh and Tong were old friends—

they had worked together on *Magnificent Warriors* (1986)—they conspired to make sure her stunt scenes weren't completely overshadowed by Jackie's.

According to Yeoh, "Stanley and I would hype each other up. 'Yes! Yes!' he would say. 'You're gonna be on the bike and you're gonna jump onto the train, because Jackie's going to be on the helicopter!' And I'm going, 'I wanna do the helicopter one!' And he'd say, 'Wait a minute! If you do the helicopter, what's Jackie going to do? You have to do the motorcycle!' And I'd say, 'Great! By the way, I don't know how to ride one!' 'That's OK! You'll learn that later!'"

The result was a productive sense of tension between the two stars, even though the characters they play are allies rather than opponents.

The final product (in its original Hong Kong version) is an extraordinarily paced nonstop ride. Audiences can get fidgety waiting for that first fight, which doesn't occur until nearly 20 minutes into the film. But, from then on, except for some brief first-rate bits of comedy, there's little letup for the remaining 75 minutes—fight at the police academy, escape from prison, comic homecoming, restaurant fight, boat chase, scuffle at the evil druglord's house, super shootout at the criminal's convention in rural Thailand, comic confrontation with Jackie's girlfriend (Maggie Cheung), and then the final 15-minute capper, involving cars, vans, a helicopter, a dirt bike, and a train.

It's worth mentioning the pros and cons of the version Miramax prepared for its 1996 American release, four years after the film premiered in Hong Kong and Chinatown cinemas throughout the world. In terms of editing, *Supercop* fares better than any of Jackie's other Americanized Hong Kong films: nearly every cut improves the movie. (Jackie says that Miramax had cut more, but he made them put it all back in.) On the downside is the new music—tedious rap songs and hack suspense music replace a perfectly effective score by Mac Chew and Jenny Chinn—and sporadically bad dubbing.

Supercop may be low in the sort of comic action *shtick* that no one can perform or stage better than Jackie. But it is continually exciting: of his 1990s films, only *Drunken Master II* matches it.

Drunken Master II (1994)

by Bey Logan

Drunken Master II is a film that should by rights be as bad as it is good, as awful as it is superb. Unusually, for a Jackie Chan production, it was film-by-committee, with the body in question being the Hong Kong Director's Guild, and it worked its way through three directors, one of them, Frankie Chan, going uncredited. It featured a now middle-aged star attempting to reprise a role he created back in his prime, in a genre he had abandoned for a decade and a half. Its script was subject to constant and radical rewrites, with characters (pop idol Andy Lau, actor/stuntman Chin Kar-lok, western bad guy Mark Houghton) coming and going at random.

Despite all of the above, *Drunken Master II* far exceeded all expectations, critical and commercial. Rather than lurching onto the screen like an inebriated Frankenstein's monster, it slides, glides, and collides across the frame with all the grace, energy, and style of its title character. Against the odds, Jackie Chan managed to distill all his talent into a film that both captures the spirit of the first *Drunken Master* and transcends it.

The idea of a sequel to *Drunken Master* was first mooted by the HKDG as a fund-raising exercise toward a planned permanent headquarters for the body. Lau Kar-leung was approached to direct the film, and it was suggested to Jackie Chan that he might be involved in some capacity. To the surprise of all, Chan offered to play the lead, returning to the role of Cantonese folk hero Wong Fei-hong, a role he'd last assayed in the original *Drunken Master*.

Production began in China, initially at a remote railway station on the Korean border, later at the Shanghai Film Studios. For reasons that remain unclear, Chan decided to take control of the film away from Lau Kar-leung, and returned to Hong Kong. He

and long-time cohort Frankie Chan proceeded to shoot and reshoot both dramatic and action scenes, including the movie's climactic duel—a showdown between Chan's character and a superkicking bad guy played by his real-life bodyguard, Ken Lo.

The plot: Wong Fei-hong (Jackie) and his father, Wong Kay-ying (Ti Lung), are returning home after a trip to buy rare medicinal herbs. The train on which they are traveling also carries the British ambassador, and his collection of purloined Chinese treasures. Wong accidentally encounters a government agent (Lau Kar-leung) who has boarded the train to reclaim an imperial seal stolen by the British. Mistaking him for a thief, Wong engages in a fast and furious kung fu duel. As a result, Wong finds himself unexpectedly in possession of the seal. On his return home, Wong finds that his fellow Chinese are being oppressed by the bullying foreigners and their locally hired henchmen. The villain's plan to export the stolen artifacts from China revolves around the local steel factory, which provides the locale for the stunning finale.

Thanks to canny casting, and Chan's genuinely youthful energy, the 40-something star manages to pull off the neat trick of becoming a kid again. It's a tribute to the acting skills of both Chan and Ti Lung, with about 10 years' age difference between them, that they are believable as father and son. Their relationship is nicely juxtaposed with the bond between Wong Fei-hong and his mischievous stepmother, played with sparkle by Anita Mui. Added to this family mix is the master/student relationship between Wong and Lau Kar-leung's patriotic kung fu master, whose sacrifice sets up the finale. These performances provide substance for the heart, while the lengthy and marvelous action sequences dazzle the eye and quicken the pulse. The final fight between Chan and Ken Lo reaches a new level of energy, even by the standards of HK's pugnacious pugilism pictures.

JACKIE'S LEADING LADIES
BY WADE MAJOR

Behind every good man, there stands a good woman. Or, in Jackie's case, a whole bunch of good women. Throughout the years, in fact, it seems that Jackie has appeared opposite nearly every major actress in Hong Kong, no small feat by any stretch considering the turnaround of talent for which Hong Kong is notorious.

Following is a profile of the best, brightest, and most beautiful of Jackie's leading ladies.

Rosamund Kwan. *Twinkle, Twinkle Lucky Stars* (1985), *Armour of God* (1986), *Project A Part 2* (1987): An enduringly popular Hong Kong actress of the 1980s and 1990s, Rosamund Kwan's fresh-faced comeliness and girl-next-door charms have appeared in some 60 films alongside nearly every major actor and actress in Hong Kong. Her roles opposite Jackie and Jet Li are noteworthy favorites. Rosie Kwan's best role opposite Jackie is as a kidnapped pop singer in *Armour of God*, though she's better known as the impossibly wonderful Aunt Yee who steals Jet Li's heart in the *Once upon a Time in China* series.

Brigitte Lin. *Fantasy Mission Force* (1982), *Police Story* (1985): Unofficially retired from acting since her 1994 marriage to Espirit clothing executive Michael Ying, Taiwanese-born Brigitte Lin is one of only a handful of female stars to have engendered a cult following akin to that of her male counterparts—an exotic beauty who excels at playing characters with a masculine or androgynous bent, especially in supernatural settings.

Amazingly, her two stints opposite Jackie Chan—as the lone female member of a zany commando squad in *Fantasy Mission Force* and as a crime boss's girlfriend-turned-informant in *Police Story*—are among her most tame. In addition to the memorable Ice Countess in Tsui Hark's 1983 *Zu: Warriors from the Magic Mountain*, some of Lin's more popular supernatural incarnations have included the castrato-sorceress Asia the Invincible in 1992's *Swordsman II* and 1993's *Swordsman III: The East Is Red*, and the titular heroine of *The Bride with White Hair* and its sequel (both 1993). American audiences are more likely to recognize her as the blonde wig-and-sunglasses-wearing star of Wong Kar-wai's *Chungking Express* (1994) or the jack-booted general's daughter in Tsui Hark's *Peking Opera Blues*.

Maggie Cheung. *Police Story* (1985), *Project A Part 2* (1987), *Police Story II* (1988), *Twin Dragons* (1992), *Supercop* (1992): One of Hong Kong's most gifted and acclaimed actresses, Maggie Cheung vaulted to stardom after portraying Jackie's girlfriend, May, in the original *Police Story*. To date, she has worked with Jackie five times, more than any other lead actress. Her function in Jackie's films tends to be a comedic one, usually panicking at the center of a chaotic situation beyond her control. She also suffered the worst injury of any of Jackie's female costars when, in *Police Story II*, a toppling metal frame struck her in the back of the head, necessitating stitches (this stunt and its aftermath are included in the PSII outtakes).

In addition to her award-winning performance in Stanley Kwan's 1992 *Centre Stage* (aka *Actress*), which Jackie produced, her credits include such classics as Wong Kar-wai's *Days of Being Wild* (1990) and *Ashes of Time* (1994), Peter Chan's *Comrades, Almost a Love Story* (1996), and *The Soong Sisters* (1997) in which she appears alongside her *Supercop* costar, Michelle Yeoh. Cheung and Yeoh also appeared alongside another famous Jackie Chan leading lady—Anita Mui—in the popular *The Heroic Trio* (1992) and its sequel *Executioners* (1993) as postmodern female superheroes. Maggie was a runner-up for the 1983 Miss Hong Kong crown (the same year Michelle Yeoh was crowned Miss Malaysia) and has won Best Actress at the Hong Kong Film Awards four times, a record.

Anita Mui. *Miracles* (1989), *Drunken Master II* (1994), *Rumble in the Bronx* (1994): One of Jackie's closest and most enduring friends, Anita Mui began her career as a recording star, acquiring the title "The Madonna of Hong Kong" for her elaborate stage shows and dynamic performance style. Her breakthrough role in the Jackie-produced/Stanley Kwan–directed award winner *Rouge* helped foster an equally illustrious career in film, where her seductive looks and ability to play a wide variety of characters quickly earned her the adulation of fans and the accolades of critics. Her trio of roles for Jackie is impressive, ranging from the glamorous young love interest in *Miracles* to Jackie's mischievous stepmother in *Drunken Master II* to the matronly acquaintance-turned-friend in *Rumble in the Bronx*.

Joey Wong. *City Hunter* (1992): Another of writer/director/producer Tsui Hark's great discoveries, Joey Wong became a household name in 1987 when she put the ghost in director Ching Siu-tung's *A Chinese Ghost Story*, slathering Leslie Cheung's milquetoast scholar with enough supernatural eroticism to supercharge a dozen Category 3 films. Like Brigitte Lin—whose *Bride with White Hair* character is, to some degree, a derivation of Wong's original Chinese ghost—she is best remembered for her various supernatural roles, which include two *Chinese Ghost Story* sequels (she plays a different character in each of the

More of those leading ladies— Chingmy Yau, Carina Lau, and Michelle Yeoh

Starlight Entertainment

three films), and *Swordsman III: The East Is Red*, in which she stars opposite Lin as a similarly androgynous lover.

Ironically, her role in *City Hunter* has none of the sensuality that audiences might have expected given her previous work. Instead, she plays a variation on the temperamental, jealous girlfriend pioneered by Maggie Cheung in the *Police Story* series, complicating Jackie's efforts to save an industrialist's runaway daughter (Kumiko Gotoh) while foiling the terrorists hijacking their cruise ship.

Michelle Yeoh. *Supercop* (1992), *Once a Cop* (1993): Malaysian-born Michelle Yeoh is the most independently successful of Jackie's leading ladies thanks to her subsequent fame as a Bond Girl in 1997's *Tomorrow Never Dies*. Remarkably, the death-defying stuntwork in *Supercop* for which she is best known—highlighted by a motorcycle jump onto a moving train—marked her comeback after what many had thought to be a permanent retirement. Her astonishing stuntwork in *Supercop* also marks the closest any leading lady has come to upstaging Jackie.

Yeoh's circuitous career trajectory was first set in motion when, while studying at London's prestigious Royal Academy of Dance, a ballet injury sidelined a promising dance career. She returned to Malaysia, where her mother had secretly enrolled her in a beauty pageant, leading to her being crowned 1983's Miss Malaysia. That success led to a television commercial with Jackie. That same year, her career as an action star skyrocketed when she appeared opposite American Cynthia Rothrock in Corey Yuen's bone-breaking action classic, *Yes! Madam*. Other classic action roles followed with *Royal Warriors* (1986) and *Magnificent Warriors* (1987), also directed by Corey Yuen. Marriage, retirement, divorce, and comeback all followed in short order as Yeoh reappeared in *Supercop*, more vibrant, athletic, and lethal than ever before. That film spawned a pseudo-sequel, *Once a Cop*, starring Yeoh and featuring a famous drag cameo by Jackie.

Since the comeback she has also appeared in *The Heroic Trio and Executioners* with friends and fellow Jackie costars Maggie Cheung and Anita Mui, and starred for director Yuen Woo-ping in the memorable *Wing Chun* and *Tai Chi Master* opposite Jet Li. Prior to her move to Hollywood, she made her dramatic film debut in the controversial *The Soong Sisters*, costarring Maggie Cheung.

Chingmy Yau. *City Hunter* (1992): An adorable pointy-chinned pixie popular for her mischief-making characters in the films of director Wong Jing, Chingmy Yau segued into films after appearing as a contestant in the 1987 Miss Hong Kong pageant (*Dragons Forever* costar Pauline Yeung won the crown). Her role as a leather-clad, gun-toting terrorist-busting babe in the Wong-directed *City Hunter* helped set the tone for a host of future performances, including the cult favorite *Naked Killer* (1992).

Yau's standout scene with Jackie in *City Hunter* ranks as a classic: a Hong Kong variation on a Fred Astaire/Ginger Rogers routine in which Jackie tosses, spins, and rolls her about, while Yau—armed to the teeth—blasts away with thigh-holstered semiautomatic fury on the surrounding terrorists.

In 1998, after nearly 50 films in ten years, Yau made the transition to more serious fare as the star of art-film director Stanley Kwan's *Hold You Tight*, in which she played a challenging double role as two separate women connected only by circumstance. The film, and her performance, won accolades that same year at the Berlin Film Festival.

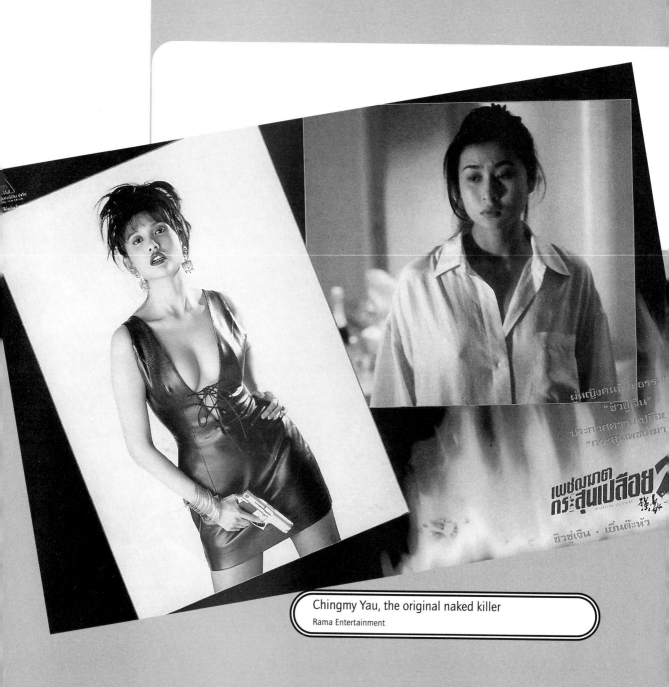

เพชฌฆาต
กระสุนเปลือย7

Chingmy Yau, the original naked killer
Rama Entertainment

bad eggs and naked killers

The dizzy joy in moviemaking, the uninhibited emotionalism, and the compulsive slapstick physicality of these Hong Kong pictures is exhilarating—even the bloodiest fight sequences feel like explosions of high spirits. The giddy, silly, headlong elements of Hong Kong cinema should be embraced, not resisted. No matter how cinematically jaded you may be feeling, these films are potent enough to reawaken the most moribund affection for the medium—and if they can't, you're probably a lost cause.

David Chute, film critic

"You are bastard! Bad eggs!"
Untold Story 2

Hong Kong filmmakers are usually less inhibited than their Western counterparts. The creativity-stifling rules and regs laid down by political correctitians and self-appointed moral guardians inhibit scripts of would-be blockbusters—rewrite-by-committee is preferred lest concepts, words, or images offend one pressure group or another. With the budget of an average Hollywood film now in excess of $50 million, producers are unwilling to chance an unruly boycott or other revenue dampers.

Not so in HK, where productions are like buzzing mosquitoes—ultralight on budget, stingers at the ready. There were predictions

When Hong Kong remade *The Witches of Eastwick*, they put a growling demon-possessed weirdo with a bunch of babes wearing Ming dynasty teddies and called it *Erotic Ghost Story*.

Photograph courtesy Media Asia. Copyright Star Television Filmed Entertainment.

that the heavy hand of mainland censorship would mash freewheeling flicks like *Naked Killer* (1992) and *Sex and Zen* (1991), squashing them into the flattened Red imagery of the Cultural Revolution (1966–1976), compressing pneumatic starlets into The Heroic Tractor Woman or something. But although Category 3 rompers are still unlikely to play cinemas in Shaoshan (Mao's hometown, in Hunan Province), there's been no posthandover attempt to curb Hong Kong's wild muse (see "Blood! Thunder! Handover!" page 138).

However, mainland China does have its sensitivities, and casting a Deng Xiaoping lookalike as "Brother Wai" would doubtless bring the noise. *Wai gor* (literally, Brother Wai—the Cantonese term for blue wonder pill Viagra) was immortalized in a leering 1998 cheapie (shot in six days), which was going to be titled *Mr. Viagra* until pharm conglom Pfizer got wind of the project. The English name of the film was then changed to *Mr. Wai-Gor*, and all images of trapezoidal blue pharmaceutical products were meticulously inked out of the promotional material with big black Magic Markers. The film features creambomb Angie Cheung as a sex-starved widow, perky Pinky Cheung as a PR girl, and Anthony Wong in a dual role as both an outsized spermatozoon and a porn star who can't stiffen unless he glimpses his wife doing the housework. Really, Pfizer need not have worried.

outrageouſ Hatſ

Naked Killer is a sort-of-famous film which has mutated into a PopCult virus whirling its way around the world. Made on a shoestring budget by producer Wong Jing and flamboyant director Clarence Ford, the film attempts to graft a star-crossed love story onto a saga of feuding deadly hitwomen. *Naked Killer* makes little sense, but no one cares—its combination of high-gloss kink, fashionable headgear, over-the-top action, hysterical violence, comminuted subtitles ("The reproductive organ was bursted by bullet"), and Carrie Ng's hellcat performance as the butch hitwoman Princess drove Western audiences wild. It seems as though most English-language HK movie books have made use of one of Chingmy Yau's *Naked Killer* publicity poses—draped in a bandolier of full-metal-jacketed ammunition with leather shorts, thigh-high leather boots, and an enormous gun. You can even spot this Yau pose in the latest Lonely Planet guide to HK/Macau/Guangzhou.

Naked Killer metamorphosed into the *Raped by an Angel* series, a bizarre appellation for a series of leering quickie-flicks starring Chingmy Yau, then Athena Chu, then the mind-boggling pairing of Pinky and Angie Cheung, then Suki Kwan as the latest nemesis in the truly warped *Raped by an Angel 4: The Raper's Union*. Wong Jing's planned *Naked Killer 2000* remains on the drawing board at press time, though given Hong Kong's rapid film-production cycles, it could well be old hat by the time you read this. In the meantime, Wong Jing had a vision of a character who would make *Naked Killer*'s Princess look tame.

Naked Killer—Carrie Ng as Princess, queen of the Hong Kong lesbian hitwoman hierarchy, smooches her muffinbutt galpal Kelly in the bloody swimming pool, post-hit.

Photograph courtesy Media Asia. Copyright Star Television Filmed Entertainment.

BLOOD! THUNDER! HANDOVER!

In the mid-1990s, the United States consulate in Hong Kong underwent a massive facelift. The huge new steel gates, blast-cushion parking lot, security guards, and metal detectors at the entrance suggest that the renovation may have been spurred by the handover hype popular during that period. Invoking a high-tech image of a fortress prepared for siege, the new consulate reflects the architecture of paranoia.

The mass media constructed an image of the heavens raining blood on July 1, 1997, and then jumped foursquare upon that image, rolling around whinnying in delight and waving their collective hooves in the air. There were rumors that China would likely break into a collection of warring states, that PLA tanks could rumble down Nathan Road at the stroke of midnight, that HK politician Martin Lee might be hurled into a dungeon and fed on rice gruel and cockroach dung. The blood-fever was contagious; in mid-1997, a Hong Kong columnist named Turtle Bunbury returned from a Phnom Penh trip and reported: "In Cambodia, I was consistently assured by backpackers, businessmen, journalists, and charlatans alike that Hong Kong was a very tense place about to erupt into total anarchy. They were telling me this in Cambodia of all places! They had cultivated these opinions from radio and press reports over the past six months."

The wet red roses so highly coveted by the Western media were on the bloom—in Cambodia of all

So far, secretive Communist organizations have not cracked down on Hong Kong ultrasleaze like *Raped by an Angel 4: The Raper's Union*, though some local filmgoers probably wish they *would*.

Mei Ah

Alas, there were no photo ops like this during the handover, or you'd *still* be hearing about them on the TV.

Lethal Panther Film (HK) Co. Ltd.

places—soon after the handover, and all the "parachute journalists" (who descend suddenly upon an unfamiliar area and are airlifted out) rushed over there to drink their fill. Soon there was bloodshed in Northern Ireland, then some other place. The story in Asia became the economic downturn initially precipitated by the breaking of the U.S. dollar currency peg for the Thai *baht*. "The Chinese" have been revisited every time the scandal-o-meter drops out of the red zone, but the handover, like an embarrassing cousin, has been stuffed back in the media closet.

One thing the parachute journalists downplayed is the economic linkage between Hong Kong and the mainland. The June 30 handover was the result of a 1984 agreement between Britain and the People's Republic of China, in which the PRC pledged to maintain a "one country, two systems" approach. This policy means that Hong Kong did not become another Chinese province at the handover; rather, existing boundaries like separate passports, currencies, and borders remain in place. The process of reunification was simplified by the Shenzhen Special Economic Zone (SEZ), an area just north of Hong Kong, which was established as a buffer zone as part of sweeping economic reforms in the late 1970s.

Shenzhen's stability and prosperity made it easier for Hong Kong companies to invest in China in joint ventures and other expansionist enterprises, a process which began before the 1984 reunification agreement. Although you'd never guess it from Western press reports, the handover was largely a "done deal" by the time 1997 rolled around.

Serious problems remain in China, which is still a developing country despite the ascendance of the coastal cities. Human rights abuses, monitoring of journalists, and crackdowns on dissidents shouldn't be ignored or glossed over. But most analysts agree that the economic reforms that have transformed China over the past two decades have improved the situation. Certainly, China is far ahead of Russia, the former "evil empire," both economically and politically.

It could be argued that necessary financial countermeasures to Asia's overall structure might have been more apparent without the red cape of the handover obscuring everyone's vision, along with the distracting shouts of the media matador. The combination of crashing currencies and stock indices has burst the Asian bubble of the last decade or so. Hong Kong has maintained its U.S. dollar peg, but the Hang Seng stock index and the SAR's property sector have been battered like dinghies in a typhoon. The ripple effect has touched all Hong Kong businesses, including the film industry.

"The world consumes your electronic products and your movies."
—Bill Clinton, Hong Kong, July 1998

The press corps, trailing the Big Creep like remora fish during Clinton's handover-anniversary visit, did not seem to react to this line. Certainly none among them bothered to pick up the *South China Morning Post* and check what was playing at the local cinemas, for among the Hong Kong movies on offer that week was a sordid little tale with a title no spin doctor could invent: *Raped by an Angel 3: Sexual Fantasy of the Chief Executive*. Thrown a batting-practice fastball like that, the presshounds whiffed it completely, preferring to claw one another for a few minutes with politician Martin Lee, whose sound-bite quotes fit precisely into their allotted segments.

The chief executive alluded to in the provocative title is of course not Clinton, but Tung Chee-hwa, an affable shipping magnate appointed by the leadership in Beijing and slated to serve as SAR head until 2002. Yet, Tung himself is not parodied in RBAA 3:SFOTCE, which depicts the misadventures of a mythical SAR chief executive of the near future. The film is less interested in politics than in displaying the charms of costars Angie and Pinky Cheung (no relation, just a shared curvy phenotype).

But here is the rub: this leering little flick, cranked out to shake a few dollars from the pockets of scattered pervies and rubberneckers, is likely to be more accurate in its political predictions than the mighty media machines frantically cranking their sirens in the spring of 1997. In RBAA 3:SFOTCE, the chief exec is elected by universal suffrage and must campaign directly to the people, an event slated for the HKSAR in 2008.

Hong Kong political maneuverings aren't histrionic affairs like those of Taiwan or the USA. People here know that HK's big trading companies and property tycoons enjoy more clout than anyone in politics, whether a British colonial government, a Beijing-installed group, or a democratically elected legislature. On this rock, consecrated to capitalism, the free market rolls on.

With its calm and orderly handover, Hong Kong has been allowed to shrink to its original dotlike shape on the media map until it gets its act together and produces some serious bloodshed. A multitude thronging that armored consulate, waving passports and portraits of Benjamin Franklin, a bit of pushing and shoving, a little air-o'-desperation . . . roll tape.

Her Name Is Cat (1998)

The guys who ran American International Pictures in the 1960s—James Nicholson and Samuel Z. Arkoff—had a marvelous scheme for project development in those pre-tie-in marketing days. They would mock up a poster for a hypothetical movie and show it to people. If they got a good reaction, they'd make the movie. "Sell the sizzle, not the steak" is something these guys could grasp without a platoon of marketing consultants whispering in their ears.

The poster for *Her Name Is Cat* is something these twin masters of film promo-tion would have appreciated. The central image—Almen Wong striding the land-scape fresh from a tussle, all lips and stare and scratches and shining plastic cladding and a big blue hog's leg—stops people in their tracks. Sizzle? Aplenty.

The film is more about imagery than coherence or character development, but its snappy action sequences are naturals for dance-floor wall-video use. Almen Wong as Cat exudes power, bringing the Cantonese title ("Panther Girl") to life. She's a ruthless titan from Northern China who works as a hired assassin for the very, very manly Sister

Kiss of death—Almen Wong distracts the victim in *Her Name Is Cat.*

Fitto Movie Company Ltd.

Shin. Cat's upbringing was harsh, and with a horror of food shortages, she stocks up on instant noodles. All this Panther Girl will eat is noodles, sometimes even the ones from the local greasy chopstick with "luncheon pork"—a greasy pig emulsion which makes Spam look like filet mignon. This supplies her nutritional needs for sweaty workout sessions and coke-dusted triad rubouts.

Michael Wong costars as police officer John Cannon. He's a cop, and guess what: she's a professional assassin, so they have conflicts in their career paths. He's getting divorced, his daughter is cute, and he's being stalked by guess-who. She becomes inexplicably obsessed with Michael and breaks into his flat to smoke his cigars, write funny notes, cuff him to the four-poster, and bite down on a big leather belt.

There's suggested kink at every opportunity: water blasting suggestively, superblack cat-burglar slinkwear, even over-the-top piped-in roaring-panther sound effects when the heroine is attacking someone sexually or homicidally. In this flick, there's little difference. Panther Girl gets to kill a bunch of people, stomp her female adversary (a too-brief appearance by Noelle Tzik) and bust through a wall to escape, waste a politician with a badass black sniper rifle, experience torture at the hands of the Hong Kong police, ride the MTR to Park 'N Shop, and rescue her pet chicken, Grandpa.

UNCLE RUSS NODS IN AVUNCULAR APPROVAL

The original *Sex and Zen* (1991) blasted into U.S. cinemas a few years after its Hong Kong release, startling and delighting exhibitors and punters alike. The film's soft-core shenanigans were packaged in Ming dynasty gauze, a layer of removal that allowed Caucasian audiences to vicariously enjoy outrageous sexual situations. Few films would dare lop off their central protagonist's precious part and replace it with that of a horse, yet *s&z* accomplishes this in the first reel. Another big plus was the breathy presence of Amy Yip, a sweet-faced starlet of Russ Meyerian proportions. Yip's notorious norks (100 percent free of silicone, she proclaimed to all who would listen) made for a fab frontispiece, but the success of *s&z* was largely due to its high production values and impressive costuming. As global audiences discovered to their delight, nothing is shed quite as sweetly as a flowing sheet of silk.

Sex and Zen 2 (1996) featured Loletta Lee, who shed the demure image she'd cultivated in films like *Shanghai Blues*, and a newcomer named Shu Qi. An attempt was made to top the amazing-transplant gag of the original *s&z*: a berserk Ming dynasty metal dork—a penile Swiss Army knife bristling with attachments—is grafted onto the protagonist. This sounds funnier than it is—even diehard Shu Qi fans prefer *Viva Erotica* (also 1996). The warm heathen touch of the *s&z* formula returned fully in the third installment.

Sex and Zen 3 (1998)

Gorgeous women in fantastic sexual predicaments, costumed stylings with dance and music, and shaven-headed superstud Elvis Tsui guzzling mystic potions and shouting "I've taken philtre! I can last an hour!"—*s&z 3*'s soft-core shenanigans include gauzy dance numbers, sexual kung fu masters, and an array of stunning starlets. The production values and cinematography are completely at odds with the absurd sex and lurid situations—how such a garishly entertaining flick could be cranked out on such a narrow budget, using centuries-old Chinese texts as inspiration, is another Hong Kong mystery.

Virtuous Susan (Karen Yeung) is a pouty and strapping young lass, but her parents are cabbage-poor, and career opportunities in rural China are limited. So they peddle her to Fragrance House, the most famous brothel in the region, for 40 *taels* of gold. Though Susan is somewhat apprehensive, she does have company: Chinyun (Jane Chung) and Fanny (Tung Yee). As the title slate appears, the three young women are perched doggy-style on a series of wooden benches for inspection by the mistress of Fragrance House, Tall Kau (Noelle Tzik).

Sex and Zen 3's poster shows Karen Yeung balancing a piece of ice on her tongue as Jane Chung wonders just what the heck she's doing.

Mei Ah

Tall Kau is the sexual equivalent of the martial arts *sifu*, assessing the girls carefully in a scene that produces a rapid-fire plethora of shredded subtitles, and outlining training techniques that will enhance their earning potential as practitioners of the carnal arts ("make men die on bed"). The scheming and competitive Fanny gets the nod from the brothel mistress: "I guarantee you'll become a famous prostitute."

Fanny is delighted. Alas, poor Chinyun suffers from an "iron vagina," and is worried that she cannot produce sufficient income for Fragrance House. Tall Kau reassures her by promising to impart rare sexual skills to her. Susan is inexplicably compared to a labyrinth, and even more inexplicably, this is regarded as a tremendous asset.

All three nascent hookers are directed to carve a wooden phallus to familiarize themselves with the tools of the trade—Tall Kau's black manservant Hark serves as model for this absurd exercise. Though the trio are supposed to preserve their virginity for auction, Fanny can't resist the obvious charm of Hark. Caught trysting, the couple is subjected to punishment. Fanny has a series of butterflies tattooed on her lower back, while Hark is gelded. Oh well.

Meanwhile, Susan is gagging on wood. Chinyun sympathizes with her and her plight. She cuddles up with buxom Susan and tells her: "We're buddies forever." The two women bond. They bond all over the bearskin rug.

Summertime is high season at Fragrance House, with visiting businessmen and scholars journeying to the capital as customers. Horse trader and pervert-with-a-heart-of-gold Lui Tan (Elvis Tsui at his scenery-chewing best) drops by, as do scholar Chu Chi Ang (Tim Shaw) and his servant Hwang Lien (Wong Pan). Sir Lui befriends the young scholar and they hoist a few cups of wine together before the showpiece Best Girl Contest. Susan bests her rivals with a shuddering onanistic performance, and the horse trader offers top *tael* for her cherry, only to cede *droit du seigneur* to his newfound drinking chum. The scholar protests that such a gift is too generous, so Lui offers to let him pay 8,000 *taels* toward the fee and graciously selects the runner-up, Fanny, to satisfy his own lust.

The scholar and the virgin whore engage in athletic vanilla pursuits while Mister Horse Trader and his tattooed companion go for the *tutti-frutti*. Lui swills down an aphrodisiac as Fanny demonstrates her Hot-Cold Eighteen Hell oral technique. An improvement on the everyday Fire and Ice Stance (alternating mouthfuls of ice cubes and hot tea), Fanny's variation incorporates mouthfuls of freshly chewed raw chilies. Lui is so impressed that he buys her out as his concubine.

Meanwhile, scholar Chu falls hopelessly in love with innocent Susan. His exam forgotten, he squanders his allowance by hanging around Fragrance House eating melon and "drowning in sex." Poverty-stricken, he's not much use to Tall Kau, who's seen plenty of these young whelps before, and she yanks the welcome mat. Chu has to hightail it to the woods and learn the 13 Virgin Tricks before his fortunes start to change.

The 13 VTs are taught by a forest-dwelling sexual wizard named Hung Chi and consist of outrageous sexual positioning with shouted titles for the various nipple-pinging stunts ("Frog popping across a river! Lighting a lamb [sic] at bedside!"). Hung Chi, energetically coupling with his four lithe wives to instruct Chu in these mystic sex techniques, is played by veteran actor Lo Mang. Those who recall Lo Mang as Toad in the Shaw Brothers' *Five Deadly Venoms* (1978) will get an extra thrill from Virgin Trick number 11: "Toad climbs the stone!"

When Chu must return to save Susan from the evil Fanny, who schemes to implicate her in a murderous plot, those 13 Virgin Tricks come in very handy indeed. A little torture, a bit of revenge, comeuppance all 'round . . . a great date movie.

Sex and the Emperor (1996)

This *yin/yang* deal is more than just the cool twirly symbol on the touristy stuff. It diagrams the duality of the universe—harmony and balance and all that. Too much *yin* is no good but that doesn't mean you get to overload on the *yang* stuff.

Yang is considered male essence, which is why female ghostresses are always sniffing after it; they are *yin*-laden and perennially seek balance. However, those who voluntarily cede their male essence can gain power in a spiritual dimension. The custom of trimming the clock-weights from young boys seems barbarous as seen from a twentieth-century perspective . . . well, it

is barbarous, but it certainly cuts down on any surfeit of *yang*. The *castrati* were often ushered into the inner circle of the Imperial Court and given opportunities denied the betesticled. Cold comfort perhaps.

Sex and the Emperor features plenty of imperial intrigue.

one of the family jewels. Li's unflagging sexual prowess proves popular in the imperial palace, where the boy-emperor (the last of the Qing dynasty) is attended by eunuchs and a bevy of chambermaids. Imperial intrigue? Not really; this film eschews historical analysis for heaps of gratuitous sex and torture, horsewhippings, mindless cruelty, and pervy situations, amid pageantry and costumes that will delight the *Sex and Zen* crowd.

When the defiled-innocent Guilian (played by Yvonne Yung Hung) is sold to the brothel, she's treated to a demonstration of the eight semi-devil sexual skills by the brothel's headmistress, Hongyi (Julie Lee). With much shouting, arm styling, and great gouts of *chi* energy blasting out of every orifice, Hongyi puts on a display of sexual martial arts skill guaranteed to ban her from every Blockbuster on the planet and draw applause from the kung fu students in the audience. Dressed in a diaphanous Qing dynasty nightie and knee-high white cloth booties, she instructs her students with exultant shouts ("Throw!" "Sift!" "Rub!" "Wrench!" "Swing!") while zealously swinging her pelvis for emphasis. She juggles a huge clay pot with her feet ("Double Slut Foot!") and hurls it in the air, then uses her bare bottom

Sex and the Emperor attempts to answer the historically important question: In the land of the eunuchs, is the one-testicled man king? Oh, no, it doesn't; this movie is pure sleaze from minute 1, flashing its celluloid panties at ya, utterly shameless.

Li Lianying is a young boy who has a date with the "Castration Master," but Li's father once saved the Master's life, so the gelder agrees to surreptitiously preserve

"You know I always like little-snaking women."
The Fruit Is Swelling

"He'll go on practicing 'Iron Scrotum.'"
Sex and Zen 2

"I want 4 lustful instruments."
A Chinese Torture Chamber Story

"If you mean tits, left or right?"
Ten Brothers

"People say one part of his body is as long as that of a horse.
Of course that part is not the face."
Sex and Zen 3

"Any pervert around?"
For Your Heart Only

"You erotic collected so many 'lewd' photos, what for?"
On Fire

"Cover the lid and press it
Then a unique, fresh virgin underwear can is created"
Shocking Asia III

"Bastard, you shouldn't shout so loudly for visiting hookers!"
Our Neighbor Detective

"Sex den, it's great!"
The Occupant

"You're a horny monk? Want to look? Pay money."
Erotic Ghost Story—Perfect Match

"Sorry, honey. I took $1,200 from your wallet for this hooker."
Task Force

"That bastard, to him sex is always more important than friends."
Stooges in Tokyo

"Yeah, me evil and you flirty. We're two of kind.
Must I reveal the monkey affairs between you and Fatty?"
The Fruit Is Swelling

"I am now going to whore in the coffee shop."
Troublesome Night 4

"You are sending your husband lunch and sex, right?"
A Chinese Torture Chamber Story

"Let me touch your nibbles."
Brother of Darkness

"Dad, mind your saliva."
Sex and Zen 2

"Kidding? Say 'Big tits baby,' 'Lustful bitch,' etc?
And 'Japanese girl VS Machine Monster.'"
Sexy and Dangerous

to scoot a series of blank sheets of paper into a huge rectangle.

Her canvas prepared, Hongyi takes an unusual nether grip on a gargantuan calligraphy brush and flows black ink over the paper, tracing characters with savage concentration. Reading out the resultant lustful ditty, she fires the inky brush into the face of a servant and caps the stunt by squeezing dry a half-meter stick of sugarcane without using her hands. As absurd as the circumstances are, Lee performs it all straightfaced, with the dignity of a white-eyebrowed *sifu* in hard demonstration mode.

株小子

Kids From Shaolin

L'il baby Jet in his *Shaolin Temple* days

Sil-Metropole Organisation

the afterburner

by Wade Major

To fans of Hong Kong films like *Once upon a Time in China (OUATIC), Fong Sai Yuk, Fist of Legend*, and *My Father Is a Hero*, Jet Li seems a born action star. His physical dexterity, matinee idol smile, stunning martial abilities, boyish charms, and seething intensity seem such a natural part of Hong Kong cinema that it's hard to believe his success was once anything but assured.

Born in Beijing in 1963, Li Lian-jie—his Mandarin birth name—began his martial arts career at age eight when he was sent to the Beijing Amateur Sports School to receive instruction in *wushu*—a regimen that mixes a variety of Chinese martial styles, including traditional weaponry training. With the help of his coach, Wu Bin, Jet's prodigious talents were realized at the tender age of 11, when he earned the national title of all-around champion. It was a title he would hold for the next five years.

Had he been born in Hong Kong, a career in martial arts films would have been the obvious next step. Transitioning to martial arts movies on the Mainland, however, was a stroke of remarkable luck and timing. By 1980, encouraged by the success of Hong Kong productions in the region, Chinese authorities finally decided to try their hand at the genre. Enlisting China's most famous *wushu* champion was a no-brainer.

In 1982, the strategy paid off with the release of *Shaolin Temple*. While the movie followed the basic plot (a young man seeks to learn the skills of the Shaolin fighting arts to avenge his father's death), it had two unique selling points: it was shot on location at the Shaolin Temple itself—and it starred Jet Li.

Jet in *High Risk*

Tai Seng Video Marketing

Despite lacking the dynamic stylistic flourishes of a Hong Kong production, *Shaolin Temple* enjoyed widespread success throughout the continent. Sadly, it was a shallow success—a noteworthy last gasp of a dying genre. By the time of the film's release, Hong Kong filmmakers were already embarking on a new path, pursuing what would become known as the bravest period of their cinematic history.

the New Wave Washes Clean

For decades, Hong Kong cinema had been ruled by mythical hero films and grittier, straightforward kung fu films. With the arrival of a new, more sophisticated breed of filmmakers, all of that abruptly changed. Seminal figures like Tsui Hark, John Woo, Jackie Chan, Chow Yun-fat, and Ringo Lam were the most recognizable personalities of a 1980s New Wave that earned the industry artistic recognition across the globe. The poor dubbing and far-fetched fights long associated with the colony's earlier movies had been displaced by a seductive cocktail of explosive action, death-defying stunts, and stylish visuals that surpassed even the most expensive Hollywood productions. But Hong Kong's new auteurs were not simply borrowing a Hollywood formula—they were improving upon it and exporting it back to America and Europe where a fan base was growing with cultlike fervor. Gangster films and the stunt-oriented action films pioneered by Jackie Chan were fast eclipsing traditional fare like *Shaolin Temple*.

Two unsuccessful *Shaolin Temple* sequels proved the trend, and Jet's celebrity began to fade as fast as it had soared. Adjusting to new genres proved equally frustrating. A debut directorial effort entitled *Born to Defence* and the obscure action/comedy *Dragon Fight* likewise failed to revive his popularity. As the 1980s drew to a close, it seemed as though only a miracle could put Jet back on top.

Then, in 1991 that miracle arrived. Its name was Tsui Hark.

ONCE UPON A TIME WITH TSUI HARK

Tsui Hark's reputation as a hit-maker mogul and popular taste-maker in Hong Kong can roughly be compared to that of Steven Spielberg in Hollywood. As a producer, writer, director, and occasional actor, the Vietnamese-born/United States–educated Tsui has conquered nearly every genre imaginable and driven the industry's defin-

ing trends for the better part of two decades. As a central figure in the move away from traditional films in the early 1980s with his company Film Workshop, it seems ironic that he would become equally central to their revival in the late 1980s. Nonetheless, his 1987 production, *A Chinese Ghost Story*, directed by Ching Siu-tung, did precisely that. An unabashedly old-fashioned mythical hero film at a time when the genre was supposed to have been dead, *A Chinese Ghost Story* was a runaway hit, suggesting for the first time that the New Wave might be reaching a saturation point.

Indeed, to longtime observers, a revival of traditional fare seemed not only predictable, but imminent. Life in Hong Kong had long been characterized as a delicate balancing act between Eastern and Western influences, particularly in the cinema. By the late 1980s, the balance had swung noticeably westward, priming audiences for yet another turnaround.

There was more to the success of *Once upon a Time in China*, however, than just the revival of a genre. Tsui Hark also revived the legend of Wong Fei-hong, one of the most revered figures in Chinese history, already the subject of dozens of films since the 1940s. A turn-of-the-century hero renowned for his abilities as both a martial artist and a herbalist/physician, Wong's defense of Chinese culture against Western encroachment, while opposing internal political corruption, continues to be seen as an atypical manifestation of Confucian values in a practical, modern setting. Wong Fei-hong was not only an emblem of what all Chinese aspired to be, but a modern example that such an ideal was attainable. With such headline issues as Chinese reunification and the perceived intrusion of Western sensibilities increasingly on people's minds, Tsui sensed that the time was right for Wong's return.

OUATIC's story finds Wong Fei-hong caught in a historic tug-of-war for the fortunes of Hong Kong—forced to battle greedy imperialist forces from England, France, and the United States, as well as corrupt local officials and anyone else who placed their own interest above that of China. But without a suitable actor in the part, Wong simply would not have resonance for audiences. For most fans, Wong Fei-hong would forever be synonymous with the great Kwan Tak-hing, who played

Jet and Tsui Hark reinvented the Wong Fei-hong legend in the *Once upon a Time in China* films.

Photograph courtesy Media Asia. Copyright Star Television Filmed Entertainment.

the part in more than 50 films during the 1950s and 1960s. And then there was Jackie Chan's immortal turn as an impetuous, youthful Wong in 1978's *Drunken Master*. Any actor seeking the part would face comparisons not only to the real Wong, but also to a pair of Hong Kong film legends.

Jettin' In

In view of these hurdles, the casting of Jet Li must have seemed foolhardy. Nine years after *Shaolin Temple*, he was still a one-hit wonder. Nor could Tsui plead ignorance, for he and Jet had already worked together on the unreleased 1988 immigrant-out-of-water tale *The Master* (finally released in 1992).

In the end, Jet was perfectly cast as Wong Fei-hong. His *Shaolin Temple* rep dated him back to a time before gangsters, gunfights, and car chases conquered Hong Kong screens. And as a Mainlander, his perceived ties to China's pure cultural heritage were stronger than those of his Hong Kong– and Taiwan-born colleagues. Jet was the nexus where Hong Kong's cinematic and historic pasts converged, a true son of the motherland who, like Wong Fei-hong, had weathered a period of Western cultural bombardment and emerged untarnished. When he appeared as Wong in *OUATIC*, it was as if audiences were rediscovering two heroes from the past spiritually joined in one movie.

To fully appreciate the magnitude of the film's impact on Hong Kong filmgoers of the time, one need look no farther than the precredit prologue. A shipboard dragon dance—attended by Wong—is interrupted by a rifle assault from a nearby French vessel. The French soldiers have mistaken firecrackers for attacking gunfire and responded accordingly. Ordinarily, audiences would expect a rousing fight to ensue, with Wong the victor. Instead, Jet Li's Wong steps in and finishes the celebration in style, ignoring the foreign interruption as though it had never happened. The movies had supplied plenty of martial heroes in the past, but none so courageous or dignified in defense of Chinese culture as this new Wong Fei-hong. In the span of only a few minutes, Jet Li and Tsui Hark had redefined Wong Fei-hong for a new generation.

So smartly conceived was the film that it seemed to have something for everyone—first-rate production values, keen writing, breathtaking choreography, an army of popular supporting cast members (Kent Cheng, Jacky Cheung, Rosamund Kwan, Yuen Biao), and a catchy theme song. Most importantly, the movie showcased Jet's acting and fighting skills to a far greater degree than any of his previous films. The package was irresistible.

Perhaps the most important aspect of the film's success, though, is the chemistry of the collaboration. It is a truism of filmmaking that good directors are as crucial to the creation of stars as the innate talents of the stars themselves. Though Jet was clearly no diamond in the rough when Tsui selected him for the role, neither was he the polished gem that Tsui would make of him. In the end, it took a director of Tsui's insight and sensitivity to isolate and magnify Jet's filmic strengths.

Whether by coincidence or design, Tsui conceived his new Wong Fei-hong as a cross between Hong Kong's two greatest action stars. Like Bruce Lee, he would be an unrepentant hero, courageous and forthright, exhibiting no fear in the face of a challenge. Like Jackie Chan, he would be a people's hero, easily accessible and not so obviously heroic. His enemies would find him easy to underestimate, making his eventual triumph all the more satisfying for the audience. Here, too, Jet's own experience seemed to mirror that of his character. For years, his gentle, boyish features had overshadowed his obvious physical abilities, making it hard to compete with more chiseled actors in the mold of the archetypal hero.

Such a contradiction, however, was precisely what Tsui needed to make his Wong dramatically viable: a boy who could become a man at the drop of a hat, a healer who could be a ferocious fighter, a figure who seemed to harmonize peace and violence. The advantages to the approach are clear in the film's famous finale—a dazzling dockside showdown between Wong and rival Iron Fist Yim. Fighting on precariously balanced ladders and swinging cargo flats, the two men engage in an epic battle made even more striking by the contrast between the two characters. While the grizzled, sweaty Yim grunts and growls, Wong remains composed and serene, suggesting that one need not become like one's enemies to defeat them.

One Directs, the Other Just Jets

Stylistically, the marriage between Tsui's visual sensibilities and Jet's physical skills proved even more formidable, establishing a recipe for staging action that most of Jet's subsequent directors—including Corey Yuen and Yuen Woo-ping—have endeavored to emulate. It was an approach that owed as much to the hyperactive supernatural films of yesteryear as to straightforward kung fu films. Tsui's natural instincts had always leaned in this direction, as evidenced by his landmark 1983 film *Zu: Warriors from the Magic Mountain*. And while there would obviously be no place for sorcery, ghosts, or flying people in a historical piece like OUATIC, other motifs and techniques could be adapted to help breathe life into an otherwise familiar genre.

It is generally taken for granted by Hong Kong movie fans that the use of wide-angle lenses, extreme angles, rapid editing, exaggerated camera movement, and wirework so prevalent in supernatural hero films are as much cinematic trickery as stylistic imprimaturs, devices used to create the impression that characters possess abilities far beyond those of mere mortals. Consequently, their use in *OUATIC* suggests careful planning on Tsui's part, a conscious attempt to marry style and narrative so as to dispel any suspicion that Jet's skills might really be less remarkable than they appeared.

In the film's tamer first half, the major action sequences are straightforward and unostentatious, relying more on realistic choreography and workmanlike editing than wirework. A brawl in an English restaurant is followed several minutes later by a fight with local thugs in which Jet uses a simple umbrella as his only weapon; these fights are showcases for Jet, not Tsui. By the time the film reaches its midpoint—an assassination attempt on Wong during a Peking opera performance—Tsui's stylistic signature is more evident, becoming increasingly so until the final face-off. Remarkably, the embellishment never seems to detract from Jet's skills: director and star so perfectly complement each other that, by the end, there seems little point in trying to discern their respective contributions.

A pertinent footnote to the collaboration is the respective foreign origins of both Jet and Tsui. A Beijing native and an American-educated Vietnamese immigrant coming together on a Hong Kong production about a legendary Chinese hero— ironic if not for the pervasive message of tolerance qualifying the patriotic theme. "Everything is changing. What will we change into?" Wong asks early in the film. The answer comes by way of his relationship with Aunt Yee (Rosamund Kwan), for whom he has obvious feelings despite the problems that her love of things Western creates for him. It is a relationship that directly reflects Hong Kong's own love/hate relationship with the West, suggesting that cultural conflicts can and must be resolved to the benefit of all parties.

The Sequel

If *OUATIC* made Jet a star, the sequel turned him into a household name. It was, in almost every conceivable way, the perfect follow-up—no small achievement in an industry known for sequelizing its franchises to death. On the one hand, *Once upon a Time in China II*, released in 1992, delivered all the requisite elements that had made the first film so successful—dazzling action, historical insight, pristine production values, and a complex story line that once again dropped Wong Fei-hong into the center of a tangled, multifactional fight for China's future. But at the same time, the new film managed to expand upon the themes and concerns of its predecessor, adding dimensionality to Wong's character and giving Jet a chance to showcase acting abilities barely touched upon in the previous film.

With two interlocking story lines and two distinct adversaries, Tsui's follow-up script maintained the original's feel for the chaos that dominated the politics of late-nineteenth-century China, but with a more accessible story line. On the one hand there is the mystical White Lotus Sect, an idol-worshipping, xenophobic cult with the bizarre dual aims of killing all foreigners and liberating the poor. On the other, there is the future president of the Chinese Republic, Dr. Sun Yat-sen, whom the government has labeled a dangerous revolutionary, entrusting his arrest to Regional Commander Lan (Donnie Yen). It is into this uncertain and volatile environment that Wong Fei-hong arrives for a Canton medical convention, accompanied by Aunt Yee and his student Fu (Max Mok replacing Yuen Biao). Ever the moral barometer, Wong wastes no time taking sides against the White Lotus Sect and befriending the charismatic Dr. Sun, putting himself on a collision course with both Commander Lan and the White Lotus Sect's secretive leader, Priest Kung.

That Wong's enemies in the sequel are Chinese, rather than foreign, is easily its most fundamental departure from the original, a thematic shift that enables Tsui to recast Wong as a more vulnerable, compassionate, compromising, and romantic hero. Because audiences had already responded so strongly to Jet's softer portrait of heroism, pushing Wong even farther in the same direction was a logical progression. He had already proven himself a hero and an unbeatable fighter. Now, Tsui and Jet would have the chance to prove him a human being.

Early in the film, when Aunt Yee reveals her true feelings to Wong, the confession stirs an almost adolescent awkwardness beneath the heroic veneer. Later scenes become irresistibly cute, with Jet evoking the embarrassment, uncertainty, and wide-eyed bliss of first love, at one point even succumbing to a mild bout of jealousy. Elsewhere, a more fatherly Wong emerges to care for and protect a group of children whose instructors have been killed by the White Lotus Sect.

A more elemental softening of Wong Fei-hong's character stems from his brief yet memorable encounter with Sun Yat-sen. When wounded Westerners are brought into the English consulate, Wong and Sun work together to relieve the suffering, bringing the best of two medical systems together: while Wong anesthetizes the patients with acupuncture, Dr. Sun performs Western-style invasive surgery. What makes the scene so remarkable is less the

awestruck reception that Wong's medicinal skills receive from the English than Wong's own awe at the wonders of Western surgery (watch for Hong Kong author Paul Fonoroff as a bearded doctor; he's the one getting his neck broken by Donnie Yen).

If one is to view the White Lotus Sect—with its empty populist rhetoric, mindless patriotism, and worship of a Mao-like idol—as a thinly veiled representation of the Red Guard, it becomes easier to read the Sun Yat-sen subplot as a comment on mainland Chinese intolerance of dissidence, democracy, and détente, embodied in the person of Donnie Yen's obsessively, single-minded Commander Lan. In the aftermath of the Tiananmen crackdown, a number of veiled, cautionary attacks on the Chinese regime had appeared in Hong Kong films, led by John Woo's 1990 opus *Bullet in the Head*. But now the OUATIC themes of pride and tolerance, which had been preached to Hong Kong's onetime colonial scavengers, were now being delivered to its future rulers by a Mainland-born actor.

Elsewhere, the messages are even more direct. The preclimax confrontation between Wong and Priest Kung that exposes Kung's "powers" as a deception ends with Kung being symbolically impaled on the finger of the Goddess. Regarding the Sect's Stalinistic idolatry, Brother Luke, an associate of Dr. Sun's, remarks, "Look at those fools. Giving up their lives for that idol. If all of us are as rotten as them, how can our country be saved?" Then, as if the message were not yet clear enough, Jet's Wong observes, "Gods are useless. You must rely on yourself."

Enter the Yuens

OUATIC 2 added the talent of Yuen Woo-ping—a well-known Hong Kong director since Jackie Chan's 1978 *Drunken Master*, and a member of the Seven Little Fortunes (see "The Seven Little Fortunes," page 110). Yuen's contribution is evident from *OUATIC 2*'s opening sequence—a strange White Lotus ritual highlighted by Peking opera–style acrobatics and choreography. Yuen's touch is again evident in the stunning Wong/Kung battle that places the combatants atop an altar of precariously balanced tables (and later a ceiling beam), requiring them to find increasingly creative ways of not touching the ground (elaborate contests and exotic set pieces are as much a staple of Hong Kong cinema as high-noon gunfights are in American westerns). But also pay attention to the symbiosis between Jet's *wushu* and Yuen's Peking opera–inspired fight choreography, the first of many subsequent collaborations with the major Yuens of the industry. Jet had already worked with action directors Yuen Cheung-yan and Yuen Sun-yi on *OUATIC* but it wasn't until *OUATIC 2* and Yuen Woo-

ping that the artful blend of techniques from supernatural films and straightforward kung fu films began to acquire the defining characteristics now considered a hallmark of Jet's work.

Today, the success of the *OUATIC* franchise ranks among Hong Kong film's proudest achievements—a triumph transcending both Tsui and Jet's personalities. Countless spin-offs and spoofs, a television series, and four more sequels all testify to an enduring legacy.

OUATIC 3 was released in February 1993. Though promising in concept, the story (detailing the Dowager Empress's efforts to turn foreign interests against one another) did little to build on the successful elements of the first two films. It also marked Jet's last appearance as WFH for a while, and a split with Tsui. It is likely, though, that a greater influence on Jet's decision to further his career with other directors was *Swordsman II*, an "interlude" film made between *OUATIC 2* and *3*.

Though Tsui Hark was still a guiding force as coscreenwriter and producer, the film—which is a sequel to the 1990 King Hu–directed adaptation of the popular Jin Yong novel—bore the unmistakable stamp of director Ching Siu-tung. Like Ching's *A Chinese Ghost Story*, *Swordsman II* was an unabashed mythical hero film, featuring an all-star cast and a wild story about a quest for magical scrolls. It was everything that *OUATIC* and its sequels were not, proving that Jet's success was independent of Tsui Hark and Wong Fei-hong.

Swordsman II is not as Jet-specific as the *OUATIC* movies. Brigitte Lin as the sorceress Invincible Asia owns the film's best moments, foreshadowing her future triumphs in *Swordsman III: The East Is Red* and *The Bride with White Hair*. Jet, despite his lead billing, often seems to be on hand largely for weapons expertise. Still, for the first time since becoming a *bona fide* star, he was working with another major director, playing a less-than-heroic character, and holding his own with an all-star ensemble; sharing screen time with such costars as Lin, his faithful *OUATIC* companion Waise Lee, Rosamund Kwan, and his future Fong Sai Yuk companion Michelle Reis.

the Legend of corey Yuen

The year 1993 was an unusually prolific one for Jet Li—he made his first foray into producing his own films, forging new alliances with directors Corey Yuen and Wong Jing. Together, the pair directed eight of Jet's next ten projects. The five 1993 films that followed *OUATIC 3* are also noteworthy for what they do and do not share with the *OUATIC* series. All are costume action films, of which four are *OUATIC*-style kung fu films centering on

factual heroes from Chinese and martial arts history (Wong Jing's film *Kung Fu Cult Master*, a loopy remake of Shaw Brothers' *Holy Flame of the Martial World*, being the one exception). Unlike the *OUATIC* films, however, most are surprisingly light and comic—as befits their directors—a conscious effort on Jet's part to forge a new persona closer to his own personality, while simultaneously distancing himself from Wong Fei-hong.

Wong Jing's *Last Hero in China* is easily the most obvious of these, a quasi-parody of the *OUATIC* films in which Jet plays a zany Wong Fei-hong as skilled in "chicken dancing" as drunken boxing. On a more serious note is Yuen Woo-ping's *Tai Chi Master*, a flashy tale loosely based on the life of the alleged originator of Tai Chi. But in the end it was Jet's first foray into producing—the Corey Yuen–directed *Fong Sai Yuk* and its sequel—that would have the greatest impact.

Fong Supplants Wong

Fong Sai Yuk is based on the adventures of a real-life Ching dynasty hero—a kindred legend to that of Wong Fei-hong, yet without Wong's imposing cinematic legacy. Jet was free to fashion Fong Sai Yuk in his own image . . . with a little help from Corey Yuen, who inaugurated the careers of Cynthia Rothrock and Michelle Yeoh with such films as *Blonde Fury*, *Magic Crystal*, *Yes! Madam*, and *Royal Warriors*.

Swordsman 2

at directing films with supernatural and mythical themes, earning a reputation as one of the most diverse directing talents in the business. Like most Peking opera–trained directors, he's expert at constructing elaborate, theatrical set pieces, highlighted by backbreaking stuntwork and a particular fondness for integrating props and exotic locales into action sequences. Like his friends Jackie and Sammo, he also viewed genre conventions with skepticism, injecting his films with a mischievous irreverence ideally suited to helping Jet swap the unflappable Wong Fei-hong for the prankish Fong Sai Yuk.

Fong Sai Yuk owes as much to Hollywood as to Hong Kong, mixing traditional elements with those of farce and screwball comedy to produce one of the most utterly original Hong Kong films ever made, an entertainment that owes as much to Billy Wilder as to Tsui Hark. It's irresistibly clever.

The ingeniously constructed story finds the Ching emperor Ch'ien Lung so haunted by fear of assassination at the hands of the Red Flower Society that he sends Governor Oryeetor (Zhao Wen-zhou) to seize the Society's list of members and hunt them down one by one. Meanwhile, in Canton, a former bandit-turned-landowner named Tiger Lu (Chen Sung-yung) looks to legitimize himself with the locals by offering the hand of his

At the same time, as an action director on films like Tsui's *Zu: Warriors from the Magic Mountain* and director of the famed *Saviour of the Soul*, he had proven his skill

daughter, Ting Ting (*Swordsman II*'s Michelle Reis), to whomever can defeat his wife Siu Wan (Sibelle Hu) in a kung fu competition. Mischief-making young Fong Sai Yuk—not realizing he has already met the real Ting Ting—almost wins, but intentionally loses when he mistakes a homely servant girl for the would-be bride. To salvage family pride, Sai Yuk's mother (played by the delightful Josephine Siao) enters the contest, masquerading as Sai Yuk's brother Tai Yuk and winning not only the hand of Ting Ting but the heart of Ting Ting's mother. Sai Yuk and his mother then cook up a story about Tai Yuk's death, hoping the whole thing will blow over. But Tiger Lu demands a substitute groom, and Sai Yuk finds himself right back where he started.

As if things weren't yet complicated enough, Oryeetor shows up to enlist the help of Tiger Lu in tracking down the keeper of the elusive list . . . Sai Yuk's father (Paul Chu-kong). As both families suddenly feel the repercussions of being on the bad side of the emperor, the film's jovial tone becomes somber, multiplying tragedy and misfortune, until the carefree Sai Yuk is forced to rise to the occasion and become both a hero and a man.

Convincingly adopting a trajectory that was the diametric opposite of Wong Fei-hong's—a boy who becomes a man as opposed to a man coming to grips with his boyish predilections—was an impressive feat, as was Corey Yuen's deft juggling of so many diverse comedic and dramatic elements. Funny, touching, thrilling, and romantic—*Fong Sai Yuk* was a cinematic potpourri that Hong Kong audiences wouldn't soon forget.

Key to the tricky execution was exploiting Jet's own charisma and personality, giving audiences enough campy action and self-referential wit to ensure that everyone was in on the joke. After an early run-in with police, Sai Yuk assuages his two friends' fears that their parents might find out, confessing that he gave false names to the police. When his friends ask what name he gave for himself, he strikes the familiar pose of Wong Fei-hong and declares, "Wong . . . Jing!" It's a ferociously funny double-joke that endears a new hero at the expense of an old one while paving the way for Jet's future transition to contemporary action films. The setting of *Fong Sai Yuk* may have been period, but its spirit was inescapably modern.

Though *FSY* is stylistically campier than anything in the *OUATIC* series, Corey Yuen's approach was essentially the same as Tsui Hark's, using the elegance and versatility of Jet's *wushu* to seamlessly fuse techniques from both traditional kung fu films and supernatural films. Many of the resulting set pieces testify to a chemistry between actor and director that surpasses even that between Jet and Tsui Hark, with the tower-top challenge a must-see. The contest has one simple rule—whoever touches the ground loses. Every imaginable possibility and combination is exploited. At one point, the furious combat shifts from the tower onto the heads and shoulders of the spectators!

Although most of the scene is wirework-aided, there is still ample opportunity for Jet to showcase the range of his martial talents. Bodies run, jump, hurl, fall, fly, kick, and spin so quickly and so elegantly that technique almost disappears. Subsequent scenes adhere to the same stylistic recipe, although with less complexity and, oftentimes, even more humor. In one such scene, Fong Sai Yuk and his mother furiously trade blows with Oryeetor, eventually backing off and simply staring as Oryeetor embarrasses himself by continuing to fight opponents that are no longer there. The joke proved so popular that it was repeated in the sequel.

And yet, it is neither action nor humor for which *Fong Sai Yuk* and its sequel—released an amazing four months later—are best remembered, but the chemistry between Jet and Josephine Siao, a onetime martial arts superstar herself during the 1960s. Together, Fong Sai Yuk and Mama Fong are more like a kung fu Laurel and Hardy—partners and coconspirators in mischief with a familial knack for kicking butt . . . and mucking up just about every-

thing else (Jackie Chan echoed the shtick in *Drunken Master II* with Anita Mui as his stepmother). Again, it was a dynamic for which Jet was uniquely suited—he played both the impulsive son and the fearless fighter with equal aplomb.

Picking up where the first film left off, *Fong Sai Yuk 2*'s one great strength is that it expands upon the relationship, further developing the character of Fong Sai Yuk in much the same way that OUATIC 2 helped evolve Wong Fei-hong through his relationship with Aunt Yee. As an internal political struggle threatens to tear the Red Flower Society apart, even threatening his marriage to Ting Ting, only Fong's relationship with his mother remains constant. In the awe-inspiring climax—reminiscent of a similar scene in the first film—Fong must balance a column of chairs to save his mother from a hangman's noose, while fending off an army of attackers. It's a magnificent tour-de-force for Jet, Josephine Siao, and Corey Yuen that proves the formidability of their collaboration and the *Fong Sai Yuk* formula.

Even if *Fong Sai Yuk* had failed to redirect Jet's career, it's certain that *Tai Chi Master* would have done the job. Jet's only collaboration with Yuen Woo-ping as a director (who has thrice served as action director on Jet Li films) bears a sharp resemblance to the style, substance, and formula of the *Fong Sai Yuk* and OUATIC films while adding enough of Yuen's own patented artistry to keep the recipe fresh.

The story is a fictionalized telling of the alleged creator of the martial art tai chi wrapped around a more conventional friends-turned-enemies morality tale. Raised from childhood to be monks at the Shaolin Temple, Tianbao (Chin Siu-ho) and elder brother Junbao (Jet Li) are the most unlikely of friends. Though technically the senior, Junbao is compassionate and forgiving to the point of naïveté, while egotistical Tianbao resents all authority and longs only for power and privilege—appetites that eventually get them both expelled from the temple and cast into the harsh world of the Ching dynasty. As the political realities of the era magnify their respective differences and ambitions, the friends part ways—Tianbao joining ranks with the powerful eunuch Liu Jin, and Junbao falling in with a group of antigovernment Taoist rebels, including a ferocious fighter/jilted wife named Qiuxue (Michelle Yeoh).

Ruthlessly determined to work his way up the imperial ladder at any and all costs, Tianbao uses his friendship with Junbao to lure the rebels into an ambush from which only Junbao, Qiuxue, and the redoubtable Reverend Ling manage to survive. The betrayal pushes Junbao into a catatonic stupor from which he emerges only after being struck by an epiphany regarding such fundamental Taoist principles as man's harmonious relationship with nature and the redeeming qualities within oneself. Dragsville.

The realization, however, does more than simply lift his spiritual burden—it prompts him to a deeper understanding of the martial arts whereby he evolves a powerful, revolutionary new style of fighting in which less becomes more as the aggressive force of one's opponents is turned against them. Or, as it were, against Tianbao during the ensuing and obligatory finale. When Tianbao finally demands to know the name of this invincible new form of boxing, Junbao proudly proclaims, "Tai chi."

Given Jet's stature as the foremost interpreter of heroes and historical figures—not to mention his broad skills with all forms of martial arts—it's hard to imagine anyone else in the lead. Indeed, his riveting demonstrations of tai chi boxing are among the film's great joys. The endbattle is a logical extension of the OUATIC finale, with Jet once again the victorious vessel of inner peace.

Like Fong Sai Yuk, Junbao is a carefree youth dragged kicking, screaming, and ultimately triumphant into adulthood through personal tragedy. Several key scenes closely parallel set pieces in the *Fong Sai Yuk* films. Junbao's rescue of Qiuxue from Tianbao is a case in point—a near-perfect duplicate of

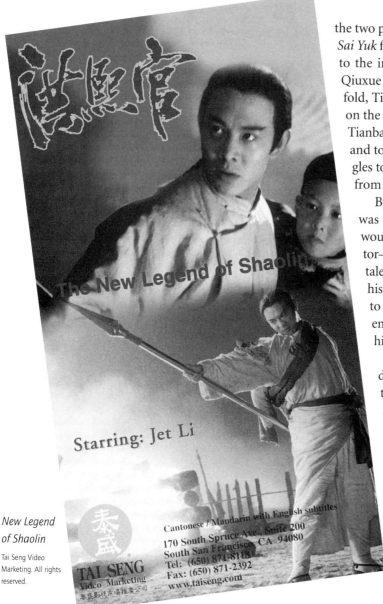

the two previous rescue scenes in the *Fong Sai Yuk* films, with additional throwbacks to the infamous tower challenge. While Qiuxue hangs from a cross atop a log scaffold, Tianbao and Junbao do battle first on the ground and then with the logs—Tianbao working to destabilize the tower and topple Junbao while Junbao struggles to free Qiuxue and keep the tower from collapsing.

By early 1994, another career shift was in the offing. But this time Jet would not have to abandon his director—he had found in Corey Yuen a talent that perfectly complemented his own—a director forceful enough to bring out his best, yet versatile enough to change and grow with him.

With Corey Yuen as action director, they next worked together on Wong Jing's 1994 *New Legend of Shaolin*, another effective exploitation of Jet's successful gentle-warrior persona. Borrowing from the popular Japanese *Lone Wolf & Cub* films (better known as the *Babycart* series), Wong's screenplay refashioned the story as a mix of *Ming Rebel* and *Shaolin Temple* genre elements, spiced with his own unique brand of haphazard outlandishness. The saving grace was the magical pairing of Jet and Tze Miu—a seven-year-old scene-stealing martial arts prodigy—as a devoted father and son kung fu team. The pairing proved so popular that they teamed up again on Corey Yuen's far-better *My Father Is a Hero* the next year.

New Legend of Shaolin is fun, but it's not a unique contribution to Jet's body of work. In contrast to his best work with Tsui Hark and Corey Yuen, there is a sense that he is no longer an equal participant in the action. Outside of some impressive spear and staff fighting, the film is so dominated by wirework and Wong Jing's signature weirdness that any discernible technique on Jet's part is lost in the shuffle. Even the humor seems oddly uninspired, highlighted by only a handful of memorable deadpan moments between Jet and Tze Miu and a closing cameo by Wong that takes a friendly swipe at Fong Sai Yuk.

Ordinarily, it would be easy to dismiss the film as an anomaly in the Jet Li corpus. But the coalescence of so many familiar elements—and cast members—from previous films, with so little additional innovation, is a sobering reminder that since his *OUATIC* breakthrough, Jet had made nothing but period hero films—a total of ten in four years. If the sheer novelty of finally placing him in a contemporary set-ting weren't enough to justify the transition now, nothing would.

My Director Is a Hero

The 12-month period between summer 1994 and summer 1995 would see the release of four (mostly) contemporary films with which Jet would further refine and redefine his image. Ironically, the new career phase followed roughly the same beat as the previous one, with Jet's grittier new persona once again shepherded by the intuitive talents of Corey Yuen and capped by a blast of Wong Jing excess (the action satire *High Risk*) to force yet another career makeover. But by that time, Jet's transition to full-fledged action hero would be complete, leaving nothing unapproached but the path to Hollywood stardom.

Though the move to tougher, more realistic contemporary films (hereafter referred to as toughies) was the riskiest step of Jet's career to date, at least three of the four films from the period—two directed by Corey Yuen—seem consciously designed to minimize potential pitfalls. Both Corey Yuen projects—*The Bodyguard from Beijing* and *My Father Is a Hero*—cast Jet as a fish-out-of-water Mainlander, while the third film—*Fist of Legend*—refashions Bruce Lee's fact-based *Fist of Fury* character as a Wong Fei-hong–style patriot, fighting for Chinese honor against Japanese aggression. All three films also feature a retreat from the high-stylization that had constrained his freedom to showcase unaided *wushu* techniques in his last few period films. *Fist of Legend* and *My Father Is a Hero* in particular contain some of the best examples of straight combat found in any Jet Li film. Best of all, the films belonged to a more generic action genre with which Corey Yuen was both familiar and comfortable.

As the first of the four toughies to be released, the success of *The Bodyguard from Beijing* was pivotal—not unlike *Fong Sai Yuk*, their last collaboration on which Jet also served as producer. An amusingly shameless rip-off of the Kevin Costner/Whitney Houston smash *The Bodyguard*, it featured Jet as a stone-faced, hotshot member of an elite Beijing Police bodyguard unit who lands the inauspicious job of protecting a murder witness named Michelle Yeung (Christy Chung), the spoiled girlfriend of a wealthy Hong Kong businessman.

Anyone familiar with *The Bodyguard* can easily fill in the rest, although in this variation, an outright romantic consummation between Jet and Chung is not to be had. The real surprise is that the film contains so little actual fighting. *The Bodyguard from Beijing* doesn't lack action—abundant gunplay and several excellent lurking-assassins set pieces give it plenty of juice. But Jet had never so much as touched a gun before—and now he was executing

attackers by the dozens. Audiences, fortunately, didn't seem to care. Jet Li the Personality had finally superseded Jet Li the Martial Artist.

Amusingly, the most memorable scene in the film is the climactic showdown—a housebound fight between Jet and Ngai Sing as a revenge-crazed assassin. The sequence is vintage Corey Yuen. As natural gas fills the room, Jet and Ngai are forced to abandon their guns and fight hand to hand. But the thinning air and risk of suffocation raises the stakes, turning an ordinary kitchen faucet into a life-saving grail. Props play a part, too—countertops, table legs, venetian blinds, and even a wet towel. In visible contrast to the fantastical spectacles of the previous years, the action was rough and realistic—a first-rate showcase for the versatility of Jet's *wushu* and the sadism of Corey Yuen's rib-cracking stunts.

More and better was the mantra of the duo's next film—*My Father Is a Hero*—their last such collaboration to date (excluding Corey Yuen's action direction and choreography on *High Risk* and *Lethal Weapon 4*) and viewed by some as the definitive example of their ability to bring out the best in each other. In some ways more reminiscent of a 1940s-era Hollywood melodrama than a traditional Hong Kong action film, *My Father Is a Hero* relates to *The Bodyguard from Beijing* in much the same way that the OUATIC and FSY sequels relate to their

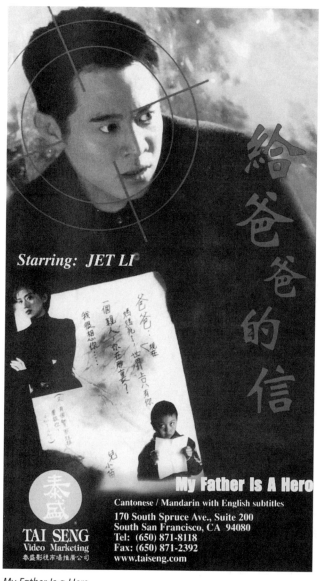

My Father Is a Hero

predecessors, broadening the emotional tapestry of Jet's character while adhering to the same narrative and character parameters established in the previous films.

The story reteams Jet and Tze Miu as another devoted father/son duo—Kung Wei and Kung Siu-ku—who, with their ailing wife and mother, Kung Li Ha, form a seemingly average Chinese family—except for one nagging detail. Unbeknownst to his loved ones, Kung Wei is an undercover police officer. "Just three more months," promise his superiors, and he'll be able to return to a normal, open life. In the meantime, one more assignment awaits: infiltrating a Hong Kong–based smuggling ring run by the psychopathic Po Kwong (Yu Rong-guang).

Shortly after he penetrates the smuggler's inner circle, however, things go disastrously awry, beginning with a semibotched heist during which Wei is identified by Hong Kong police inspector Fong (Anita Mui). Believing him to be a mainland criminal, Fong travels to China to insinuate herself into the friendship of his family. But her heart is softened upon meeting Siu-ku and Li Ha—now severely ill—who dubs her "Auntie Fong" and, on her deathbed, entrusts her with returning the boy to his father after she has died. Suspecting that Wei may be an undercover police officer after all, Fong returns to Hong Kong with Siu-ku and works to fulfill her promise to Li

Ha by reuniting the boy with his father and helping extricate Wei from an increasingly dangerous predicament. Wei, meanwhile, fights a complicated battle of wits with the crafty Po Kwong, struggling to maintain his cover while protecting his son from escalating jeopardy. The film culminates in a gripping clash of titans as father and son fight side-by-side against Po and his henchmen.

Despite a higher action quotient than *The Bodyguard from Beijing, My Father Is a Hero* is actually the dramatically riskier of the two, a mix of sentimental melodrama and action that relies heavily on the abilities of Jet and Corey Yuen to work within the confines of more serious material. Thanks to their versatility—and the smart casting of Anita Mui—many of the film's most memorable scenes involve neither action nor comedy.

When Siu-ku sends an emergency page to his father, alerting him to Li Ha's death, it is Jet Li the actor—not the fighter—who rises to the occasion, wrestling with his emotions, trying to contain his grief for fear of revealing himself to Po Kwong and his gangsters. Corey Yuen then pushes the emotional envelope even farther, plunging the audience inside Wei's mind and heart by intercutting his memories of a happier time with the present, and muting the soundtrack so as to create a surreal sense of immediacy. More harrowing still is a later scene in which Wei and Siu-ku must feign ignorance of one another to keep from disclosing Wei's identity to Po Kwong, even as he resorts to beating Siu-ku to within an inch of his life.

The same strain of immediacy runs through the film's many impressive action scenes, most of which place a stronger emphasis on character and relationship than on traditional thrills. In the first major set piece, in which Wei battles a pair of assailants on the catwalks of a sports arena while Siu-ku participates in a martial arts competition below, the sophisticated intercutting between Wei and Siu-ku delivers a stern announcement to the audience that there is more at stake than Wei's life—if he loses, Siu-ku may be deprived of a father before his very eyes. It is the beginning of an unabashedly sentimental undertow that governs virtually every scene in the film. It is not simply the triumph of good over evil for which audiences are being prompted to root, but the reunion of a fractured family's two remaining members.

Only during the finale—a shipboard auction of rare artifacts which Po Kwong hopes to hijack—does a recognizable Corey Yuen emerge to indulge more playful instincts with his star of choice. And what indulgence it is. The thunderous clack and clatter of colliding clubs jump-starts the finale as Jet disposes of the first wave of henchmen before moving on to Po Kwong and his lieutenants (*TBFB*'s Ngai Sing and Jackie Chan regular Ken Lo). Several bone-crushing minutes later, after Tze Miu joins the fray, the action shifts to Corey Yuen's beloved props—auction artifacts and the ropes suspending them suddenly transformed into weapons of destruction. By the time Wei finally ties Siu-ku to a rope and uses him as a kind of human bola/yo-yo, the audience is having too much fun to object to the shift in tone.

In a sense, it could be argued that the scene is a throwback to the Iron Fist Yim finale of *OUATIC*, a sudden burst of mythical hero film madness purchased with the preceding 90 minutes of relative realism. But by the end, the scene proves to be substantially more daring than derivative. After five years of defining the quintessential gentle hero for Hong Kong audiences, one aspect of Jet's heroism had remained unimpeachable—none of his characters had ever had to rely on luck, good fortune, or the good will of others to disentangle themselves from a dilemma. Not so with Wei, who, despite his better efforts, is unable to finish off Po Kwong until the nick-of-time arrival of Inspector Fong. Throughout the film, Wei's fate is more often out of his hands than in, marking an ironic counterpoint to Jet's own career at the time—an actor finally gaining control of his own destiny, opting instead to portray a character so loosely in control of his.

Surprisingly, the most interesting of the toughies for many fans—and martial artists in particular—is the only one of the four with which Corey Yuen was not involved: 1994's *Fist of Legend*, released during the period between *The Bodyguard from Beijing* and *My Father Is a Hero*. But *Fist of Legend* featured more than enough Yuen-power to compensate for the absence of Jet's most trusted confidant and director. Written and directed by TBFB coscreenwriter Gordon Chan, the picture's action team represented a virtual Yuen family reunion from the first two *OUATIC* films—Yuen Woo-ping heading a team that also included two of the original *OUATIC* action directors, Yuen Cheung-yan and Yuen Sun-yi.

The result—a loose remake of Bruce Lee's *Fist of Fury* and Jet's last effort as a producer to date—was nothing short of spectacular—a rough-and-tumble fight film that plugged his realistic new contemporary persona into a more traditional *OUATIC* template

Based on factual events that transpired in Japanese-occupied 1921 Tsingtao, *Fist of Legend* details the quest of a renowned martial artist named Chen Zhen to expose his master's killers and seek appropriate vengeance. Beginning with the Japanese karate master alleged to have defeated his master in a challenge, Chen follows a conspiratorial trail that finally leads to an epic confrontation with the (seemingly) invincible General Fujita (Billy Chow), a hulking wall of a man hell-bent on humiliating the Chinese into submission by any means necessary.

The obvious hurdles were not unfamiliar—Jet was again playing a revered historical hero with cinematic baggage, a character that most movie fans would forever identify with Bruce. And *Fist of Fury* was anything but obvious source material for a Jet Li film. Bruce's smoldering sexuality and bad-boy arrogance ran counter to everything that audiences had ever responded to in Jet Li. Worse was the film's vicious anti-Japanese rhetoric, anything but reflective of the OUATIC message of patriotic tolerance. In the end, however, the contrasts worked in Jet's favor, for they were precisely what gave *Fist of Legend* a revisionist identity all its own.

Not surprisingly, the new and improved Chen Zhen emerged as a slightly more modernistic reflection of Wong Fei-hong—a wise and true patriot who opposes the Japanese aggression against China, yet refuses to project indiscriminate hatred against all Japanese. By no coincidence, the point on which *Fist of Legend* differs most dramatically from *Fist of Fury* is also its most revealing point of commonality with OUATIC, namely the decision to give Chen a problematic girlfriend. The girl, a fellow student from the University of Kyoto named Mitsuko, plays a role similar to Aunt Yee, helping soften Jet's heroic edge, while calling attention to the need for cultural détente between the warring factions. She is, after all, Japanese.

Such considerations, however, played a small role in earning the film its current cult status. For fans, *Fist of Legend* is most revered as a virtual clinic on the martial arts, with Jet demonstrating a mastery of nearly every imaginable fighting style in the world. This is why the Yuen Woo-ping team was assembled, less for the theatricality of their staging than for their encyclopedic knowledge of the varied fighting styles that Jet would be required to master and convincingly execute.

Mere minutes into the film, when Chen is attacked by antiforeign demonstrators while still a student in Kyoto, he defends himself with Japanese-style locks, traps, and throws such as one might expect to see in a jujitsu or aikido demonstration. Then, halfway through a challenge with his deceased master's son (*Tai Chi Master*'s Chin Siu-ho) for the headmastership of their school, he abandons traditional kung fu for a cocktail of tactics borrowed from western boxing, Thai kickboxing, and Korean tae kwan do. A later challenge with Mitsuko's karate-expert uncle, Master Funakoshi—played by real-life karate master Shoji Kurata—goes a step farther, with each man fluidly adopting the style of the other.

Finales, of course, are what Jet's movies are made for, and here's where *Fist of Legend* attains the status of legend. The towering, knock-down-drag-out brawl between

Chen and General Fujita is marked by nearly 15 minutes of combative physical abuse so relentless that, at times, it almost doesn't seem to belong in a Hong Kong movie. The contrast of styles so prevalent in previous fights literally disappears in the heat of the anything-goes free-for-all. For once, there are no fancy props, no clever visual gimmicks, no furniture gags—just two outstanding martial artists (and a team of expert choreographers) working at the peak of their abilities to create what still stands as one of the most blisteringly visceral hand-to-hand confrontations ever recorded.

Jet's farewell to the toughies was also his final Hong Kong collaboration with Corey Yuen and Wong Jing—the Wong-directed 1995 action film satire *High Risk*, in which he played an unsung and underappreciated movie stuntman who emerges from the shadow of a fading action star (Jacky Cheung) to become the hero of a *Die Hard*-style hostage situation. It was a strange—if predictable—case of history repeating itself, with both Jet and Corey Yuen (as action director) again overshadowed by the excesses of Wong Jing's style—excesses which, as before, capped an era and helped launch a new one.

Identity Crisis

In five years, Jet had made 15 films, reinvented his image (twice), incarnated some of the most cherished figures in Chinese history, and worked with a host of prestigious filmmakers, adapting to and excelling under a diversity of directorial styles. As far as his audience was concerned, he had proven that he had nothing left to prove.

Ironically, Jet's final four Hong Kong films—made between 1996 and his 1998 departure for the financially greener pastures of Hollywood—speak less of a star entering his prime than of a creeping identity crisis; a celebrity seemingly more at ease with himself than with his image. Now in his early thirties, he still possessed the innocent, youthful demeanor needed to power the dichotomous characters that had defined his place in the movies. But something had begun to change. Characters once deceptively easy to underestimate were giving way to characters that were simply deceptive.

The 1996 film *Dr. Wai in "The Scriptures with No Words"* is the story of a newspaper serialist who guards an imaginary secret life, fancying himself the hero of his own wild 1930s-era adventures. A cross between *Raiders of the Lost Ark* and *The Secret Life of Walter Mitty*, the Ching Siu-tung–directed film also reunited Jet with Rosamund Kwan for the first time since *Swordsman II*.

Later that same year, a reteaming with producer/writer Tsui Hark and action director Yuen Woo-ping on the Daniel

A 1999 double-feature at a Tokyo cinema showcases the versatility of Mister Li.

Asakusa Kinematik Eigakan

Lee–directed *Black Mask* took the premise a commercial step farther. This time Jet's secret superhero alter-ego was real, not imagined, taking its cues from comic book and science fiction influences in America and Asia. In the tradition of *The Heroic Trio* and Corey Yuen's *Saviour of the Soul*, it featured Jet as a seemingly mild-mannered librarian by day, chemically engineered supersoldier by night. Like *Dr. Wai*, it was high-concept and big-budget, long on effects and short on kung fu. High style,

however, seemed to make up the difference, with many viewers content to simply soak in Jet's cool new look, complete with trenchcoat, black hat, corrugated-steel mask, and accompanying James Bond–like guitar theme.

Five months later, it was back to the past as—at long last—Jet rejoined the series that made him a star, playing an amnesiac Wong Fei-hong stranded in the American West in the Sammo Hung–directed *Once upon a Time in China and America*. Unlike in the previous four WFH films, Jet as Wong wasn't just pretending to be someone he wasn't—he truly believed he was someone he wasn't. This time, there was no missing the obvious real-life parallels, which mirrored Jet's own efforts to escape from and forget the character of Wong.

Just months before Jet's Hollywood debut, the most telling portrayal of all unspooled in director Stephen Tung's *Hitman*, in which Jet played a kindly would-be killer-for-hire who had actually never killed anyone. Once again, he was pretending to be something he was not, only this time Jet was flirting with the line separating bad guys from good guys. Unlike the undercover policeman in *My Father Is a Hero*, his *Hitman* character—Tai Feng—really does intend to be a killer-for-hire. While both characters endeavor to conceal an underlying goodness from their criminal cohorts, Tai Feng's moral barometer is more ambiguous than Kung Wei's. And though the character is never less than endearing—thanks to the contributions of comedian Eric Tsang as Tai Feng's bumbling agent—there is no escaping the fact that for the better part of the film, Jet is playing a character on the verge of doing the wrong thing.

Unlike Jackie Chan, whose most popular characters are nearly all variations on himself, Jet had built a career playing individuals whose personalities often contrasted sharply with his own, characters frequently at odds with their own natures. It's clear that as the struggle became an increasingly redundant part of his roles, it spoke to something more personal in his career.

Taken as a group, Jet's last four Hong Kong films cast valuable insight into what may have been transpiring for him professionally and personally. In a seeming attempt to counter the influx of Hollywood product that had begun crippling home-grown product in the late 1990s, the emphasis is on special effects and stylization at the expense of inspired action choreography. Also a factor was the absence of Corey Yuen's guiding influence to help Jet transition once more to a new level in his career, a career built as much on his versatility as an actor as on his martial artistry. By 1998, it was obvious to many that he was no longer being challenged as either.

But these films are not lacking in entertainment value. *Black Mask* remains a popular favorite, particularly among non–Hong Kong audiences more likely to be seduced by the cyberpunk style than the handful of Yuen Woo-ping–designed fight scenes. *Hitman* too has its share of impressive moments, including a nail-biting battle with a gunman in an elevator shaft and an explosive fists-and-bullets climax that keeps audiences guessing to the very end. But the singular attributes of Jet's *wushu*—his capacity to adapt to any style, to do anything asked of him, to fluidly and artfully accommodate the most demanding action directors, to give the camera precisely the dynamism it needs at any time and from any angle—were no longer being maximized. It was, by all accounts, the right time to move to Hollywood. And, more importantly, Hollywood wanted him.

Lethal Hollywood

Given the experience of making his final quartet of Hong Kong films without Corey Yuen, it's not surprising that Jet would make his involvement in *Lethal Weapon 4* contingent upon Corey Yuen's participation, ensuring that he and his favorite collaborator would have as much control as possible over the choreography and staging of his action scenes. The fact that he was playing a villain opposite a superstar like Mel Gibson meant that he would need all the help he could muster in making a positive impression on American audiences. Ironically, it wasn't Corey Yuen's choreography that won audiences over, but the magnetism of Jet's presence, the same fearless intensity behind the youthful, innocent face that Asian audiences had known and loved for a decade. Critical response was fast to embrace Jet as well, with most reviews citing him as the film's sole redeeming element.

What the film did not provide was a clear-cut indication of where exactly Jet's Hollywood career might lead. That he was able to rise above *Lethal Weapon 4*'s preponderance of offensive stereotypes and Asian clichés—at times appearing so dignified as to almost redeem them—was an undeniable positive. But Hollywood's track record with Asian material being as dismal as it continues to be, there could be no assurance that future roles would offer any hope for improvement.

The good news is that, as of this writing, the momentum seems to be swinging in Jet's direction, no doubt aided by the recent success of fellow Hong Kong émigrés Chow Yun-fat, Michelle Yeoh, Sammo Hung, and Jackie Chan. Soon after the release of *Lethal Weapon 4*, a bidding war erupted for rights to Jet's next film. At press time Jet is set to star in a modern-day action variant on *Romeo and Juliet* entitled *Romeo Must Die*. In the film, Jet will play a New York businessman whose brokering of a peace between Italian and Chinese mobsters is complicated when he falls in love with the daughter of an Italian don.

Jet as a peace-making hero caught between feuding factions? Complicated by an unlikely romantic involvement? For anyone who has seen *Fist of Legend* or *Once upon a Time in China*, the similarities are titillating. For those who haven't, the best is yet to come.

The master at work

Photograph courtesy Media Asia. Copyright Star Television Filmed Entertainment.

10

between the bullets: the spiritual cinema of john woo

by Michael Bliss

John Woo has a thousand faces. He's the romantic Christian idealist who loves guns and explosions. He's the man of peace who choreographs death and destruction better than anyone working in movies today. He's the action director who numbers among his favorite films *Citizen Kane*. He's the Hong Kong auteur who made the Hollywood system listen to a truly ethical voice for the first time since the heyday of Griffith and Stroheim. So who, exactly, is John Woo, and why should we be talking about him?

For one thing, we're talking about Woo because he's the most important director to emerge from Hong Kong cinema. In fact, he's the most popular Asian director since Kurosawa. Like Kurosawa, Woo is a difficult fit because he blends Western humanism with Asian attitudes. And like Kurosawa,

he's a man who knows that, often, violence and peace are inextricably linked.

Just about everybody has seen, or heard about, *The Killer* and *Hard-Boiled*, and most agree that nobody since Sam Peckinpah has stylized violence the way that Woo does. But unlike Peckinpah, whom Woo greatly admires, Woo isn't a pessimist. Peckinpah was a disgruntled man who thought that most people were a disappointment. Woo believes in people and feels that faith, redemption, and friendship aren't just ideals (as Peckinpah did) but realities.

There's a classic moment in Peckinpah's *The Wild Bunch* to which Woo often refers (he even resurrects it in the last minutes of *A Better Tomorrow II*). The Bunch, tired of running from bounty hunters and the law, hazard their lives by going back into the middle of a small Mexican town to rescue their friend. Woo would have shaped Peckinpah's film a bit differently, though. In Woo's films, characters don't just do the right thing when their backs are to the wall—their morals are *always* on display.

Most likely this is because in Woo's universe, everyone is always close to the end of the line. Woo probably wouldn't admit it, but he's apocalyptic. For him, life is short and unpredictable, so we have to act conscientiously always, not just when we're forced to do so. In addition to all of the delirious gunfire in Woo's films, there's always a powerful morality operating. Where did this philosophy come from, and how did it get into the films? To answer that question, we have to go back to Woo's childhood.

genesis

John Woo was born in 1946 in China's Guangdong Province, which is only 70 miles upriver from Hong Kong. Woo's father didn't like living under Communist rule, so in 1951 he moved the family to Hong Kong. But in 1953, after a terrible fire, the family found itself homeless. They lived in the streets for a year, then in a slum. Woo's father contracted tuberculosis and was unable to work; the family was too poor to

send Woo to school. Fortunately, an American family's donation through a church was used to send him to a Lutheran school. Woo never forgot this generosity. He planned to become a minister so that he could in some way repay it.

After his father's death, Woo became interested in film, but he had to be self-taught because there were no film schools in Hong Kong. In 1969, he became a production assistant at Cathay Studios. In 1971, he began work at the Shaw Brothers studio as an assistant to the studio's most prolific director, Chang Cheh. One of the most important things Woo learned from Chang was to be honest in films. Woo says that Chang was quite like Peckinpah, especially "in his unrestrained way of writing emotions and chivalry."

Fists, Kicks, Laughs, and a Redemptive Return

As a Shaw employee, Woo realized that he would have to make films in line with the studio's emphasis on formulaic martial arts dramas. Woo directed his first film, *The Young Dragons*, in 1975. *Dragon Tamers* was next, followed by *Hand of Death*, in which Woo directed a young Sammo Hung and an even younger Jackie Chan. He then turned to comedies with *Money Crazy* (a big hit) and *Follow the Star*. He tried to branch out with the heroic *Last Hurrah for Chivalry*, but the studio wasn't pleased with the film's serious tone, so Woo, who had been dubbed the "new king of comedy," was encouraged to make the lighthearted *From Rags to Riches*, which was followed by 1981's *To Hell with the Devil*. Unfortunately, THWTD's mix of comic and serious elements didn't please the studio either. Nor did a film called *Sunset Warriors* (1983), a story about modern-day mercenaries trying to topple a drug lord. (The film was shelved, although it reemerged in 1987, recut and retitled as *Heroes Shed No Tears*.)

The following years, 1984 and 1985, were the worst in Woo's career. Dubbed by the studio as old-fashioned, he was sent to Taiwan, where he was able to direct only two films, *Run, Tiger, Run* and *Time You Need a Friend*. It was a time when Woo really needed a friend, and one came through for him: Tsui Hark, a young director whom he'd helped years before. Tsui had started his own studio, Film Workshop, and offered Woo the chance to direct something he really believed in. The result was the astounding *A Better Tomorrow* (1986).

If you want to find the starting point for this excitement, you don't have to go back much farther than *To Hell with the Devil*, which is the first *real* John Woo film. It's a story about an aspiring pop singer (played by comic actor Ricky Hui) who sells his soul in exchange for fame. Two men fight

for the singer's soul: a newly-made devil and a bumbling priest (Paul Chun-pui), who will get into heaven only if he wins the battle. *THWTD* is a Hong Kong Faust story with touches of Brian De Palma's *The Phantom of the Paradise*. The task for Woo seems to have been: How do I tell people how easy it is to endanger one's soul without boring everyone to death? A comedy was the answer. Woo had made plenty of them before. Now, he realized that he could use low comedy to serve a high purpose. There are silly bits involving video games, lasers shooting out of the priest's eyeballs, and the devil getting his head knocked off and running around looking for it, but eventually, the singer is saved.

Just like Woo was saved by Tsui Hark. When Tsui gave Woo the chance to direct something with heart, something he really believed in, how else do you suppose Woo saw it if not as a miraculous rebirth? When Woo returned to Hong Kong to make *A Better Tomorrow*, he must have felt like *THWTD*'s pop singer: back from damnation. Woo put everything he had into his comeback film, bringing with him a slew of ideas born out of his personal, difficult experiences. He took stories from his childhood, blended them with his notion that the triads were morally eating away at Hong Kong society, and wrote a scenario. Then he called up a television actor who'd had a bit part in _THWTD_, Chow Yun-fat. The result was the most influential Hong Kong film ever made.

trenchcoat icon

A Better Tomorrow revolutionized Hong Kong filmmaking, not only by taking swordfighting and martial arts interplay and updating them to men with guns, but by blending together high moral codes, chivalry, Chinese opera, and the notion of the knight errant. As you might expect, this is no mean trick. Woo didn't flinch from violence or humor and he wasn't afraid to be sentimental. Reaching deep down inside himself, he gave his film history, soul, and an unabashedly romantic story. The characters in this film shed tears from the very beginning; they sweat out their anxieties about family and friends. Although there are nods to earlier Woo films (the slapstick comic business with Leslie Cheung's Kit and Kit's girlfriend, Jackie), _A Better Tomorrow_ is mostly a story about a man and his brother, on opposite sides of the law, who come to a painful reconciliation thanks to the intercession of a triad figure of epic proportions: Chow Yun-fat's Mark Lee.

Use the term "heroic bloodshed" to describe the film if you like, but make sure you understand that Woo means it literally: that's a _hero_ shedding his blood. Mythologist

Joseph Campbell says that the hero is the man who undertakes a dangerous mission for the sake of his race; that he must go through a perilous night journey to bring back a message that will heal us. In Woo's opinion, Hong Kong society, torn by the actions of gun-running gangsters, needed a healing. _A Better Tomorrow_ brought it in fictive form. Its central character is a man you feel compelled to admire. Suave, debonair, spirited, Mark enjoys himself, but we know that his type of playful insouciance can't last. Schmoozing with street vendors and cops and lighting cigarettes with bogus hundred dollar bills are actions that signal a high lifestyle bound to be toppled. Mark's friend Ho (Ti Lung) is headed for a similar fall. His secret grief and fear is for his brother Kit, who doesn't know that Ho is a triad. After a shootout, Mark is crippled, reduced to wiping off the windshields of triads' cars for money thrown onto the sidewalk. Kit is passed over for promotion; Ho is betrayed by a typical Woo villain—an amoral triad-aspiring punk—and is jailed. When he's released, he's greeted by a cop (played by Woo) who tells him that redemption won't come easy. But it does come, thanks not only to the help of some ex-cons but to Mark reconciling Kit and Ho and then shooting his way into myth. _A Better Tomorrow_ uses the typical Woo film plot: harmony to destruction to restoration. Perhaps not coincidentally, it borrows ele-

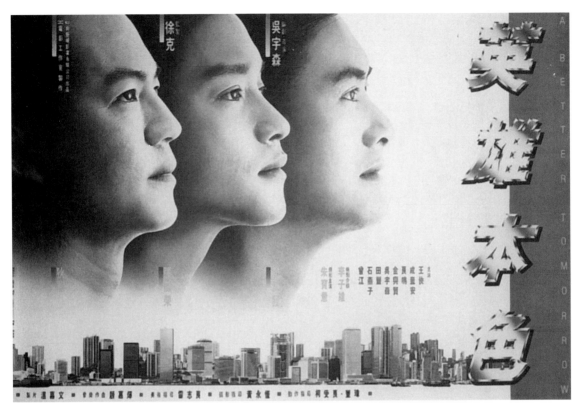

徐克　吳宇森　　　　　　　　　　　　　　　　　　　　　　　　　　　　　　　　　A BETTER TOMORROW

A Better Tomorrow

Photograph courtesy Media Asia. Copyright Star Television Filmed Entertainment.

ments from the classic story of the resurrected god, from Adonis to Jesus.

Look for Woo in the film and you don't have far to go. He's more than just the cop in the scene outside the prison: he's Mark at the beginning, loving life; he's Mark midway, down and out, crippled, in decline but never despairing. When Mark is given a chance by an old friend to redeem himself, that's Woo in Taiwan getting the call from Tsui to come back into real filmmaking. And when Mark goes out in a fiery gun battle, that's Woo devoting himself totally to this film.

Much of Woo's attitude toward the characters in this and other films is based on the traditional Chinese emphasis on loyalty and family. At the beginning of the Chinese epic novel *The Three Kingdoms*, which takes place in the third century during a time of political chaos, three men meet secretly in a peach garden, swearing to come to their war-torn country's aid. Here's their oath:

> We three, Liu Pei, Kuan Yu, and
>   Chang Fei
> Though of separate birth,
> Now bind ourselves in brotherhood,
> Combining our strength and purpose
> To relieve the present crisis.
> Thus we may fulfill our duty to home
>   and country
> And defend the common folk of
>   the land.
> We could not help our separate births,
> But on the selfsame day we mean
>   to die!
> Shining imperial Heaven, fruitful
>   Queen Earth,
> Witness our determination,
> And may God and man
> Jointly scourge whichever of us
> Fails his duty or forgets his obligation.

That's Woo's creed in a nutshell. His heroes are devoted to doing the right thing, to restoring order and balance to a troubled world. They are determined to fight to the death; and allegiance to the oath is more important than anything else.

Unfortunately, Woo comes dangerously close to enshrining *A Better Tomorrow*'s Mark as a figure to be emulated. In fact,

youths all over Hong Kong started imitating the way he talked and dressed. Woo tried to make amends for this reaction, not only in the 1990 film *Just Heroes* (in which a young man's glorification of triad life is repeatedly debunked) but also in *A Better Tomorrow II* (1987). The film is about not only redemption but resurrection, most notably via the appearance of Mark Lee's twin brother Ken (also played by Chow), whose character leaves us with ambivalent feelings. Apparently Woo felt that given Mark's popularity, he couldn't completely kill him off, yet he was obviously reluctant to bring Mark back and once again risk glorifying him. There's an interesting scene in the film in which we meet a sketch artist who has turned Ho and Mark's exploits into illustrated adventures. Talking to Ho, with the movielike storyboards all around them, the artist says, "Many things are memorable. I put down all the incidents of your life into many stories." When Ho protests that his life is "nothing much worth writing about," the artist replies in just the way that Woo might. "It's not true," he says. "The world nowadays no longer has people who are friends like you are."

It's to Woo's credit that when Ken dons Mark's sunglasses and duster, and puts a toothpick in his mouth, thereby reviving his brother's character, Woo underplays the moment's drama. Like *A Better Tomorrow*, though, *A Better Tomorrow II* still manages, in spite of itself, to add a dangerously compelling sheen to its shootouts. Often Woo seems to be a victim of his cinematic talent. But maybe Woo's gun battles can be understood better if they're seen as the director wants them to be.

The person of whom Woo is most reminiscent is American southern writer Flannery O'Connor, an avowed Catholic whose stories are filled with violent characters. O'Connor once used a quote from St. Cyril of Jerusalem that works to highlight Woo's use of violence as a cinematic motif. "The dragon sits by the side of the road, watching those who pass. Beware lest he devour you. We go to the Father of Souls, but it is necessary to pass by the dragon." Woo may be trying to direct people toward the Father of Souls, or God if you will, but he knows that you can't talk about Heaven without talking about the dragon's province, Hell; that you can't talk about peace without talking about violence. In fact, Woo would probably say that it's not only important to do so, it's necessary. O'Connor adapted one of her books' titles from Matthew 11:12: "from the days of John the Baptist until now the kingdom of heaven suffereth violence, and the violent bear it away." For Woo, part of the kingdom of heaven is the real world, and it always suffers violence. Will the violent bear the world away? Not if Woo and his tarnished heroes can help it.

Predominantly, Woo is a religious filmmaker. Remember, it was religion that got Woo off the streets, and he's never forgotten it. As he notes, "I still think a person's faith will transcend over everything at all times. As long as you have confidence and faith, you will overcome all kinds of difficulties and can have a breakthrough." For Woo, religion is much more than sermons and rituals: it's also the important things that happen between family members and friends and lovers. In Martin Scorsese's *Mean Streets*, the main character, Charlie, says it best: "You don't make up for your sins in church. You do it in the street. You do it at home. The rest is bullshit, and you know it." Woo admires Scorsese (to whom he dedicated *The Killer*), doubtless because Scorsese puts his religious attitudes and his upbringing (with all of its conflicts and problems) into his films. Woo does the same thing. What are movies for, Woo would ask, if not to entertain, educate, and improve people?

It's a shame that Woo has been saddled with the designation "action director," since it lumps him in with men such as Hal Needham, Don Siegel, and Steven Seagal. Woo may direct films in which there's action, but he's hardly an "action director." If Woo is like anyone in American films, it's Paul Schrader. A Protestant like Woo, Schrader makes films in which violence is always religious violence. It was Schrader who gave us *Taxi Driver*'s Travis Bickle, the prototypical urban demented loner: self-inspired, agonized, a man nailed to a cross of madness and pain. And it was Schrader who at the end of *American Gigolo* turned a meeting between the lady and the hustler into a scene of confession and absolution.

St. Augustine said, "that which is not of the city of God is of the city of the Devil," which is where Woo's unrepentant triads live, men whose only concern is their self-aggrandizement. Splitting the world into two camps is a pretty harsh and exaggerated view, yet to a great extent, that's the way Woo sees things, perhaps because those years when he was living in the streets taught him a simple lesson: live or die. Just look at the exaggerated way that he opposes

characters in his films. On the one side are his all-too-human heroes: *ABT*'s Mark, *Bullet in the Head*'s Ben, *The Killer*'s John, *Hard-Boiled*'s Tequila. On the other, there are street scum elevated to the level of high-living thugs: *A Better Tomorrow*'s Shing, *Bullet in the Head*'s Paul, *Hard-Boiled*'s Johnny Wong, *Hard Target*'s Fouchon. Woo knows that there's great entertainment value in bad characters, and he's smart enough to exploit them for this quality. But he never commits the mistake of making these characters attractive: they're all unctuous sons of bitches who deserve to die and, usually, do. The meting out of a rude form of justice is what makes the deaths of Paul and Johnny Wong so appealing. These men never showed mercy to anyone, and their righteous executioners, Ben and Tequila, show them no mercy. Paul isn't killed; he's executed—just as are Shing from *A Better Tomorrow* and Johnny Weng from *The Killer*, both of whom flaunt the fact that they're going to get away with murder. The latter two are slain by a silver bullet of righteousness fired from a cop's gun, which means that for Woo, the cops are doing God's work on earth.

As an artist working in a popular medium, Woo sees himself as something of a messenger. That's why he occasionally appears in his films in the role of a spiritual and moral adviser, as in his bit part in *A Better Tomorrow*. In *Hard-Boiled*, he plays

Hard-Boiled's scummy Johnny Wong (Anthony Wong) hones a theological point as Tony (Tony Leung Chiu-wai) puffs a cig.

ex-cop Mr. Woo, the owner of the Jazz Club where Tequila plays clarinet. When Tequila isn't sure if he should risk his already precarious position for Tony's sake, he goes to Mr. Woo for advice. "Mr. Woo, he's a true friend," Tequila says. "He and I are both in serious danger right now. In my position, what would you do?" Woo makes his answer simple: "If he was really a friend, I wouldn't hesitate, whether he was right or wrong. Even if I was still a cop, yes, I'd help him." "Such character," Tequila says. "Not me, old buddy," Woo says, pointing upward; "It's the guy up there." In the hands of any other director aside from Kurosawa (who with the exception of *Ran* was never this explicit about religion), this scene would be preachy or embarrassing at best. Woo makes it work because he delivers the lines sincerely; and as we know from watching his other films, Woo not only means what he says about trusting oneself to a higher power, he proves it through the convincing actions of his characters.

Woo is also a master choreographer. His choreography is based either on the music of violence or counterpoint music that connotes peace. Of all of Woo's films, *Bullet in the Head* is the one that is most like a piece of music. It starts out with a dance in a Christian school gymnasium that is cued to the tune of the Monkees' "I'm a Believer." Prominent among the dancers is Tony Leung Chiu-wai's Ben. What's appealing about dance is its innocent depiction of a wedding between grace and passion. Dance scenes also have power because often they're without words. Woo's dance sequences link up with his action scenes, which draw heavily on Chinese opera's insistence that all actions be stylish enough to be dancelike. Not surprisingly, at *Bullet*'s beginning, Woo cuts from the gymnasium dance sequence to a gang fight in which Ben and his friend Frank participate, making us draw a connection between the two scenes. Essentially, we're in Martin Scorsese's mean streets, places where if you don't have courage and integrity you're not only a fool, you're a dead man. Remember, though: Scorsese got his idea of mean streets from Raymond Chandler, who wrote, "But down these mean streets a man must walk who is not himself mean." That sums up the type of person that Woo elevates to the status of a modern-day knight: the one who fights for justice and isn't afraid to get a bit bruised in the process.

Throughout *Bullet*, we see various kinds of battles: the one in Saigon; the one at Frank's house; the one between Frank and Ringo, the street punk who tries to steal his money; the ones among the friends over the gold that the third friend, Paul, covets. Mostly, though, these external wars reflect each character's warring passions. Paul puts it best when the trio, with a café singer in tow, are trying to escape from Vietnam. He wants to take along his cask of gold leaves, even though it weighs him down. "All I want in this life is simple: just this box of gold. Is that too much to ask?" Paul says, which tells us what a pathetic state he's been reduced to. *Bullet* does something that Woo has never since attempted. It shows us how one becomes a triad: by abandoning not only one's friends but one's better instincts, opting instead for money as the measure of self-worth. The fact that Paul comes from a family whose father is a self-described failure, and who tells his son that in this world, only money counts, demonstrates that Woo knows how family can mold your attitudes. Paul's counterpart is Ben, who Woo says is based on himself. An admirer of Elvis and the Beatles, Ben has a loving mother and is the only one of the three friends who seems to have a girlfriend (he envisions her, in slow motion, walking to the strains of a tune stolen from George Harrison's "Do You Want to Know a Secret"). What alienates the trio is greed and war (for Woo, the two are the same). What destroys the trio's closeness are the destructive forces Woo saw operating in contemporary politics.

Skull Communions

The Tiananmen crackdown of June 4, 1989, upset Woo greatly. He recalled this event

not only in *Bullet*'s riots (which mirror the violence of the PRC's Cultural Revolution during that period), but also by replaying the famous image of a lone protester facing down a tank; and he dramatized the exaggerated emotions associated with high-tension confrontations by reworking the Russian roulette sequence from *The Deer Hunter*. *Bullet*'s Saigon section, which features a café that has a suave tough guy with a wide-yard sentimental streak (the wonderful Simon Yam), seems to take on elements from *Casablanca*. Ultimately, though, like so many Woo films, *Bullet* is about loss: loss of friends to crime or drugs, near-loss of family. More devastatingly than gunfire, selfishness tears *Bullet*'s people apart (Frank says to Paul at one point, "Are you putting this gold before your friends? You're pointing your gun at a buddy of over ten years. Do you measure your friendship in gold?"). It's a bittersweet film about devotion and abandonment, and it ends on a bloody, flaming wharf in a showdown between Ben and Paul, with the dead Frank's skull bearing witness to a final retribution that could only occur in hell.

Stealing a Laugh

It's understandable that after *A Better Tomorrow* and *A Better Tomorrow II*, *The Killer*, and *Bullet in the Head*, Woo would

THE LEADING MAN

The icon:
Chow Yun-fat

Ikebukuro Bungei-za

Someone once observed that Cary Grant looked like how Alfred Hitchcock must have felt inside. The connection between Chow Yun-fat and John Woo is something like that. Woo has even made the connection explicit, saying of Chow, "He's so natural. He looks great, too, like a dream hero. Chow and I have a lot in common. We have similar thoughts about the world, about people, about life. And we're both old-fashioned."

Chow Yun-fat was born on Hong Kong's Lantau Island in 1955. Like many others, Chow began his acting career at TVB, Hong Kong's biggest television studio. He was a soap opera idol as a result of his role on the *Shanghai Bund* TV series, which brought him to the attention of film directors. In 1982, Ann Hui cast Chow as the lead in *The Story of Woo Viet*, which remains among Chow's personal favorites. But despite the attraction of Chow's performance, the film didn't advance his career much. That didn't happen until Chow's appearance in Woo's *A Better Tomorrow*.

Chow is tall, handsome, and stylish; he carries himself well, handles a gun as though he were born to it, and can successfully play both comedy and drama. All these qualities were necessary for the role of *ABT*'s Mark. Yet you have to appreciate what Chow brings to all of his roles—be they gangster, fool, loser, street punk, homicidal maniac, or sad-eyed lover—a warmth and vulnerability born of skill.

Chow's resume goes way beyond his work in Woo's films. After the Wai Ka-fai–directed *Peace Hotel*, he too relocated to Hollywood, chalking up 1998's *Replacement Killers* and the far-superior 1999 film *The Corruptor*. He's charmingly quirky in director Mabel Cheung's *An Autumn's Tale*, touchingly paternal in *All About Ah Long*, and romantically tortured in *Dream Lovers*. Behind all of these characterizations is the same personality: unlucky in love, gentle, kind, humorous, and irresistibly charming. What Chow conveys is genuineness, and he does so in such a convincing manner that you can't help but be attracted to him.

Off screen, he's apparently the same way. Director Wong Jing has said of Chow, "All Hong Kong knows that every day he goes to the market, buys fish and vegetables, takes them home and cooks them for his mother." Try out that scenario featuring the average Hollywood superstar and you'd laugh yourself silly. But Chow is real, direct, and incredibly focused. As an on-screen gangster, that's what makes him so dangerous; as an enemy, that's what makes him so formidable; as a friend, that's what makes him so valuable. And as an actor, that's what makes him so rare.

Once a Thief marked Chow's return in a John Woo film, to the delight of Japanese fans.

Ikebukuro Bungei-za

atmosphere. Yet things are never unmixed in Woo's universe; even the brightest sunlight casts dark shadows somewhere, and Woo was careful to balance this film's frothiness with a grim back-story about good and bad parenting.

Borrowing elements from Hitchcock's *To Catch a Thief*, Woo makes Chow a high-class robber à la Cary Grant's John Robie. Chow's partners, Jim and Cherie, are played by Leslie Cheung and Cherie Chung. All three were originally street kids raised by a Fagin-like manipulator (Kenneth Tsang) who had them steal for him. This sinister father has his counterpart in a local street cop who tries to reform them. Again, we see Woo splitting the world into diametrically opposed camps. Naturally, this set of conflicting allegiances influences the kids, doubtless much as Woo was in his own life faced with a similar choice: a life of crime in the streets or the more difficult road, moral behavior. Because *Thief* is a comedy in the classic sense, Woo is able to blend both worlds. The kids grow up to be professional thieves, but they're good-hearted ones.

The emphasis in the film's first half is on fun; the thefts are carried out skillfully,

want a change of pace; he found one with *Once a Thief*. With its Mediterranean setting and sunny atmosphere, the film gives off a glow that provides a nice contrast to his previous films' predominantly gloomy

with great humor. Yet, as he did with *A Better Tomorrow*'s Mark and *The Killer*'s Sally and John, Woo invokes handicap as a cinematic motif. In *A Better Tomorrow*, Mark's response to his debilitating leg injury was to refuse any sympathy regarding his affliction. Sitting with Ho and Shing in a nightclub, Mark at one point hoists his bad leg onto the table, pours whisky over it, and says, "To Shing and my leg. Happy?" As Joe in *Thief*, Chow seems to be even farther away from self-pity. Injured and then (presumably) confined to a wheelchair, Joe at one point goes to a ball and has a lovely *pas de deux* with Cherie. He's so adept at using the chair—spinning, turning, at one point leaning as far back in the chair as you think is possible—that you forget he's in a wheelchair and tend to see the chair as merely a small part of the dance's greater mechanism.

The film holds out many surprises, not least that Joe's crippling is a ruse to draw out the returned bad father so that the trio can have their revenge on him. The scene in which the bad father shoots at Joe's legs, after which Joe lifts himself up out of the hollow casts his legs have been hidden behind, is more than just a great moment in cinema: it's also another of Woo's thinly veiled resurrection references, meant to show us once again that well-intentioned people will always triumph over the world's debilitating effects. What we have here is

serious business in the midst of comedy, a lesson Woo learned from classic literature.

For a while toward the film's end, it looks as though this lovely trio is going to be dissolved. Jim and Cherie have gotten married; where can Joe fit in? Instead, in a wonderful final scene, we see Jim and Cherie at home. Jim is in slacks, his wife's hair is in curlers, and Joe, in an apron, is tending to the housekeeping and babysitting chores. While the parents look on, Joe gets so involved in dusting objects and then tossing them aside that after picking up various stuffed animals, he picks up the baby, dusts him, and then tosses *him* aside, while the parents look on stunned. The film closes on one of those classic Hong Kong comedy freeze frames, but its exuberance flows on long after it's over. More than a film, *Once a Thief* is like a prayer: John Woo's hope that for once, everything will turn out all right.

Ninety-seven reasons

Woo's two most stylish films work as companion pieces, even if they do span a period of three years. In *The Killer* (1989) and *Hard-Boiled* (1992), Woo not only made two of the most important films in world cinema, he also upped the stakes. Why had the stakes been upped? In a simple phrase: 1997. Remember, Woo views things from an apocalyptic point of view. He also sees the world as divided into two opposing camps: good and evil (although he is keen enough to know that many of his characters have both traits). When Woo saw reunification looming, he saw it in terms of the destruction of the colony he'd grown to love. These feelings came out in *The Killer*, which reflects Woo's political anxiety, and *Hard-Boiled*, his metaphor about Hong Kong threatened by the takeover.

The Killer uses blindness as a metaphor for various kinds of vision: seeing the world, seeing what one's values are, seeing what you mean to other people. More so than the film on which it's based, Jean-Pierre Melville's *Le Samourai*, *The Killer* is a film whose world is spiritually played out. This quality of Woo's films can't be overemphasized. The exhilaration that comes from watching Woo's action scenes is counterbalanced by the sense of letdown experienced when you start to recover from the rush of excitement that the shootouts cause.

The same thing happens to the characters involved in the action. After all the excitement, one begins to think about the implications of what's happened. This is precisely what happens in *The Killer* to Chow Yun-fat's John: he comes to see that all of his rationalizations for his assassin-for-hire lifestyle don't change the fact that he's killed a great many people, most of

whom he didn't even know. Yet Woo is also aware that you can take this response too far. In *Hard-Boiled*'s hospital shootout, Tony (as Tequila had done earlier in the teahouse) accidentally kills a cop. Both men feel a sense of terrible regret, but unlike Tequila, Tony is stunned by his guilt. Tequila snaps him out of this response with some very practical advice: Tony must continue to function because mistakes happen. What we see here is Tequila acting as priest to Tony's penitent parishioner, cautioning him not to overindulge his grief. Chow's Ken doles out the same advice in *ABT II* to Lung (Dean Shek), who also collapses because of the slaughter around him. In each case, Woo tells us that indulging our grief is not only selfish but, especially if one has heroic qualities, a waste of time.

One wonders, though, if audiences actually react to Woo's violence as many of his characters do. Sam Peckinpah thought that audiences would be able to see that his exaggerated action scenes were meant as a condemnation of violence; Martin Scorsese hoped that people would see *Taxi Driver*'s final shootout the same way. But as Peckinpah and Scorsese came to understand, and as Woo doubtless realizes, people don't always recoil from violence. Sometimes they get caught up in a film's excitement, and morality seems to get left behind. That's why Woo puts so many scenes involving healing between his shootouts: to give the audience a chance to reflect, and perhaps realize that we need to resist the pleasure that violence can create.

The Killer seems to have been prompted by Woo's thoughts along these lines. The film's beginning and end take place in a church, because that's where Woo's heroes go for refuge, as does the director. "I never feel as completely at peace as I do after I go to confession," Woo has said. You can read *The Killer* as one long confession on Woo's part about his obsession with violence. The film tells us a story about a man who tries to free himself from a fate that's self-woven. And it's full of irony. John takes an assignment for a mob hit while staring at a giant cross; he comes to see himself only after

accidentally blinding a cabaret singer, Jenny (Sally Yeh). Jenny realizes who John really is only after she loses her sight. John's friend Sidney regains his dexterity with a gun shortly before he is killed. The cop on John's trail (Danny Lee's Inspector Li) becomes aware that rather than hating his prey, he admires him. "He's different from other murderers," Li says at one point. "He doesn't look like a killer. He comes across so calm; it's like he has a dream . . . eyes filled with passion." In fact, the whole film is drenched in passionate feeling, much of it having to do with the pain of loss and physical damage, and the consolation that having true friends can bring. In the midst of a world dominated by triads who only believe in

The Killer— Woo got the pistol cross-pointing idea from *Mad* magazine's "Spy vs. Spy."

Photograph courtesy Media Asia. Copyright Star Television Filmed Entertainment.

Ok, you've seen this classic shot a million times, but you didn't know that *Hard-Boiled* translates as *À Toute Épreuve* in French, now did you?

Photograph courtesy Media Asia. Copyright Star Television Filmed Entertainment.

UN FILM DE JOHN WOO

A TOUTE EPREUVE

HARD BOILED

materialism and money ("I don't trust anyone, including you," gang boss Johnny Weng says to Sidney), *The Killer* gives us many examples of strong friendship: Sidney and John; John and Jenny; Li and his partner, Chang.

Unfortunately, most of the time in *The Killer*, good intentions come too late: John intends to donate his corneas to Jenny so that she can see again, but in the film's concluding shootout, he's blinded. One of the film's final images shows us Jenny and John, both now blind, crawling toward each other—but they can't see, and miss each other completely. Does this mean that the film has a despairing point of view? Only if you think that the slippage between intention and action is inevitable. Woo doesn't believe this. That's clear from *The Killer*'s counterpart, *Hard-Boiled*.

Hard-Boiled is John Woo's farewell to Hong Kong filmmaking. By the time he began production on *Hard-Boiled*, Woo and his producer Terence Chang had already decided to leave Hong Kong, so Woo made *Hard-Boiled* his magnum opus. It's the most apocalyptic, violent, and emotional of all of his Hong Kong films. Chow's character, Tequila, is a maverick cop on the trail of triad boss and gun-runner Johnny Wong (Anthony Wong, at his smoothest and creepiest). Tequila is professionally impassioned but emotionally flawed. He's on the outs with his girlfriend (Teresa Mo) and at odds with his superior, Pang (Philip Chan).

The opening shootout takes place at a teahouse, where triads come to sell guns that are stashed in the false bottoms of birdcages. This metaphor of corruption underlying innocence and things of the spirit appears many times in the film, especially in the form of a hospital (like churches, for Woo symbols of spiritual succor) in whose basement Johnny Wong has his arms cache. The hospital comes to represent Hong Kong society: on the surface, clean, attractive, promising peace; underneath, riddled with moral depravity.

The film is a series of enormous set pieces best described, in Woo's words, as "operatic." What Woo means, of course, is Chinese opera, the stories of which are well known, and in which performers have to be adept not only at acting but at gesture, singing, and, perhaps most significantly for the film linkage, dance. Tequila doesn't just shoot people: he's as graceful as a dancer when he does so, like Fred Astaire with a .38. Many of Tequila's movements also involve moving down into a scene, as when he half-leans on and slides down a banister while firing his guns during the teahouse shootout, or when he rappels into an arms warehouse fracas like an angel of fiery retribution.

Tequila's problem is that he's too passionate in his hatred of evil. Pang cautions him to act with restraint, but he can't. Tequila's impulsiveness is counterbalanced by the cool veneer of undercover cop Tony (Tony Leung Chiu-wai), who's as conflicted an individual as Tequila, but hides it, partly by necessity. Conflicted characters are nothing new in Woo's films, but no one approaches the intensity of conflict that Tony must undergo; he's a nowhere man, trapped between the world of the cops and the world of the triads. As a result, he's more of a ghostly figure than anything else, living in a universe of cloudy uncertainty, only at peace when on his boat, which is moored in the aptly named Clearwater Bay.

If Tequila's fault is that he too strongly believes in everything, his nemesis, Johnny Wong, believes in nothing. Like *Bullet*'s Paul and *A Better Tomorrow*'s Shing (both played by Waise Lee), Johnny is an unrepentant bastard with no values or allegiances. Johnny gets into an argument with his right-hand man, Mad Dog, during the hospital shootout that concludes the film. Mad Dog says that Johnny is wrong to endanger the patients, that he's out of line. "What's this about out of line?" Johnny asks. Like a textbook sociopath, he knows what this morality business is all about, but he doesn't give a damn. Johnny's also a bit of a drama addict. On the way to raiding a rival gang leader's warehouse, Johnny, attempting to hand Tony his gun, says,

"Either we conquer the world or you kill me tonight with this."

You have to wonder what men like Johnny Wong, Shing, or Johnny Weng do for fun, since they never seem to enjoy themselves. Perhaps they're all a bit like *Hard Target*'s Fouchon and *Broken Arrow*'s Deakins, taking pleasure in destruction, and attempting to profit from it. Essentially, they're angels of death feeding on negation. They're also a lot like John Milton's Satan, who says with both pride and regret, "Myself am Hell."

Opposing these forces are the ones oriented toward life and regeneration. That's where Woo's use of Chow Yun-fat comes in. A reviewer once said that Jackie Chan made sweeping his change off a dresser look graceful. Chow is the same way, except that Chow commands more integrity than Jackie can muster because he's not only graceful, he's more beautifully chiseled. Chow's leaps in *The Killer* and *Hard-Boiled* are more than examples of operatic choreography: they also show his joy in living. As a consequence, in *Hard-Boiled* you can sympathize with Tequila's need to get along with Teresa, his desire to make Tony his friend.

Hard-Boiled's end is as grim as that of *The Killer*. The hospital is decimated, perhaps to make way for a new society (the same idea is in *The Killer*, whose church is

The magnificent Tony Leung Chiu-wai in *Hard-Boiled*

Photograph courtesy Media Asia. Copyright Star Television Filmed Entertainment.

in a symbolic state of disrepair). Woo seems to be saying that at least part of Hong Kong, the part that houses criminals, has to be destroyed in order to save the rest. It's a typical Christian conceit: something must die in order to be reborn. These are fairly weighty concepts for a popular art form to bear. Woo gets away with this kind of film-making because he entertains us so well. In a sense, he's like a medieval troubadour: his set pieces are his songs, and the Christian ethics are his lyrics.

Woo traffics heavily in Christian symbols, among which are birds, representations of the spirit. In *Hard-Boiled*, the most recognizable bird forms are the paper cranes that Tony makes each time he kills someone. The film's most indelible image occurs when Tony is sitting in the boat's cabin; the smoke from his cigarette wafts up, billowing among the cranes, which seem to be swimming in an ethereal fog. It's an image that comes back to haunt us at the film's end, when Tony (who, like a true hero, has sacrificed himself so that Johnny Wong can be shot) sails off into the white mist of that cold region to which he's been headed all along. Death? Antarctica? You can't say for sure which. (Woo refuses to comment on this issue.) What we do know is that the film's end recalls the mournfulness of much of *The Killer*. The echo of Tequila's clarinet wails in the distance; the boat silently cuts through the water. Tony, his head bandaged (why, if he's dead, would it need to be?), sails away into a white nothingness.

The melancholy at *Hard-Boiled*'s end is central to Woo's filmmaking. Woo seems to be acutely aware of the distance we've come from Eden, where everything (supposedly) was harmonious. We already know that he believes in a savior of souls, so this melancholy must come from the disappointments people sometimes subject us to, and also from the continual presence of evil, compromise, and deceit. Ideals in Woo's world make sense not only because they're the opposite of corruption, but because they just seem right. But even a life well lived can be riddled with doubt, and Woo

wouldn't be the complete filmmaker he is if he didn't show us that at times, even people of great faith undergo empty moments when the exhilaration of action gives way to a terrifying silence.

exoduſ

Apocalypse may never be far from Woo's mind, but not even he could have foreseen the Armageddon that he was getting himself into when he went to Hollywood to make 1993's *Hard Target*. Fearing that this Asian maverick might run amok, Universal assigned eight producers to keep an eye on Woo. The studio wasn't as savvy as it thought it was, though. One of the producers was Chuck Pfarrer, the film's screenwriter, who was only too glad to see Woo bring his story to life. Two others were Robert Tapert and *Evil Dead* director Sam Raimi, admirers of Woo, who said that they felt lucky to be paid to sit back and watch Woo work. But things still didn't turn out smoothly. Woo was given quotas as to how many people could be shot. Try to picture the scenario: "Mr. Woo, we're from the MPAA. You killed 27 people in the last scene, so by our calculations you can only kill 16 in this one."

Woo also had to deal with Jean-Claude Van Damme, who got the notion that he should be allowed to have a say in the film's final editing. Whether he did is doubtful. If you compare Woo's cut of *Hard Target* (available from sundry video sources) with the film's released version, you'll see that aside from a few lost pieces of business (Lance Henriksen's Fouchon saying that his men are "as dumb as a sack of hammers," Van Damme and Yancy Butler playing out a very restrained love scene), the film is relatively intact.

Many Woo fans don't like *Hard Target*, but the film shouldn't be underestimated. Woo and Terence Chang recognized that it would be a wise move to make a film that blended American patriotism with a none-too-subtle critique of the way that America treated its Vietnam veterans. The film's focus on homeless vets, with Van Damme's Chance Boudreaux fighting on their behalf, is rousing. Better yet, because *Hard Target* is set in New Orleans, a great deal of its action takes on the atmosphere of a homicidal carnival run amok. Woo makes Boudreaux a Bayou native (which neatly glosses over Van Damme's Belgian accent) and focuses on Jean-Claude's athletic ability. Woo repeatedly photographs Van Damme so that light haloes around him, and often features him in graceful slow-motion shots with steel guitar music in the background. The "muscles from Brussels" is turned into an avenging god.

Woo gives Van Damme a delicious set of gangster types to react against. Fouchon,

who runs a *Most Dangerous Game* hunt-a-guy-for-dollars operation, is so smooth and sleek that you love to hate him. Henriksen cleaves to the role, gleefully wasting people with a big-bore, single-shot Thompson Contender pistol. Fouchon's sidekick, Pic Van Cleve (Arnold Vosloo), is decked out with a punk haircut. Woo has Van Cleve scowl a lot, look at people through his eyebrows, and deliver monosyllabic dialogue (if you're trying to identify his accent, it's South African). In one scene, Fouchon and Van Cleve walk into the Mardi Gras graveyard warehouse where the film's final showdown is to take place. Van Cleve looks around, obviously doesn't like the setup, and, ever so slowly, says, "This . . . is . . . not . . . good." Fabulous.

Much of *Hard Target* is a replay of bits from Woo's Hong Kong films (in fact, the film is like a John Woo primer for the uninitiated). Boudreaux gets to jump over and slide around pieces of Mardi Gras floats and use the Chow Yun-fat two-fisted, two-gun salute on plenty of bad guys. In a wonderful improvement on the scene in *Hard-Boiled* in which Tequila descends from the rafters into the fray, Boudreaux drops down into the midst of Fouchon's men while perched on the back of a gigantic sculpted crane. Woo has Yancy Butler reprise a Teresa Mo bit from *Hard-Boiled*: a thug calls her a bitch, so she shoots him. Woo says that he was glad to have the

生き残るのは
ただ一人…。

ジョン・ウー監督作品

フェイス/オフ

FACE/OFF

Visage swap—
flyer for a
Tokyo showing
of *Face/Off*

Ikebukuro Bungei-za

opportunity to redo these pieces of business, like the one (again from *Hard-Boiled*) in which two opponents (this time Van Cleve and Boudreaux) walk parallel to each other on either side of a wall, all the while firing their guns. Aside from an embarrassing performance by Wilford Brimley, *Hard Target* is a wonderful romp.

Unfortunately, after *Hard Target* Woo was unable to get funding for some of his other pet projects, including *King's Ransom* (which he wanted to have Chow star in) and *Tears of the Sun*. To keep his hand in, Woo and Terence Chang took on *Broken Arrow*, which Chang refers to as "a popcorn movie." Written by

Speed's Graham Yost, *Broken Arrow* is little more than *Speed* with stolen nuclear weapons instead of a runaway bus. Since the film is driven by its special effects, Woo has little to do other than orchestrate the work of technicians. The film did accomplish two things, though: it demonstrated that Woo could helm a big-budget Hollywood production, and it brought Woo together with John Travolta, which made *Face/Off* possible.

Mr. Woo Makes the A-List

To understand *Face/Off*, you have to go back to the notions of melancholy and loss in Woo's films. ABT's Mark puts it best. Staring at the nighttime Hong Kong skyline, he says, "I never realized that Hong Kong was so beautiful at night. It'll vanish one day. That's for sure." True enough— material things never last. That's why Woo places his trust in a higher realm. The things that we take with us from Woo's films are qualities that we can treasure forever but that we can't touch: love, honor, devotion. We believe in them; we live our lives by them, not only because they matter, but because, not being material, they can't be corrupted as long as we aren't. And for Woo, what protects us from that corruption is not only our resolve but our faith.

Face/Off's Sean Archer (John Travolta), an FBI agent, tries to compensate for the death of his son Michael by fixating on his work, not as a source of comfort but as a font for pain. Obsessed with revenge against the man who shot Michael, terrorist Castor Troy (Nicolas Cage), he's unable to feel pleasure, is incapable of relating emotionally or sexually to his wife, Eve (Joan Allen), and is unsuited to be a father to his daughter.

Castor, on the other hand, revels in the sensuous and shows almost embarrassingly tender affection toward his brother and partner-in-havoc, Pollux. The face-touch gesture that Sean uses with his son during the film's opening carousel ride disappears from Sean's life until the film's very end, but Castor has a form of this kind of intimate bonding, and he displays it all the time: he repeatedly bends down to tie Pollux's shoes. In a strangely perverse way, he's far more of a caregiver than Sean seems to be. Though the two characters are on opposite sides of the law, the situation is ripe for their bonding.

Of course, there's been bonding between characters in previous Woo films, but not like this. The ads for *Face/Off* put it succinctly: "In order to trap him, he must become him." But not quite. Even after a high-tech operation during which Castor and Sean literally trade faces, Sean is still Sean; he's just in a body that looks like Castor's. For Sean, this transformation is hellish, as we see when he wakes up from the operation and smashes the mirror that shows him that physically, he's now his evil twin.

Transformations have occurred in other films before, sometimes with comparably gruesome results. John Frankenheimer's *Seconds* is about a man who trades in his old body for a new one, only to discover that he liked the way he'd been before. The process in *Seconds* can't be reversed. For Sean, after he's trapped in Erewhon prison, reversal also seems impossible. After he escapes, he must rely on Eve's believing that he's still himself in order to survive. With the strength that her faith gives him, he's able to defeat Castor.

Face/Off is a major triumph, not just because it's so entertaining, but because of what it represents. It's a film with the usual Woo pyrotechnic muscle, but it was made in the United States, in English, with American actors. Too many people fail to realize how difficult it is for foreign directors to work in another language, in a new country, and still retain their traditional themes. Great directors such as Jean Renoir and Wim Wenders were broken by Hollywood and returned to their home countries. Woo mastered the filmmaking process long ago; now it seems that he's mastered "the system" (meeting after meeting about what he intended to do, studio interference, market research pressures) too.

Woo got out of Hong Kong with his innocence intact, yet he hasn't given up on violence. In *Face/Off*, though, the real violence isn't the shootings: it's the violence done to the idea of harmony, of heaven. It's Castor accidentally shooting Michael, or blaspheming to music from Handel's *Messiah*; it's Sean doing himself violence by holding fast to the scar of his pain over his son's death instead of, as Castor suggests, getting some fun out of life. Aside from Sean and Castor (both before and after their operations), many of the people in the film wear false faces. Sean's daughter retreats behind a painted punk veneer meant to mask her grief over Michael's death (as Castor-as-Sean tells her, "you haven't been the same since Mike died, hiding behind someone else's face, hoping you wouldn't feel the pain"). Eve adapts to a marriage without love by being cool and professional. Ironically, when Castor-as-Sean reads in Eve's diary that Sean and his wife haven't made love for months, he says of Sean, "What a loser," not realizing that he's correctly identified the source of Sean's sexual problem: loss. So Sean, like Tequila, becomes a wild avenger.

Face/Off isn't the seamless piece of work that *The Killer* is, but it's close enough to show us that even in the midst of all the Hollywood bullshit (Woo wanted to have the opening run without titles, but the studio nixed the idea), Woo was still able to make a sincere film about pain, suffering, and their antidote, love and devotion. *Face/Off*'s heavenly theme of reunification seems to heal the wounds that Woo has been carrying ever since he lived in the slums of Hong Kong. Music critics have said that the notes of fate sounded at the beginning of Beethoven's Fifth are banished by the "Ode to Joy" in his Ninth. At *Face/Off*'s end, Woo takes the sense of doomed foreboding from *The Killer* and *Hard-Boiled* and turns it into its opposite, hope and wonder. The film's opening music returns, but in a lighter key. Sean emerges out of gauzy, bright light as though seen through tears of joy, comes to his house's door, and integrates Castor's orphaned son Adam into his family. The moment is touchingly beautiful and tremendously moving. The family unit—for Woo the repository of a peace that really surpasses understanding—is restored. Having taken you up with the film's exciting opening, Woo takes you even higher at its end.

It's very rare to go to a film and feel uplifted. Sometimes, movies are so bad that they paralyze you with their stupidity, as though someone injected novocaine into the old cerebral cortex. But Woo's films invigorate you. His films have the same effect as Kurosawa's *Red Beard*. A vain young doctor who's been assigned to a poor clinic run by a doctor known as Red Beard (Toshiro Mifune) rebels at the clinic's crudeness and what he feels is his low position there. But by the end of the film, he's come to see in Red Beard a man of passion, tenderness, and wisdom; as a result, he vows to follow Red Beard for the rest of his life, to give back to people what he's learned. This master/disciple tale gets to you, so much so that you feel that you, too, would give up everything for even a little taste of the young doctor's discovery of the true meaning of existence. Woo's films are like that. Not only by his stories but by his powerful artistry, Woo makes you come away from his films energized and hopeful, trusting that somehow, what will win out over what *Hard-Boiled*'s Tony refers to as "all this darkness" is a goodness that anyone can reach.

Dramatic stunts like this one (from *Devil Hunters*)
have helped make Hong Kong films world famous.
Gai Ngap Films

11

aiyaH! that Had to Hurt . . .

by Jude Poyer

"**W**hat the hell are you doing? Don't waste my time if you're scared!" "Sorry. I don't want to jump out of frame," replies the hesitant stuntwoman. "Are you out of your mind?" barks the action director. "Roll camera!" Ah Kam peers down from the concrete overpass to the freeway meters beneath her. It has taken enough courage for her to stand precariously on the ledge, but now she must dive from it onto a truck passing below. "Action!"

In the film *Ah Kam*, the stuntwoman lands successfully. In real life, the leap sent actress Michelle Yeoh to the hospital.

For every film student who's drawn to Hong Kong cinema by the twisting narratives and visuals of Wong Kar-wai's pictures, for every perv in a raincoat who sneaks into a late-night screening of *Sex & Zen 2* to mar-vel at Shu Qi's curvy assets, there are 10 other Hong Kong movie devotees who became converts when they discovered the meaning of "Action" with a capital *A*.

Hollywood satisfies the insatiable international hunger for bullets and body blows by churning out buddy-cop flicks; big-stomping monster flicks; and movies where a mad terrorist group takes over a high-rise, airplane, or other self-contained structure. But for all the high-tech explosions, computer-generated thrills, and glossy stylization, no high-concept actioner can compete with the underlying reality of an action scene in a Hong Kong movie.

Now, the film itself might stink. Its poor excuse for a plot may be as recycled as the notepaper it was jotted down on. We may not care whether the characters live or die, *but* we know that the actors playing them (and the stuntmen doubling for them and being clobbered by them) went through hell to bring us our 90 minutes of escapism.

How can these action stars (and starlets) keep their teeth when getting kicked in the jaw? How come Jackie Chan and his team didn't slice their arteries demolishing every pane of glass in the shopping mall of *Police Story*'s manic final reel? Why didn't Yuen Biao break both legs cartwheeling off a burning building in *Shanghai Express*? How can Ching Siu-tung make a motorcycle somersault its way across the screen (in *The Heroic Trio*)? And how the hell do they make those shirt-tearing bullet hole effects where blood bursts forth like bored oil from some anonymous victim of Chow Yun-fat's twin Berettas, right into the camera lens?

the power and skill of Hong Kong stuntwork

As he clings to the ledge of the Statue of Liberty in *Judge Dredd*, it takes all of Sylvester Stallone's acting ability to convince us that he's not really dangling from a model on a soundstage, a few feet above a green screen which will later be digitally replaced by a vertigo-inducing aerial view of the fictitious Mega City. But in Jackie Chan's *Project A*, we see Jackie summon all of his rapidly depleting strength to hold on to the hand of an enormous clock on a tall clock tower. The camera, positioned directly above him, shows the star and then a drop of about 40 feet to the ground below. There's no green screen, no airbag to cushion him should he fall—all that stands between Jackie and the hard ground are a couple of flimsy window-awnings. For a dreadful interval he battles to hold on, then the last of his strength leaves his arms, and so he loses his grip, and falls.

In *Shanghai Express*, Yuen Biao's only possible escape from a burning building is down. We watch him drag a rug from a washing line and lay it over the blazing edge of the building's roof. He stands on the rug, pauses for a split second, then nimbly cartwheels down to earth! Anyone who's watched one of those *Hollywood's Greatest Stunts* shows knows how a high fall *should* be done: with a stuntman falling through the bottom of the frame and onto an unseen safety-rig, followed by a separate shot of the actor making the remaining few feet to touchdown. But in *Shanghai Express*, the camera follows Yuen Biao—the lead actor—all the way down to the ground, where he dusts himself off and delivers a line of dialogue!

The list of eye-popping moments in Hong Kong action scenes is virtually endless. Whether it's the slow-motion spectacle of Sammo Hung punching Australian martial arts actor Richard Norton square in the jaw in *Twinkle Twinkle Lucky Star*, or in

Pantyhose Hero, a speeding Saab sweeping the burly Sammo off his feet, into the windscreen (which he smashes) and back onto the road, all in one spine-splintering shot, no words on a printed page can do justice to the spectacle of Hong Kong's stuntmasters at work. Once witnessed, though, on video or (better still) cinema screen, you'll be fascinated by what's emerged from Hong Kong action movies, particularly in the last two decades. We'll endure the nonsensical plots and cranky subtitles because these scenes of cinematic carnage and chaos are downright mesmerizing—and often appear to have been downright life threatening to their participants.

But is what we see really that hazardous? Are the men and women who seemingly put their lives on the line in these films relying on their own guts and fate alone? Yes and no. For example, it's true that Michelle Yeoh learned how to ride a motorbike for the scene in *Supercop* where she rides one onto the top of a moving train. It's also true that Yeoh's bike was lowered onto the train from cables attached front and rear. Audiences accept that in the world of celluloid Jet Li can really do those "no shadow kicks," and many swallow the real-world hype of press agents. It's often difficult to separate myth from reality, so don't believe everything you hear about Hong Kong stuntwork in books, in documentaries, in interviews, and on the Web.

"your skill is your safety"

For almost as long as films have been made in Hong Kong, people have been fighting in them—according to the HK Film Archive, the first Hong Kong martial arts film was 1938's *Fong Sai Yuk: Battle in the Boxing Ring*. The source of these films is the territory's rich heritage and affection for martial novels and the different regional forms of Chinese opera (both of which placed an importance on physical action), as well as genuine styles of kung fu: Chinese martial arts.

Sifu Yam Yu-tin (who worked on the Mainland as well as in Hong Kong) was the first action choreographer of Chinese cinema. In addition to staging the fights for many black-and-white films of the time, Yam also directed films and oversaw the martial art training of his daughter Yam Yin. The popular fictional tales of Wong Fei-hong were adapted for the screen by director Wu Pang from the late 1940s, and Ms. Yam often played the female lead. But Wu soon found that unlike Ms. Yam, regular actors were incapable of performing the fight scenes—a main attraction of the series. Wu had hired some genuine kung fu practitioners to work on the films on account of their direct teacher/student lineage to Wong. It was hoped that their proficiency would bring some level of authenticity to the action of an otherwise fantastic set of tales. To find the remaining fight performers—Hong Kong's first stuntmen—the filmmakers looked to the opera schools.

opera training

In Chinese opera, the theatrical tradition of China, performances consist of not only storytelling and singing, but also exhausting and elaborate fight sequences and displays of acrobatic skill. Expertise requires years of rigorous, almost sadistic, training. Stuntman turned action director Tony Leung Siu-hung recalls his childhood Cantonese opera training, under his father Leung Ban: "He used to make me hold a handstand position, with my feet touching the wall, while an incense stick burned away completely—45 minutes to an hour! If you tried to get down too early, *'BOOM!'*—you'd get hit. For the splits, I'd sit with my back against the wall with one leg attached to a bamboo stick, and the other attached to a rope which he would tighten, pulling my legs towards the wall. I used to cry!" Many kung fu films (starring former opera students) contain torturous training scenes showing how their characters achieve such a high level of physical skill.

While Hong Kong films were in their infancy, their action scenes were unsophisticated. As more and more younger opera players began to enter the scene, however, things began to change. Fights evolved from loosely choreographed movements executed in long static takes (with minimal camera movement) into something more cinematically refined. By the late 1960s there were four opera schools in Hong Kong. Three were for part-time students—kids who would head there after school for several hours' practice, followed by a nighttime performance for the paying public. One institute, run by *Sifu* Yuen, was for girls and boys who lived, trained, ate, and slept on the premises five days a week, for a contract period up to seven years. Parents were paid a monthly sum by the money-minded master who, in return, pocketed the profits from their children's appearances on stage and in motion pictures.

Alex Law's 1989 film *Painted Faces* depicts life at Yuen's school and focuses on a group of the most gifted students, the Seven Little Fortunes (see sidebar, page 110). Law's film is not an attempt to accurately represent the school, its performers, and the times and circumstances in which they found themselves at the close of the 1960s. The film shows the Seven Little Fortunes turning to film stuntwork as opera's popularity in the colony declined—though Chinese opera retains a degree of popularity in the SAR even now. The stars of the stage, having graduated from the academies, were attracted by the rapidly growing kung fu film industry.

It was much more lucrative than their stage work, and stuntwork was a vocation in which their hard-earned physical wizardry could be put to use.

An introduction to the industry was easy to come by for a gifted opera player, since the films' fight choreographers tended to be opera masters. The schools had become surrogate families for the performers, and besides, nepotism is perennial in the motion picture industry. But gifted martial artists, gymnasts, and even trampolinists found that they too could earn their keep being slaughtered by invincible heroes or standing in for somersaulting, sword-wielding heroines.

"Maſter!!!!"

A fortunate stuntman might find himself serving as apprentice to an action director. The stuntman would learn the "trade" of action direction by performing and assisting with numerous fights and stunts over the course of many productions. If he was good, he might gain the status of assistant action director, where his job would be to demonstrate exactly what the coordinator demanded of the stuntmen performing an action. The assistant is also relied upon to provide the action director with new ideas for choreography. Naturally, many stuntmen eventually tire of seeing someone else rejecting their ideas or worse, taking credit for their ingenuity, and many aspire to be action directors themselves.

Tony Leung Siu-hung spent several years as one of Ching Siu-tung's assistant choreographers, but he parted ways with Ching when he felt he had enough ideas of his own worth filming and receiving credit for. Not all *sifu*/student relationships are so businesslike—they can be more flexible, with the assistant gaining more responsibility on smaller-budgeted films, then returning to assist his master on a large-scale film when needed.

Stuntman-turned-director Ridley Tsui is one of the last generation of opera students. Tsui, a stuntman from the age of 12, followed *Sifu* Lau Ka-wing (brother of Shaw Brothers' Lau Kar-leung; see page 82), acting as his assistant on films like *Tiger on*

The chapter's author takes flight on a wire while rehearsing an explosion stunt.

Jude Poyer

the Beat 2. His tie to Lau wasn't exclusive, though. Following an introduction to Sammo Hung from Lau, Tsui worked as a member of Hung's stunt team and even choreographed and doubled Sammo in the Lau-directed *Skinny Tiger & Fatty Dragon*. But up until the late 1980s, stuntmen tended to stick to their designated teams—on Jackie Chan's self-directed films, he uses his JC Stunt Team, while on the ones Sammo directs, it's his boys who take the knocks. It wasn't until the formation of the Hong Kong Stuntman Association in 1994 (see "Club Mad," page 231) that things became less restricted.

Aiyah!

It was Ridley Tsui's job to demonstrate to actor Conan Lee how a stunt should be performed in *Tiger on the Beat 2*. This was no simple fall. Pursuing a pickpocket (played by Tsui) on a busy pedestrian overpass, Lee's character takes a running leap over the side fence toward a lamppost, intending to slide down it to street level. Before he would allow the actor (who rejected the idea of being doubled) to attempt it, action director Lau Kar-leung had Tsui and his other assistant demonstrate the stunt. Take one—pickpocket Tsui jumped off the overpass, landing safely on the back of a passing goods vehicle. Then Conan Lee made his leap.

What followed is ingrained in the memories of all those present: Lee clears the fence and falls toward the lamppost below. He grabs it but instantly loses his grip. His body twists in the air as it spirals downward to the asphalt 30 feet below. There's no airbag, box-rig, or mattress—nothing but hard Hong Kong road. "Everybody was shocked," remembers Tsui. "How did it happen?"

Amazingly, Lee didn't break a single bone. He did, however, spend a considerable amount of time in the hospital, and filming ground to a halt. Did letting his leading actor perform such a hazardous stunt constitute gross irresponsibility on Lau's part? Ridley Tsui believes not. "He's an actor. He didn't have to do that [stunt], but [Lee was] like: 'I want to be Jackie Chan!'" In Tsui's eyes, Lee would have been better served by following Lau's direction and the assistants' examples. Rather than grabbing the lamppost and sliding down fireman-style, Lee "grabbed the wrong part. He tried to grab the horizontal arm that holds the light, like a gymnast. You can't hold it! [The way we showed him], you can use your arms, your whole body, not just your hands."

Lau was not very happy with Lee's boldness, but rather than reshoot the stunt, producers included the botched jump into the film's final cut! "He was bleeding from the mouth," recalls Tsui. "He's so lucky he didn't die."

Death did occur during the filming of Sammo Hung's *License to Steal*, which features a protracted action scene at a building site. At one point, two pole-wielding gangster thugs pursue comedian Richard Ng and are about to catch him when two planks of wood spring up from a workman's pit in the ground. The cronies run straight into them and fly violently back. To the viewer it looks like a simple stunt, but the stuntmen were not completely relying on their own agility. Each was wearing a harness attached to a wire fed through a slit in the back of his jacket. The wire trailed back several feet, where it ran through a pulley at ground level. Behind the pulley stood members of the stunt team who yanked on the wire, hurling the stuntmen backward.

It took the combined strength of four men to pull back each stunt performer. The force of their tug, and a misjudged angling of the pulley, meant that one of them (to the left of the screen) was jerked back violently into the ground. Not onto his padded back, but instead, onto the back of his skull. However, despite misinformation to the contrary, a stuntman's death is a far-from-typical Hong Kong action movie set occurrence (the *License* fatality being the only one in recent memory).

full flame contact

Accidents, though, are not rare in the HK movie world where time is money and productions are in limited supply of both. Stunt performers the world over know that bruises and cuts are *de rigueur*, and most seasoned pros have the odd horror story to tell. Hong Kong stuntmen are no exception.

Ridley Tsui lists his ankles, back, nose, and jaw as vocation-battered body parts. But his worst experience was no fracture or sprain. Tsui was part of a team of stuntmen assembled in Thailand by Lau Ka-wing for Ringo Lam's dark crime thriller *Full Contact*. In the film, Chow Yun-fat's character takes cover from gunfire by diving through the open kitchen windows of a riverside house. A rocket is fired through the same window, and the whole place is instantly ablaze.

Chow Yun-fat is one of Hong Kong's tallest leading men and since six-foot Ridley Tsui was the only tall member of Lau's team, the job of doubling Chow fell to him. Tsui positioned himself on the floor, facing away from the windows. On action, fire tore through the house and licked at Tsui's exposed right shoulder. As directed, he bolted out of the house and out of frame, but not exactly intact. "My shoulder was like a banana: yellow, with the skin all peeling down. Chow Yun-fat threw a bucket of water over it, but the pain was too much and I dived into the [nearby] river."

Several factors limited Tsui's ability to protect himself during the stunt. As his upper body was covered only by a leather waistcoat and tight T-shirt with rolled-up sleeves, his arms and shoulders were

exposed to the oncoming flames (the heat alone could cause injury even with no contact). His costume did not allow for him any protective fire-resistant clothing (like a Formula-1 driver wears) underneath. Another factor was Ringo Lam's auteuristic approach to filmmaking. In most instances, Hong Kong action directors enjoy high autonomy when filming action scenes. The action director is usually given control of choreographing the physical movement of the performers and rigging whatever special equipment might be required, not to mention the positioning of the camera and sometimes even the editing of the finished scene. Because of this freehand approach, the Hollywood work of Hong Kong action directors rarely resembles the homegrown product.

Ringo Lam is one of the few Hong Kong directors who hire stunt coordinators to rig and execute his vision for a scene. Lam usually tells the action director what he wants to see, what he doesn't like, and what he wants changed. He also maintains strong control over the camera and the editing process. Lam's vision for the burning-house scene in *Full Contact* dictated that the kitchen go up in flames in the same shot as Chow's character gets up and out. In instances where the action director has control, he is freer to devise safer ways to bring the script to life. It's evident in *Full Contact* that the stunt team was well aware that the shot was hazardous—all the other "actors" are dummies!

Where's Your Tool?

Just as foam dummies often substitute for the bodies of actors, Hong Kong stuntmakers employ a variety of different devices to make their action scenes both safer and more spectacular. Some of these props are as old as action cinema itself and have remained pretty much unchanged since those early days. New devices, or new ways of utilizing old ones, are constantly dreamed up by the innovative minds of competitive choreographers. The minds that create these tools (and stuntmen bold enough to work with them) leave spellbound audiences asking, "How the hell did they pull that off?"

Taking a Knock

Although their films contain the occasional neck-risking stunt, most Hong Kong stunt performers and directors pay considerable attention to safety. But since Hong Kong action films can't compete with Hollywood flicks on scale, budget, or built-in hype, they must have a unique selling point. Often, this hook is stunts of the kind that American filmmakers could never dream of executing, for fear of accidents, death, rocketing insurance premiums, and litigation. Due to time and money pressures, though, HK filmmakers can't take the same amount of time in preparing and executing those stunts as Western filmmakers would.

Unlike a major studio film from America, which is often guaranteed global distribution through cinema chains and video labels, most Hong Kong films rely on international distributors acquiring the territorial rights for a movie to make money. Distribution throughout Asia is essential if a production is to be profitable. Distributors (and their audiences) from Thailand, Malaysia, Indonesia, and the Philippines want as much bang for their buck as they can get. It's often not the Jackie Chan/Jet Li/Chow Yun-fat flicks but the Hong Kong movies featuring less-exalted names that contain the craziest stunts—the ones that had to hurt.

Hong Kong filmmakers aren't crazy, though, and as much attention to safety is given as time and budget will allow, as long as it's not at the expense of the action's excitement factor. Any actor or stuntman about to engage in a bout of fisticuffs will be padded up. Slipping a cotton and foam

Sometimes budget-conscious filmmakers use bottles molded from thin wax. Then they get busted over people's heads.

Fung Ping Films

pad over a forearm and under a jacket sleeve is quick and enables the wearer to block an oncoming kick, punch, or club without fear of serious bruising. The audience also gets to see contact being made between the strike and block. Similarly, if a performer is to receive a kick to the torso, he'll likely be padded under his costume.

The Western tradition is to use false perspective to give the impression of a hit. Hong Kong fight scenes often favor camera angles that clearly capture the impact of a strike. While most fight performers have sufficient enough control to enable their strikes to touch but not to injure (pulling punches), some techniques call for padding.

There's a scene in *Dragons Forever* where Sammo Hung is held by gangsters and villain Benny Urquidez plants a running sidekick in his chest. Benny "The Jet" is a real-life undefeated kickboxing champion, an immensely powerful fighter who used to yell, "The power of Jesus is in my hands!" as his opponents crumpled unconscious. Needless to say, Sammo (also the film's director) sensibly opts to wear a large protective pad over his sizable abdomen. Watching the scene, it looks like Sammo's reaction to the kick, and that of the stuntmen meant to hold him up, is genuine!

The kinds of pads worn in stuntwork vary from the elastic cotton-and-foam variety worn in semicontact karate tournaments to harder ones like hockey or rollerblading pads worn over the elbows and knees. For really serious falls or reactions, motocross

There's no faking a kick like this! You can be sure that the victim is wearing a pad.

Ridley Tsui

rider padding is used—back and chest protectors made of hard, articulated plastic. Sometimes these are worn over the karate pads—the soft pads absorb the impact; the hard pads protect the bones.

Fight scenes have become bolder as films have moved away from the "stripped to the waist" kung fu duels of yesteryear. At one point in Jackie Chan's fight in the *pachinko* amusement parlor in *Thunderbolt*, the doors of a steam bath open and out rush several near-naked, tattooed attackers—mostly HK stuntmen playing Japanese *yakuza*. Note that those who receive the hardest punishment from Chan (thrown violently to the floor or onto one of those "test your strength" metal striking points intended for mallets) are the ones who put on jackets before fighting! While he's dealing with this bunch, one assailant clad only in his underwear (stuntman For-Sing Mars) grabs Chan from the front. Then Japanese actor Ken Sawada proceeds to clobber Chan's back with a metal chair. Look closely, and the outline of Jackie's back-pad is visible through his loose-fitting jacket.

To further enhance the effect of hard contact between combatants and object, Power Powder (a better name for talcum powder) is sometimes used. For example: before a kick, powder is sprinkled on the target area of the person to be kicked and on the shoe of the kicker—creating a shower of dust on impact. Likewise, the floor may be sprinkled with powder prior to a fall. Although unrealistic (where does it come from?), it is surprisingly effective: the finales of such films as *Once upon a Time in China 2*, *Eastern Condors*, *The Iceman Cometh*, and *Tiger Cage 2* bear this out.

It's easy to imagine a heavily padded actor enduring retakes of a kick to the chest, but what about those head shots, where an expertly placed right hook sends sweat flying from the face of a screen star? We've seen Jackie Chan getting booted in the cheek in *Project A Part 2*, Sammo Hung delivering a jump-roundhouse kick to some guy's head in *Lucky Stars Go Places*, and Yuen Biao planting a tornado kick on the jaw of Melvin Wong's double at the end of *Righting Wrongs*. All of these had to hurt! There are some measures that can be taken to lessen the damage of such blows, though. A mouth guard (the kind worn for boxing or rugby) or a mouthful of cotton wool helps an actor keep his teeth. Recently, action directors favor shooting punches thrown at slower-than-real speed, which make contact with faces yet inflict almost no damage. This already slow action is then shown in slow motion: The viewer's mind subconsciously accepts that the slow-motion strike and impact occurred in real(istic) time.

Close-ups of kicks to the face are less problematic. Usually a stuntman will put his arm through a trouser leg, put a sock and shoe over his hand, and then give a

SEVEN LITTLE STUNT NUGGETS

Not all great films, but, for various reasons, of stunt interest.

Painted Faces

Alex Law's moving dramatization of life for the Seven Little Fortunes of *Sifu* Jim Yuen's opera school. We see little Jackie ("Big Nose"), Sammo, and Biao shed tears of pain at the hand of their master's beastly training and beatings. We shed tears of our own as we see the extent of the bond of brotherhood between the *sifu* (portrayed by Sammo Hung) and his opera buddy-turned-stuntman (the performance of the late Lam Ching-ying's career): a man who's endured one stunt too many.

The Chinese Stuntman

An unsuspecting insurance investigator lands himself a career as a Hong Kong movie fall guy. Worth watching not only to see Bruce Li (real name Ho Chung-tao) in a role in which he doesn't exploit his namesake, but also for the props used in action sequences of different genres, as Ho fights his way through period costume dramas and contemporary (1970s) cop flicks. Rumor has it that the plot device of gangsters rigging stunt equipment to cause "accidents" is based on fact. True to life or not, you're sure to wince when Ho dives onto a mattress, only to discover someone's planted metal spikes in it!

Runaway Blues

Starring Andy Lau in one of his signature rebel-without-a-cause roles, what sets this gangster film apart is its crazy stunts, handled by veteran Blackie Ko. In one shot, a guy slides down the side of a moving bus, onto the road, and into the pathway of a rush of oncoming traffic. With just inches to spare, his legs narrowly avoid being mangled by one car's wheels. Another scene sees an unfortunate gangboy set on fire. Why this burn differs from other fire stunts is that this human torch is tied up and only wearing a pair of shorts!

No Regret No Return

There's little new in terms of plotting in this medium-budgeted hitman caper starring Max Mok, but there's plenty to recommend. Stuntman-turned-director Ridley Tsui delivers a terrific action film, especially remarkable as he was just 26 when he made it. Tsui not only directs, stunt coordinates, and costars, but also performs some unbelievable stunts, including using an ambulance roof to break his fall as he jumps from a second-story light slap to his screen-opponent's face. If the shoe has some Power Powder sprinkled on it prior to shooting, the "kick" can appear even more punishing.

Wired for Action

Wires and mini-trampolines often lend actors superhuman skill. Mini-tramps aid stuntmen in aerial kicks and acrobatic maneuvers. They're popular in the fantasy genre—whenever masked swordsmen somersault over low-angle cameras, it's likely they've leaped off a mini-tramp. In contemporary action films, mini-tramps are used to project stuntmen into the air as if thrown by explosions, a primitive (but safer) alternative to the air-rams used in Western stuntwork, which use compressed-

window ledge! The best stunt, though (guaranteed to have you reaching for the rewind button in disbelief), comes near the film's start, when Mok's double, speeding on the back of a motorbike, is plowed into by a car.

Extreme Crisis

While Ridley Tsui draws upon his acrobatic and martial-arts skills to design and execute his action scenes, Bruce Law's action is influenced by his pioneering (for Hong Kong) use of technological stunt apparatus, as well as his willingness to study Hollywood "Making of . . ." documentaries. Law's first film as director is an ambitious Asian reworking of *Die Hard* and *The Rock*, which packs in enough explosive action set pieces to distract the viewer from the script's shortcomings. Lorries explode, Rolls Royces flip in the air, Shu Qi negotiates an out-of-control car

(despite the actress not owning a driver's license), Theresa Lee falls from studio scaffolding, and Julian Cheung goes airborne. It's no wonder Law calls his company Stunts Unlimited.

Ah Kam

Although incorrectly referred to as *Ah Kam: Story of a Stuntwoman*, the misnomer's a pretty accurate one. Sadly, the schizophrenic end product can't decide whether it's a serious, true-to-life drama or an action film. This is partly because shooting ground to a halt when lead actress Michelle Yeoh was hospitalized performing a fall. Footage showing the aftermath of the accident is included in the closing credits and generates more pathos than the preceding 90 minutes of film. Worth seeing, though, for its portrayal of the loyalty (both good and bad) that exists in the Hong Kong stunt cir-

cle, and the notions of hierarchy and brotherhood found there. Sammo Hung is appropriately cast as the patriarchal stunt coordinator, and real stuntmen play members of his team.

Jackie Chan: My Stunts

Jackie Chan, the stuntman success story, talks, leaps, and punches his way through the history and development of fight and stunt sequences, displaying many of the tricks of the trade as he revisits locations from his movies to show how he pulled off some of his most famous work. In addition to the new video footage of the camera-friendly Chan, this fully sanctioned one-of-a-kind documentary uses furiously edited montages of the actual film fights to good effect, bringing the man's words to life. Just don't expect Jackie to reveal all of his stunt secrets. He's far too smart to do that!

air pistons to catapult the stuntmen. In Hong Kong films, the stuntman will run toward the off-camera tramp, jump on it, and go airborne as the effects crew triggers the explosion behind him.

The use of wires in Hong Kong films is an art form in itself, making the gravity-defying shenanigans of such films as *Swordsman II* and *Zu: Warriors from the*

Magic Mountain possible. Cloak-clad eunuchs take to the sky to dispatch a dazzling array of darts at a noble horseman, an Ice Queen glides along the heads of her assembled courtiers before assuming her throne, or (as in 1998's *Storm Riders*) a pair of dueling warriors spiral down hundreds of feet toward a crashing waterfall, their combat set against a breathtaking Buddha

Air-rams are seldom used in HK stuntwork, but here's a member of Bruce Law's team being catapulted.

Bruce Law Stunts Unlimited

statue carved from the surrounding cliff face. You don't see stuff like that in Hollywood's summer blockbusters!

Wirework is also in (less obvious) evidence in modern-day films. Steel cables (thin enough to be largely undetectable on screen, but strong enough to support the weight of a person) perform a dual purpose in present-day films. As in the swordplay and fantasy flicks, they are sometimes used to enhance the physical skill of the performers' leaping and kicking, but they also perform a vital safety function. Most viewers know there's more than just martial skill in evidence as Jet Li bounces his way across the evil White Lotus Sect's temple (in *OUATIC 2*), unleashing flurries of kicks. But not all Hong Kong film aficionados are aware of the degree to which wirework is used in a contemporary spy film like Jackie Chan's *Who Am I?*

A wire rig works by using a pulley system to make an actor or stuntman travel upward and/or backward. Beneath his costume, the performer wears a harness around waist and thighs or waist and shoulders. The wire leads from this harness, passes through a hole in the costume, and leads to a pulley attached to the set or studio ceiling. If the scene is being filmed outdoors, the pulley is attached to scaffolding or the arm of a mobile crane. The wire runs through the pulley and back down to the stunt team, who hold a rope attached to the wire—the combined strength of the team pulling on the rope lifts the performer up off the ground. If the ascent is intended to be more forceful, the stuntmen holding the rope may stand on a ladder. When they jump off the ladder down to the ground a few feet below, their combined body weight will jerk the harness-wearer off his feet.

In *Thunderbolt*, car mechanic Ah For (Jackie Chan) is visited by gangsters intent on bribery, and a long-haired goon produces a wad of cash. Cut to a wide shot and Ah For front-kicks the money from the thug's hand with his right leg, then delivers a jumping left-leg, right-leg combination of two more front kicks. The three kicks are basic ones and wouldn't pose a problem for any Hong Kong stuntman, but a wire is being used here to make the technique appear more powerful. If the stuntman performing a jumping kick doesn't have to expend energy to gain height, he can deliver the kicks with more power and more dramatic impact.

To the viewer, the three kicks appear skillful but not fantastic or unrealistic. That's because action director Sammo Hung knows that when working in the modern-day genre, audiences won't accept the degree of wire lift they would in a fantasy flick. Likewise, in *Who Am I?*, when Jackie (his hands cuffed behind his back) springs off the floor onto his feet, leaps through his cuffed hands so that they are in front of him, then delivers a jump-roundhouse kick to a spy's head—all in one continuous shot—the wire lends lift to his leaps, making him appear superphysical, not superhuman.

In Hong Kong films, most actions using wires will have the performer attached to a single wire. With just one cable, the stuntman can coordinate his ascent (the job of the team pulling the wire) with his body rotation by using his shoulder muscles to generate spin. This is how the spiraling/corkscrewing effect of swordplay films is achieved. More than one cable would get hopelessly tangled.

Double wires are worn at either hip if the stuntman is to perform a somersaulting motion. Yuen Biao's backflip kicks to the jaw of his foe in *The Iceman Cometh*'s final reel are examples of these "double-acro" wire rigs. If his body is to spend more time horizontal than vertical, the stuntman may find that double wires aid balance. In the scene in *Hard-Boiled* where Anthony Wong's gang shoots up a rival's warehouse, we see Mad Dog (Kuo Chui) slide in on his bike and spray a bunch of suited triads with Uzi lead. One of the mobsters is shown in slow motion, flying horizontally over a desk and into some boxes. Yes, he's wired: one cable between the shoulder blades and one near the spine.

One reason why Hong Kong filmmakers seldom use more than one wire on a person is for fear of the wires being visible in the completed film, as they are for brief instances (watch the above-mentioned scene in *Hard-Boiled*). Because of visibility problems, wires used in Hong Kong productions are thinner than the cables used in Hollywood. Stateside, actors and actresses can perform an action with two or more strong, thick cables, which are later painted out with sophisticated,

Bruce Law, wearing a wire harness, holding a spool of wire and a pulley

Stefan Hammond

expensive computer-editing equipment. In HK, a popular wire used for flying effects is just 1.5 mm in diameter, but it can easily support a "flying" performer.

Wires also act as safety tools. In *City Hunter*, Jackie Chan leaps over a balcony onto a model dolphin suspended by a cable from the ceiling. He then swings on it, firing happily away with his machine gun. In the end credits of the film, though, we see an outtake where Jackie does lose his grip. But the prudent Mr. Chan was wearing a harness, with a wire running through his sleeve that was attached to the prosthetic porpoise. With wires running through jacket sleeves, stars and stuntmen alike can cling onto buildings, helicopters, and ground vehicles for long periods without fear. They know they won't fall, because they're bolted in tight.

Just as wires lift people up, they can help them descend safely as well. For a good

example of wires aiding a fall, look to *Royal Warriors* and Michael Wong's sacrificial dive to save lady-love Michelle Yeoh. We see Wong, who's hanging over the side of a building by a rope around his ankle, untie himself. Cut to a medium shot showing Wong falling out of frame. We are then treated to wide shots from a low angle (emphasizing the height of the building) and see Wong's double falling on a wire. Because it's in slow motion, the descent does not appear staggered—rather, it's extremely dramatic, especially when crosscut with shots of onlooker Yeoh's reaction. For the last portion of the fall, a drop through a glass canopy, we actually see a separate fall altogether. Here the stuntman is bereft of wires to slow him down.

Boxing Clever

Of course, when jumping off buildings without the aid of wires, something has to cushion the impact. In the West, airbags are used for high falls, but falls from heights requiring an airbag are a rare occurrence in Hong Kong films. What do Hong Kong's stuntmen choose to take a dive into? Cardboard boxes. It's not as unsophisticated or as unsafe as it may first seem. The world record, set by a Czech stuntman, for the longest fall into a (cardboard) box-rig was from 200 feet!

Here's how Yuen Biao did that spectacular fall to earth in *Shanghai Express*: After cartwheeling off the burning building, he's seen dropping all the way to the ground, not out of frame or onto cushioning. How did he avoid injury in this unprecedented stunt? He's falling into a dugout: a trench in the ground into which a box-rig has been placed. When the rig is covered over by sand and straw, it's camouflaged level with the ground and largely undetectable. "That [rig] was just one box deep, with one layer of foam mattresses covering the boxes," recalls Yuen (a ready supply of foam mattresses is always on hand during action filming, to cover box-rigs, or for stuntmen to rehearse low falls). Yuen is still proud of his cartwheel into stunt history, and rightly so. When describing the safety precautions taken for the stunt, he's quick to add, "At that time, I'm the only one in Hong Kong who will do it!"

Box-rigs aren't always 100 percent efficient. In the UK, the top layer of boxes will have their upward-facing corners cut off (to avoid gouging the stuntman upon impact). Care is taken to make sure that all the boxes are tightly packed together. The latter of these two time-taking measures might have spared Michelle Yeoh her hospital stay following that jump from the bridge in *Ah Kam*, an Ann Hui film about a (fictional) stuntwoman's experiences. After stuntwoman Ah Kam fails to jump on the first take, the action director (played by Sammo Hung) gives her a helpful push

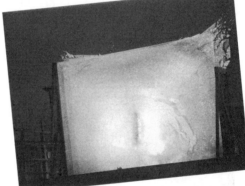

Law doing what he does best: incorporating a moving vehicle and an explosion to create spectacular devastation. Note the mosaic appearance of the glass as it explodes—it's real glass that has been pre-shattered by a detonator.

Bruce Law Stunts Unlimited

for the second. In the final release print we see her sail onto the back of the moving truck. Yeoh's on a wire but her leap is a swan dive, and on a single wire it's hard to maintain a horizontal position. As she falls, her body pivots upright. Another shot—a low angle—was to capture Yeoh (sans wire) swan-diving off the bridge and out of frame onto a box-rig. The boxes weren't packed together tightly enough and instead of absorbing the force of her landing, they shifted apart. Just as the single wire was against her, so was the position of Yeoh's body for the stunt: Landing on the front leaves the spine especially vulnerable. Yeoh was lucky to escape serious injury.

Another bad landing, this time on the 1987 smash fighting-femmes flick *Angel*, put one stuntman in a wheelchair and his coordinator, Tony Leung Siu-hung, in court. The stunt required that two stuntmen perform a 25-foot fall onto a box-rig. Leung was confident in the stunt's safety, enough to choose his own brother as one of the stuntmen: "This stunt's actually very simple for every stuntguy, especially for the injured guy (who was doubling for the actor). He was my assistant, very professional and experienced. He permanently injured his backbone because he did the wrong landing: He landed on his bottom, not his back." Leung found himself in court since the production company that had hired them for *Angel* had dissolved (a common practice in Hong Kong, which allows producers to avoid any financial responsibility after shooting has ended). "There's a regulation for those bankrupt companies that all damages they owe can be refunded by the government. The stuntman wanted money from both the government and me. We went through the civil court. My lawyer advised me in advance that if I lost I'd have to pay HK$5,000,000. I'd [already] spent over HK$250,000 just for lawyers. Finally the government paid [in line] with their bankrupt company regulation." By then Leung had already spent a considerable amount on legal fees. Discouraged from spending more trying to get his costs refunded, Leung (a devout Buddhist) accepted this unfortunate turn of events as part of his karma. The silver lining was that the accident and its ensuing litigation was one factor that made him an active participant in establishing the Hong Kong Stuntman Association. The mishap, which had left one stuntman paralyzed, could hardly be blamed on Leung. ("I'm very concerned about safety.") The accidents on *Angel* and *Ah Kam* have to be seen in context: two injuries for the hundreds of times box-rigs have been used in Hong Kong films.

A Pane in the Glass

Wires, boxes, and pads are the responsibility of the stunt team, but there are other instances when the team must work in conjunction with the film's effects crew. If a stuntman is to be torched, exploded, riddled with machine-gun fire, or sent crashing through a window, then he has to have faith not only in his coordinator, but also in whoever is responsible for handling the various props that facilitate the stunt.

Princess Diana once demonstrated to the world the safety of a sugar-glass bottle by smashing one over her spouse's head at a James Bond exhibition. But sugar isn't always the answer, and not all the glass used in stunt sequences is phony. Sometimes budget-conscious filmmakers use bottles molded from thin wax. But in Hong Kong, if an actor or stuntman is to smash into a picture frame or cabinet, the chances are that it'll be made from sugar.

That's how Jackie Chan's stunt team keeps their arteries intact at the end of *Police Story*. Sugar glass is safe enough that actress Brigitte Lin rather than a stunt double was hurled through the odd store display too. But sugar-glass sheets aren't cheap, and sometimes (especially for actions involving large windowpanes), real glass is used. Of course you don't crash straight through: The effects department attaches an explosive charge to the pane of glass, and the charge is triggered an instant before the performer hits it. The glass (the reinforced kind used for car windshields) shatters into thousands of tiny fragments. "Charged glass," though relatively safe, can inflict small cuts. Few action directors expect

A fall through a window—because the glass looks so real as it shatters, you can be pretty sure that it's fake, and made from sugar.
Ridley Tsui

actors to work with it: a small cut to the face isn't a serious health risk but could cause major continuity problems. Stuntmen can travel through charged glass without too much worry. Naturally, if he's traveling through it face-forward, a stuntman will close his eyes and try to shield his face with his arms. He may also put cotton wool in his ears to prevent any small fragments getting trapped there. All should be safe, so long as the effects man doesn't detonate the charge too late!

It's generally easy to distinguish between sugar glass and real (charged) glass. If it's genuine, the glass will have a mosaic appearance to it just prior to its being broken, because the charge has been detonated. Sugar glass, ironically, breaks into real-looking shards when smashed. In *Task Force*, a bold raid on a triad hangout is executed by a stunt double crashing through the locked front doors, which are solid glass. The doors are charged, so when they break, they shatter, and the stuntman can safely roll over the debris without sustaining serious cuts. By contrast, the display cases that Yuen Biao and Yuen Wah send each other into at the end of *The Iceman Cometh* are made from sugar glass—that's why they look so real!

Going Out with a Bang

How do filmmakers create the illusion of bullets tearing through clothing and flesh? Through ingenious devices known as squibs. In Hollywood films, one has to look back to James Caan's execution in *The Godfather* or the bloody battles of Sam Peckinpah films to see the kind of devotion to the squib now only found in marvelously politically incorrect Hong Kong cinema.

Squibs are small plastic packets (condoms can be used) filled with fake blood—a mixture of food coloring, for redness, and cough syrup, for texture—and linked to an explosive charge. They are most commonly placed under or in the lining of clothing. When detonated, the explosion tears through the material and glorious red goo gushes forth. In Hong Kong, squibs are just part and parcel of creating a gunfight scene. Single-squib rigs are quick to prepare. Usually these are detonated by the effects crew, and it's the job of the actor or stuntman wearing the squib to react as if shot,

in time with its detonation. For the simplest single-squib rigs, the explosive charge is attached to a pair of electrical wires trailing down the trouser leg of the performer. If one squib is to be set off in a given take, the crewman may be exploded by touching the wires to a battery's terminals, causing a short circuit.

If the performer is wearing multiple squibs, the wires usually lead to a detonating board, where they're set off in a preset sequence. The performer knows the sequence and can jerk his or her body appropriately. That's how the effect of several bullets hitting the chest, stomach, and arms of a person can be achieved in a single shot.

Both camera crew and performer must take care not to make the trailing wires visible. During Chow Yun-fat's warehouse raid in *Hard-Boiled*, there's a memorable moment just after Tony (Tony Leung Chiuwai) has told Johnny (Anthony Wong) to leave. Tony, armed with two handguns, comes from behind a car to face Chow. One gangster in a light jacket and dark pants is in front of Tony—he's ready to shoot Chow but gets blasted in the chest by Chow's pump-action shotgun. In the shot that established this unfortunate triad just seconds earlier, the camera (following Tony) tilts low enough for us to see a large group of wires trailing out of his left trouser leg. Thankfully, though, the action, camera movement, and editing in the scene is so

BALLERINA DANGLE

A total disregard for human life sometimes appears to be the hallmark of a good Hong Kong action director. Based on one infamous scene in *Fatal Termination*, a femme-fightin' flick starring Moon Lee, Philip Ko Fei seems to fit the bill. Moreover, he seems a prime candidate for an injunction forbidding him from working with children, for in this movie he appears to put the life of a sweet little girl on the line.

The scene is a favorite among Western fans of Hong Kong action as it typifies the films' blatant disregard for all that Hollywood codes hold sacred. Moon Lee's cute daughter (about six or seven, it looks) is dressed and ready for ballet class. Unfortunately, no sooner has she parted with Mom than she's kidnapped by smirking crims, planning to bring a whole new meaning to the term "snatch and grab." The baddies' car speeds past the girl. From the backseat, a demented hairy *gwailo*—think: Chewbacca on crack—reaches out of the window and picks up the child by her hair! The vehicle takes off at high speed and races down busy streets with Moon's speeding-away daughter held inches above the asphalt. Audiences can see that it's a real girl whose kicking ballet booties are traveling at high speed over real highway.

"The critics wrote, 'Those filmmakers are crazy! How can they hang a little kid like that?'" remembers Ridley Tsui, who was working under Ko for that film. "But they didn't know that we set things up very safely." Of course it wasn't a human arm holding the little girl, but a metal bar "wearing" a jacket sleeve. The bar was securely attached to a sturdy metal cage inside the car, like the ones fitted inside racing cars. The little girl was wearing a wire harness, with a strong metal wire trailing up her back and onto the metal. The wire is concealed by the tuft of the girl's hair in the "hand" of the bar. Locked into place, she was as snug as the proverbial bug in the rug.

The girl's parents were on hand to oversee the execution of the sequence, which turns into a fight scene, with Moon Lee battling on the hood while her ballerina babe dangles from the side. Tsui adds: "Of course she was ok. The little girl was very relaxed, just pretending to be crying when we needed her to." In between sniffles, she's vigorously clawing at her tormentor's eyes. This ferocious pint-sized cutie has been awarded the special Toughest Tiny Ballerina in a Hong Kong Film award in perpetuity.

Fatal Termination's jaw-dropper—there's no truth to the rumor that Hong Kong taxi drivers have resorted to similar tactics to resolve fare disputes.

My Way Films

Bang!
Karel Wong Chi-yeung

fast and furious that such oversights tend to pass undetected.

Squibs are, on the whole, safe. As with any action tool, though, there are safety measures that lessen the chance for mishaps. With multiple squibs or powerful single squibs, closing the eyes keeps them clear of any nasty flying (fake) blood. If the squibs are on the chest, one's arms should be kept clear—one *Thunderbolt* actor's biceps was badly scarred by the flames of his exploding squibs. Accidents involving squibs are rare, but stuntmen tend to do the most squib work since they're not expected to waste as much time as actors with "NGs" ("No Good" takes) or predetonation nerves. Actress Shu Qi was reportedly in tears when Ching Siu-tung required she be rigged with multiple squibs in *The Blacksheep Affair*—rather ironic, since most Hong Kong stuntmen (who think nothing

of reacting to squibs) would never have the guts to pose for the kind of photographs Miss Shu is famous for!

Some action directors don't hesitate before attaching squibs to the heads of actors and stuntmen (see Yuen Wah's slow-motion demise in *On the Run*, or Theresa Lee paying the price for indecision in *Extreme Crisis*). But care should be taken that the squibs aren't too heavily charged.

Ouch!

Karel Wong Chi-yeung was eager to please on the set of the 1989 Ocean Shores production *The Last Duel*. Having won a much-coveted television acting contract with TVB, the 22-year-old hoped that he could create an equally impressive impact in his big-screen debut. He was therefore willing to perform whatever hazardous actions stunt director Lau Chi-hon (*The Killer*) required from him without using a double. When the time came to film his character's justly grisly demise, Lau decided that Wong should take a bullet through the head. Two squibs (loaded with ample fake blood) were attached to the back of the actor's head on either side. The camera was overcranked (so that the image—giving the impression of the bullet tearing through Wong's skull, and his reaction—could be shown in slow motion) and began to roll. "Action!"

"It felt like two baseball bats smashing the sides of my head," recalls Wong. "I was weak, I was deaf—I mean I thought they'd deafened me. It wasn't until three hours later that I started to hear again."

Wong is careful not to lay any blame on Lau. "Often, it's not the stunt director's fault. It's the effects guys that you've got to be careful of. Maybe for an explosion they are afraid to NG and be told off for not using enough explosives, so they overcharge the bomb." After this experience, Wong became more cautious about what he'd agree to perform without the aid of a stunt double. "Back then I was young, so I would say 'Yes! Yes! Yes!' to whatever they asked. I was young and new [to the film business] and wanted to make a good impression."

In Hong Kong, an actor (unless already established as a box office draw) cannot afford to be unaccommodating. If he's perceived as "trouble," producers know they'll have no difficulty finding a willing replacement. Yet even little-known actors have it easier than stuntmen who (as individuals) are largely anonymous to the moviegoing public. Ridley Tsui explains: "If they ask you [a stuntman], 'Can you do this?', you don't have time to think about it. Just say 'Yes.' If you say 'No' someone will replace you and you will lose your chance." Unfortunately, if a stuntman backs out of a stunt, he runs a serious risk of never being employed again. While Hong Kong stuntmen are as competitive as any group of peers, most undertake hazardous work less for glory and respect than for a pragmatic desire to be regarded as employable by stunt coordinators.

bruce Law: He's the firestarter

One stuntman brave enough to turn down a job is Bruce Law. A former tae kwan do champion and motorbike enthusiast, Law spent much of his youth speeding around the streets of the New Territories in not-quite-legal races. Law's introduction to the film business came in 1985 when stunt riders were needed for a chase scene in Sammo Hung's *Heart of the Dragon*. Several stunt jobs later, Bruce Law was asked to be the stunt coordinator on a film.

The honeymoon period ended when Law balked at producers telling him he had to hurry preparations for a speedboat-crash scene. "The last time that a scene like that was tried, the stuntmen were injured. So I planned how it should be done safely and the producers said it was too time-consuming and expensive. They asked me to change it and I said 'No.' They kicked me out and got someone else."

For any other stunt coordinator, the dismissal would have badly marred his career, but Law had found himself a niche in the world of action filmmaking. The industry had realized that for stunts involving moving vehicles, fire, and explosions, Law was the man for the job. By the way, when the speedboat sequence was attempted without his tutelage, all the stuntmen got hurt.

An avid follower of Western stunt technology, Law has educated himself in Hollywood's latest and safest methods of onscreen destruction. Directors such as Ching Siu-tung and John Woo started counting on his expertise beginning in the late 1980s. It was Law who masterminded Michelle Yeoh's riding-a-motorbike-onto-a-moving-train-roof sequence for *Supercop*, and he even doubled the actress for some of the more hazardous shots. "For one shot, I asked to have ten thousand cardboard boxes alongside the train for me to land in. On the day [on location in Kuala Lumpur], they told me that they only had five thousand. When I did the jump, I missed the boxes." Despite a hard landing, Law would not allow himself to be confined to his Malaysian hospital bed: "I wanted to try jet skiing, and you can't do it in Hong Kong. So I had to do it while I was there, even though my back was quite painful!"

Law (unlike many other Hong Kong stunt coordinators) likes to leave nothing to chance, and his intricately designed car rigs and explosive devices are often tested days prior to filming. Law is keen for actors to safely perform their own stunt sequences if possible. How did he convince Stephen Chiau to have his arms set ablaze in *The King of Comedy*? Law led by example: "I just stood there, with my arms on fire, for over a minute while chatting with him. I said, 'Do you trust me?' and he was ready to do it."

To execute safe body burns, Bruce Law uses flammable liquids or glues, which burn with a cold (yellow) flame while emitting minimal smoke to limit the risk of harmful inhalation. The performer wears fireproof clothing under his or her costume, and protective gels over the exposed skin and hair to prevent singeing and blistering. For explosion effects, Law likes using propane gas flames, which are controllable, allowing actors to work outside the (predetermined) distance of the flames' reach. That's how Jackie Chan can jump out of the window of an exploding hut (in *Supercop*) and be closely followed by tongues of flame, without being exposed to serious risk of burning. "Of course, I had him wear a fire suit anyway. You cannot injure a star!"

Law's company, Stunts Unlimited, is located in the New Territories town of Yuen Long, not far from the Chinese border. Several cargo containers house his stunt equipment and welding gear, and it's also here that Law parks his personal collection of police vehicles and trucks specially rigged to accommodate camera crews. "A guy from the States came here. He's got thirty years' experience with the fire department there, and he regulates all the L.A. stunt workshops. He said mine's as safe and as well maintained as any U.S. outfit, if not better," boasts Law, whose Hollywood-inspired professionalism seems somewhat out of place in the maverick Hong Kong movie scene. His safe approach keeps him and his stunt crew busy.

"Where's Your Permit?"

In early 1997, an assistant propsman was killed by shrapnel from an exploding car on the location of *Downtown Torpedoes*. While the press and police criticized the filmmakers for not clearing the set of all personnel not integral to the stunt, the film community retorted by saying that if permits were granted for such explosions, time could be taken to carry out such safety measures. Although Bruce Law didn't oversee that explosion, he knows all too well that in Hong Kong, rather than have a permit request denied, it's easier to just film and hope the police don't interfere until the footage is in the can. Amazingly, according to Law, that's how the car and motorbike chases for *Thunderbolt* and *Full Throttle* were achieved. The death on *Downtown Torpedoes*, however, led Law to demonstrate to government officials the safety of his explosive equipment, in the hope that a system of regulating stunt facilities might be introduced, leading to permits being made available to those demonstrating responsible techniques.

In 1998 came the release of *Extreme Crisis*, Law's directorial debut. Although even Law himself is quick to remark on the shortcomings of its script, the film showcased his approach to stuntwork. In shooting the film, Law used sophisticated Hollywood stunt gadgets and digitally removed all visible traces of them by means of computer editing. Crash-mats, wires, and air rams mysteriously disappeared while the stunts they facilitated remained.

In one scene, filmed under strict secrecy in the wee hours in Hong Kong's Central district, an explosion sends several parked cars into the air, where they corkscrew a full 360° before landing. Law managed to avoid a run-in with officers of the law, but on returning home after that 30-hour shift, he found a photo of the acrobatic vehicles adorning the front page of the *Oriental*

Corkscrewing cars from *Extreme Crisis*—Bruce Law's preplanning not only made this spectacle of stunt technology a one-take success but made it safe enough for him to position the actors in the same shot.

Bruce Law Stunts Unlimited

Daily News. "Later that morning, the police called me down to the station for a chat."

Another highlight of the film is a scene in which several SDU officers are ignited by a Japanese terrorist's flamethrower. Law's stuntmen are engulfed in flame yet simultaneously react to squibs and keep firing their machine guns. "Dangerous?" remarks the man with more than 170 films under his belt, "Not at all!" Naturally, Bruce Law is selective when it comes to choosing who will execute his stunt sequences: "I want stuntmen who are smart and clear-headed, not crazy. Those crazy guys will kill themselves."

Acting in Peril

It's a widely perpetuated myth that all actors in Hong Kong do all their own stunts. It is true, though, that they are expected to perform more hazardous work than their counterparts elsewhere. Often, if a role in a film is particularly action-oriented, rather than casting an actor (who will either have to be exposed to possible dangers, or doubled extensively), a stuntman will play the part. When Anthony Wong torches his *mahjong* buddy in the opening scene of *The Untold Story*, the audience can see that the guy getting toasted is the same character who was earlier spouting colorful abuse at Wong. That's because he's played by a stuntman—James Ha, also the film's stunt coordinator. Likewise, when a bunch of opium dealers are set alight in Kirk Wong's *Gunmen*, they are all played by stuntmen. Actors can't be so easily trusted to hit their marks and deliver their lines correctly while ablaze.

Finding the Face That Fits

If a movie features terrorists, gangsters, robbers, or hitmen, there's a good chance they'll be played by stuntmen, especially the characters required to kill (or be killed) rather than speak. For example, the disloyal triad boy getting a pounding from Roy Cheung in the opening scene of *Young & Dangerous 3* is a stuntman.

The casting process in Hong Kong is not as arduous as in other countries. Stuntmen rarely attend casting sessions—the action director hires them based on his familiarity with them and their relative merits. When they do attend casting sessions, it's to see whether they are suitable to play more substantial character parts, or if they must convincingly pass off as a certain nationality or type of person. In the summer of 1997, casting personnel visited Hong Kong Stuntman Association rehearsals for a handover spectacle, in order to find action men who could pass for Korean terrorists in the movie *Option Zero*.

Some unimaginative casting finds Bruce Law playing a car mechanic in *Thunderbolt*, a motorbike racer in *Full Throttle*, and an SDU chief in *Extreme Crisis*. Stuntman/assistant action director Chan Man-ching plays a dreadlocked assassin for his mentor Tung Wai in *Downtown Torpedoes* while almost a decade earlier he dueled with Moon Lee for Stanley Tong in *Angel 2*. "I was too baby-faced then!" says Chan, but what action director wants, action director gets.

It's not unusual for a stuntman to be cast in a major role in one film, only to return to regular stuntwork in the next, as did Benny Ko—the superkicking deaf-mute in *Police Story 2* who also had minor stunt roles in *Twin Dragons* and *Thunderbolt*. Some lucky stuntmen do find steady acting work later in their careers. Veteran kung fu movie villain Li Hoi San is now a contract player for TVB, regularly appearing in their soap operas. Former top stuntman Chin Kar-lok's acting was criticized in reviews for films like *Operation Scorpio*, which attempted to make an action star out of him. Just as his body was tiring of taking knocks, though, he showed impressive dramatic sensitivity in a major role in Derek Yee's *Full Throttle*. By the time he played a romantic, nonaction part in the female-driven drama *Intimates*, he'd proved that he no longer needed to kick and flip to be worth watching.

future kicks

It's ironic that HK action directors now enjoy unprecedented status and demand in Hollywood, while in Hong Kong the stuntmen's legacy risks extinction. Even if the Hong Kong film industry does manage to overcome its current rapid decline, action Hong Kong–style may not, and diminishing box office returns aren't alone to blame.

The Chinese opera schools are essentially extinct in the former colony, so that fertile pool of talent has dried up. Aspiring young stuntmen keen to break into the business are few, and ready jobs are similarly rare. In status-conscious Hong Kong society, many parents discourage their children from pursuing careers in the entertainment industry, which they regard as insecure and even disrespectable. Many Hong Kong youngsters can easily earn as much in less strenuous fields like retail and banking. Even if the kind of training that Jackie Chan, Tony Leung Siu-hung, and Ridley Tsui underwent were readily available today, it's unlikely that many of today's MTV and Internet-weaned Hong Kongers would be willing to endure it.

The new blood entering the action-film industry in recent times tends to be *wushu* athletes from mainland China or Western martial artists keen to get their mugs on Eastern screens, sometimes perceived as a stepping-stone to Hollywood careers. These days, though, they are seldom given the opportunity to show off their skills. There was a time when an agile villain could make a hero of the kung fu–fighting lead actor, but nowadays, the villain would likely demonstrate that the lead is more at home in the recording studio than in any gymnasium. Clever choreographers can make popstar-actors appear capable combatants, but this requires that their opponents restrain themselves and eschew their full repertoire of moves.

Perhaps Hong Kong action films, like the gallant swordsmen and swordswomen they used to portray in abundance, can narrowly avoid plummeting into oblivion and return to their heroic, mythic status of old. Perhaps there's hope.

The annual dinner of the Performing Artists' Guild of Hong Kong, held toward the end of 1998, saw Jackie Chan telling members of the Hong Kong Stuntman Association how he hoped to make things better. The action icon, enjoying his greatest success ever with *Rush Hour*, had made time to assume a post on the association's board and helped devise a Stuntman Diploma Training Course for 1999. The course—aimed at interested youngsters—is designed to teach prospective stuntmen various skills related to the job, such as kicking, gymnastics, trampoline work, and fight scenes. The course's creators (and thousands of Hong Kong action film lovers worldwide) hope that this scheme will provide a new generation of stuntmen for tomorrow's action directors to put through their paces—and wow audiences with—in years to come.

club Mad

This chapter avoids the terms *stunt person* or *stuntwoman* not to avoid political correctness, but because the Hong Kong Stuntman Association only has two women members (one is former Shaw Brothers queen Yeung Ching-ching and the other is named Li Fai). If a slight starlet needs doubling, more often than not, a slender stuntman will do the job.

The HKSA was established in 1994 to help unify stunt performers from different groups and to protect their interests (examining issues like insurance and production companies covering medical costs for those injured). Unlike the entertainment industries of the United Kingdom or the United States, Hong Kong has very little union regulation. While (in theory) anyone can undertake stuntwork in Hong Kong, the HKSA attempts to grant membership solely to competent professionals. Potential members must be approved by a number of

HKSA chairman Tony Leung Siu-hung (at right) poses with a bevy of sword-wielding beauties. Can you spot the stuntman?

Jude Poyer

established action directors and, once accepted, agree to work only for pay and under conditions set by the association.

While its membership once numbered close to 300, the current figure is almost half that. In addition to its two women, the HKSA also boasts four *gwailos* and one Japanese member. Key HKSA figures include action directors Tony Leung Siu-hung, Ridley Tsui, Steven Tung Wai (*Hitman*), and Yuen Bing (*Lifeline*) as well as Jackie Chan, whose *Drunken Master 2* helped raise funds for the association.

Ben Ng Hydes out in *Red to Kill*.
Martini Films

Hewn and Scattered

The only film that an independent can make and survive with is a film that the major producers cannot or will not make . . . if you cannot titillate them with production value, you titillate them with something else.
Director Herschel Gordon Lewis

extreme cinema used to be the province of farsighted fringies like Lewis, whose *Blood Feast* (1964) established precedence for Grand Guignol cinema. Lewis made movies where people died with their eyes open, and pioneered nontoxic stage blood that actors could ingest. Nowadays, even mainstream guys like Spielberg pass up cute aliens in favor of the literal visceral.

Even so, Hong Kong is far less inhibited when it comes to entertaining the troops. With a population of 6.8 million living on top of each other, the real-life struggles that spring from the pages of Hong Kong's *Apple Daily* provide plenty of raw material for splatterific plots.

Many of the industry's notorious tales of grue are taken from actual cases. Herman Yau's *The Untold Story: Human Meat Roast Pork Buns* (1993) was based on a Macau restaurateur who slaughtered an entire family, ground their bodies into meat-bun filling, and sold the resultant snacks to patrons. Another true story was filmed by Clarence (*Naked Killer*) Ford as *Remains of a Woman* (1993). The plot was simple: Boy meets girl, boy meets other girl, boy gets first girl to help dismember new girl, boy becomes a born-again Christian in jail because of new

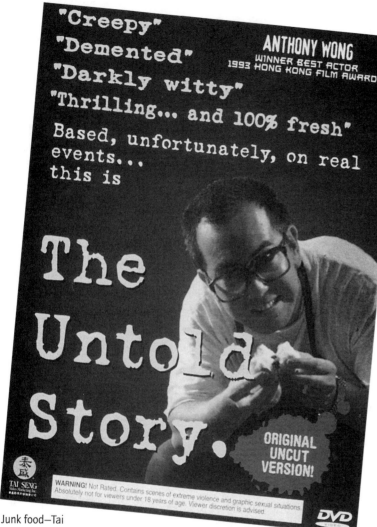

"Creepy"
"Demented"
"Darkly witty"
"Thrilling... and 100% fresh"
Based, unfortunately, on real events... this is

ANTHONY WONG
WINNER BEST ACTOR
1993 HONG KONG FILM AWARDS

The Untold Story.

ORIGINAL UNCUT VERSION!

DVD

Junk food—Tai Seng Video's release of the uncut *Untold Story*

Chuck Stephens described it best: "Lam manipulates the body like a marionette, antically squeezes and jiggles her breasts, then saws her into pieces, spattering his face, the room, his fishtank and the camera with geysers of gore. Expressively underlit, Lam's miniature charnel house becomes a theater of blood for Yam's manic performance: he twitches, minces, puckers his lips like a fruity goldfish and pathetically barks at the moon. Eventually, Lam (himself a virgin) finds an innocent nursing student on which to enact his darkest desire: the (sweaty, grunty, lovingly filmed) necrophiliac conquest of a fellow innocent." *Arrgghhh!*

Many HK actors have a laudable appreciation for the ghoulie/roughie/kinky tradition and appreciate that the villainous roles are the plum assignments. Ben Ng shudders and strips. Lily Chung screams and strips. Anthony Wong does everything short of grinding his murder victims up, baking them into pastries, and serving them to the investigating cops.

evangelist girl and is acquitted, leaving surviving first girl to take the murder rap. *Dr. Lamb* (1993) presented Simon Yam as a serial maniac, again based on an actual case.

Wait a minute—he does that too. All of these performers are willing to do whatever is necessary to vibrate that taut metal wire in the collective belly of their quivering audience. Hong Kong filmmakers don't shrink from a juicy story—even if the juices don't run clear when pricked with something sharp.

These films are sometimes referred to as "guilty pleasures," but guilt is a useless emotion. There's nothing wrong with vicariously enjoying depictions of nastiness one would never perpetrate. There *is* something wrong about wasting 90 minutes on a film that thinks it can cover up laziness of plot and characters by dumping a few gallons of red corn syrup over everything, which is why you're not being steered toward *Horrible High Heels* (1997) or *Bloody Mary Killer* (1994). If you lean toward the extreme, you'll enjoy these films. Load up on too much caffeine and peek through your trembling fingers. Go ahead.

ebola /yNdrome (1996)

Watching this oozing chunk of splurted-out HK splatter is akin to viewing a particularly poignant and repulsive traffic accident in hyperslow agony-vision—a violent half-second impact expanded to 90 torturous minutes—in sum, a free-form charnel funhouse thumbing its nose at its meager budget and leaving no avenue unexplored in its relentless quest to assault sensibilities, insult everything and everyone, and send the stomach contents of every single viewer whooshing out in a collective geyser. *Ebola Syndrome*'s bratty, anarchic vileness dwarfs the efforts of such notorious filmmakers as Lucio Fulci, Jess Franco, Joel M. Reed, or Jorg Buttgereit, or the coprophagic excesses of John Waters's 1970s films.

By the five-minute mark, ES's protagonist Kai (Anthony Wong) has performed a lifetime's worth of evil. After being caught *in flagrante delicto* with his boss's wife, he penitently offers to castrate himself with a pair of garden shears—those curved, one-handed jobs that can amputate a small branch. Instead, he stabs the boss's stooge with the shears and strangles his boss (Shing Fui-on, the actor known as Big Sillyhead) with the folding legs of a *mahjong* table. After slicing off the wife's tongue with the bloody shears, he turns his homicidal attentions on Lily, the cute daughter of the freshly splattered couple.

As the girl cowers, Kai douses her with gasoline and starts fumbling with his Zippo. He comforts the weeping, terrified girl by telling her: "Don't worry, it won't hurt." But before he can torch the lass, a neighbor comes knocking on the door, wondering what in the heck is going on. Kai's line, delivered as he saunters out, sets the tone for his character throughout the film: "I'm killing them, what's wrong?"

Unlike anything you've ever seen—Herman Yau's *Ebola Syndrome*

If you have figured out by now that *Ebola Syndrome* is a black comedy, bonus points for you. But there are no brakes; you hop on this toboggan and you're going all the way. Next stop is South Africa, where

Kai the exile is working in a Chinese restaurant, hacking up live frogs with a cleaver. Kai is under no vegetarian delusion that "meat is murder"—he knows that meat is meat, and murder is murder.

Kai is being exploited by his employers, a Taiwanese couple engaged in the time-honored trade of the overseas Chinese: running a Chinese restaurant. They pay him a pittance and hurl abuse at him. There's little sympathy for Kai, though—he's a disgusting human being, the type who refuses to bathe lest it wash away the aroma of the slaughtered pigs he carries into the restaurant. Pork is his metaphor—Kai gets his kicks by listening to his employers have weird wild sex while masturbating with a puce-translucent piece of purloined pork loin from the larder. The "marinated" pork is later served to an obnoxious *gwailo* customer. Kai is plagued by lust, but the local hookers won't touch his custom.

An opportunity occurs when he and his boss (Lo Mang) drive to a village to buy a couple of pigs at discount rates. The natives are infected with the Ebola virus, but our heroes escape with the precious carcasses and start driving back across the veldt. When the truck breaks down and Kai spots a native girl collapsing by a nearby riverbank, of course he's gotta run over and take advantage.

She explodes mouthwise in a milky geyser, drenching Kai in body fluids and, you guessed it, she's got the dreaded bug. And though it's fatal and there's no cure, one person in 10,000 is immune and survives, only to become a carrier of the most hideous make-ya-bleed virus ever. And what are the chances that Kai, miserable chunk of humanity that he is, just happens to be a carrier, spreading horrible convulsive death by contact with *any* of his bodily fluids?

But before he even figures out that he's got this perverse Midas touch, there he goes again: cruelly slaughtering his employers and stealing their cash. Then it's back to Hong Kong, to look up his ex-girlfriend.

Wong and Yau's demented comedy picks relentlessly at the viewer's fevered brain. If a taxi pulls up to a curb in *Ebola Syndrome*, it runs over a rat. Wong misses no opportunity to sneer, wear pompous hats, grab his crotch, or toss extra cash at *gwailo* hookers to avoid condom use. There are even "Mouthcam" shots like some mutant dental-hygiene industrial film. Seldom does an audience laugh, moan, and scream so ardently for biohazard-suited cops to open fire. No sequel to this one; handover crackdown? Not exactly—as Yau said: "I like this kind of movie. But it didn't make money. Too bad!"

Jekyll . . .

Martini Films

red to kiLL (1996)

How exactly to best describe Billy Tang's *Red To Kill* . . . hmmm . . . phrases like "scurrilous, pot-boiling mayhem" and "obscenely twisted squirtin' excess" aren't quite strong enough. Let's just say that if the Romans had invented film as a device to wean their citizens from bloody spectacles pitting humans against wild beasts, they would have come up with something like *Red to Kill*.

This film is wild at heart and guaranteed to offend. It hurls itself headlong at HK's dirty secrets—the stigma of mental illness, the desperately cramped quarters of public-housing estates, and the mob mentality of their residents—uncaring if it shatters its pate in the process. Stacked on top of these serious social issues are unforgettable portrayals of predator and prey by Ben Ng and Lily Chung, respectively.

Ng plays a Jekyll/Hyde rapist-murderer, and his depiction of tortured humanity is

THE SCENE OF THE CRIME

Some of these horrific films aren't defensible as a whole. Yet, knowing how much you rubberneckers want to know just what was hewn off and where it went flying, here's a listing of some especially ripe scenes.

Skin Striperess (1992)

Poor Chi (Chan Wing-chi) is a pale lovely from mainland China who's forced to entertain a corrupt official named Yung (Stuart Ong). When she's accidentally disfigured, her pimp (Billy Lau) hires a rogue wizard to make her lovely once again, a process that requires a busted snake's head, the chewing of a live frog, and the entire peeled skin of a female victim. Of course, it works like a charm, and Yung gets his jollies.

But just then, a group of teenagers accidentally dig up the victim's body, removing the protective Sacred Salt. Chi morphs demonoid and turns the tables on the terrified Yung, ravaging him impolitely as the walls and ceiling manifest dripping blood. She tosses him through a glass wall and goes to find the wizard, who beats a big drum and shakes his jowls. This Stoogian defense fails him as the monster he created reaches right out with her claws and peels his bark off.

OCTB Case—The Floating Body (1995)

Ex-con Li Chien-wan (Ben Ng) finds himself with an unexpected corpse (Lily Chung) to deal with. After meditating over it, he arranges a number of totems on the living room table: a bottle of xo, a couple of bombers, and a Makita electric chainsaw. Ng fires up one of the joints and starts smoking it through his nose in a fit of predismemberment whimsy. Amplified heartbeats mix with elephant trumpetings as he crunches a few potato chips, rips the cork out of the xo, and guzzles. By the time he tenderly deposits the corpse in the bathtub and starts the blade whirling on the Makita, most viewers will be sufficiently creeped out to mash the eject button, but it's only 15 minutes into the movie!

A Chinese Torture Chamber Story (1994)

Poor Little Cabbage. Humble and righteous Little Cabbage ("Baby Bok Choi") is the daughter of a Ming dynasty–era silk-maker. Her bound feet render her attractive to concubine-minded scholar Yang Ni-mu, who is also righteous. Not so Mrs. Yang, whose licentious bent drives her into the arms of her lover Hoi-ning, but lessens not her jealousy for hubby's *petit chou*. While Yang is away on a business trip, his wife marries Little Cabbage off to Got Siu-tai, a tofu maker who is a pleasant fellow, but whose member is described not with words, but by elephant impersonations. Shy and retiring Little

gobstopping. Ng's hands and muscular forearms lurch into frames like vengeful snakes. Low-angle shots of his distended mouth quivering in the grip of reptilian-brain *lustmord* are spookier than any writhing data-drawn beastie. Chung is even scarier in her simplistic portrayal of a woman described as having the mentality of a 10-year-old. People suffering from mental or emotional problems are stigmatized in Hong Kong society, and although strides have been made in recent years,

Cabbage, tofu lad with his big swinging trunk, and one tael (a goddam *tael*—that's five times the usual dose) of aphrodisiac . . . we're set.

As the aphro courses through Got's veins, he levitates the dining room table with his trunk, turns crimson and weird, then hoists flustered Cabbage from the ceiling with red silk. Temporarily regaining his senses, he insists she tie him up for her own protection. Coitus an impossible dream, she attempts to provide hand relief, as the anthem of their forlorn affection (a Muzak instrumental version of "Unchained Melody"—you know: "Ohhhhh, mah love, mah daaaarlin', I hunger, for, *your touch* . . .") drenches the scene in unexpected pathos. The principals involved (flat-faced Tommy Wong as the supine victim, and luscious Yvonne Yung Hung as the star-crossed cutie) deserve special acting awards for their straight-arrow, sweat-crunged performance in this harrowing bishop-flogging scene. Regrettably, as Got achieves orgasm, his gargantuan penis detonates in a slow-motion room-filling red mist.

many of the old prejudices remain. By presenting a mentally retarded character as a victim in such a violent film, Tang twists the knife in these outmoded beliefs. Like Stravinsky's *Rite of Spring*, *Red to Kill* delights in stepping on everyone's toes.

A human beast is stalking a Hong Kong housing estate, which also contains a hostel for people being rehabbed prior to being moved back into society. The hostel inmates are a cheery bunch, yet the bickering and vengeful residents of the estate are convinced that they are responsible for a series of recent crimes: women wearing red are ending up as violated corpses. The residents are convinced they've nabbed the "sex lupine" when hapless Brother Chubby trips drunkenly down the stairs late one night . . . but he's a red herring.

Real red rage continues to surge as Chan Chi-wai (Ng) relieves and re-creates bloody childhood trauma. Eventually the violations reach the door of Ming Ming (Chung), who was moved into the hostel by social worker Miss Cheung (Money Lo) after Ming Ming's father was killed in a car crash. The beast corners Ming Ming and does his vile thing, but is attracted by her lunacy, lunatically declaring it a match for his own, and (delusions of matrimony ringing through his festering skull) spares her.

Mistake? Ming Ming 'fesses up with the help of Cheung, and the authorities clap the beast in irons. Justice? Chan's scumbag lawyer viciously cross-examines Ming Ming in the courtroom, painting her as a demented slut. She freaks out, the judge throws the case out, and the beast walks. But in Hong Kong, the color of revenge is consistent.

Chan has developed a monster crush on Ming Ming, and he is heading over the edge (for a guy whose hobby is psychotic rape and murder, this is remarkable). Cheung, enraged by Chan's disregard for human dignity or life, dolls up in red and yanks his chain by taunting him sexually.

Chan rushes around like a dog coated with raw meat, dumps a pail of ice down the front of his jockstrap, then shaves his head and dons a pair of skintight biker shorts for the final confrontation with the vengeful social worker and her charge. The floor slick with blood and broken glass by film's end, it's thumbs-down for Ng's sociopathic lust-killer, but despite the Grand Guignol red-daubed finale, no one is particularly happy by film's end.

When RTK hit Hong Kong screens, the first two weeks brought plenty of box office action, but revenues started to sag during week three. Martini Films' quick-thinking boss Kimmy Shuen came up with a strategy straight out of the AIP/Nicholson-Arkoff playbook. Shuen replaced the film's newspaper ads with plain red text on a black background—a message from Lily Chung claiming that a certain scene would be trimmed from the video release, and if the audience was interested, they were best advised to see it while they had the chance. Cha-*ching*!

tHe uNtolɗ ʃtory 2 (1998)

The original *Untold Story* was a raging tale of meat and murder based on true accounts of necrophagic antics in Macau. Anthony Wong's clenched teeth and cleaver work as the murderous antihero earned him the

Carnal suffering is the lot of everyone trapped in *The Untold Story 2*.

Mei Ah

Best Actor award at the Hong Kong Film Awards of 1993, a well-deserved prize.

Five years later the sequel comes thudding into the grindhouses of Mongkok like a sodden pork bun from Hades's own steamer. This film's Chinese title translates roughly as "Human Barbecue 2: Suffer in Hell," and it has little in common with its prequel save carnal revels and the presence of Anthony Wong. It's a tightly wrapped tale of sexual jealousy, murderous intent—walls of flesh, and wanton lust for more sex, more money, and more freshly roasted meat.

Cheung (the actor's name is Emotion Cheung) is a nice-guy proprietor of a Hong Kong barbecue restaurant. Both Officer Lazyboots (Wong) and the local triad boss (played by *Robotrix* director Jamie Luk) hang out chatting over plates of crisply roasted pork and "4 treasures rice." The shop employs a few locals like Third Aunt (Helena Lo), who pushes a mop and chit-chats with the customers, and the cash drawer is full of greasy red banknotes at the end of each long workday.

Cheung has problems. Number 1 is his wife Kuen (Yeung Fan), who is young, gorgeous, abusive, spiteful, greedy, selfish, and sexually insatiable. Her constant drains on his money, incessant sexual demands, and wanton demeanor have embarrassed him throughout the neighborhood and rendered him impotent. She literally kicks him out of bed when he fails to perform, then spends the shop's earnings on lingerie, fixing to incite her goldbricking supercreep boy-toy—a studpuppy named Fai. Kuen enjoys hard-drinking sessions and returns to the apartment only to spew vomit and moan for more of Fai's ghastly caresses.

Henpecked Cheung is retreating into a pathetic shell. He's still human, but functions more as a cash register and beer disposal unit. Greasy and apathetic, he numbly chops up slabs of flesh as his wife flaunts her ripe cleavage in the customers' faces and scoops up the cash to finance her trysts. "You are thirst in sex," observes the triad boss, leering. "I'm not free now," she responds.

Cheung's savior arrives suddenly: Fung (Paulyn Suen), Kuen's visiting cousin from Guangzhou. She's a bit of a plain Jane, but Cheung is attracted by her shy and sweet manner. When he spies her lathering up in the shower, he "experiences priapism." But she's no artless bumpkin, as we find out when she walks in on Cheung's bath to seduce him.

The lead returns to Cheung's pencil. Of course, this sets off his wife's alarms—she rapidly figures out the new arrangement, and hell hath no fury. Fung deals with the situation by skewering her screaming cousin repeatedly with a 13-inch metal rod. Cheung dissolves into a quivering jelly as his wife's body slides to the floor, but Fung softly reminds him of her promise: "I will be the last woman in your life." His terror is palpable.

She fills the bath, deposits Kuen's wide-eyed, stark naked corpse in the tub and nonchalantly disassembles it with a heavy-duty electric knife as Cheung cowers, feckless, reddening from the spray as the murderous Mainlander's vorpal blade goes snicker-snack.

Resigned and petrified, he fires up the barbecue. Closeups of Fung's delighted face are intercut with closeups of sizzling grease and flesh, eliciting groans from the audience. When the red, succulent barbecued rib-slab is hoisted onto Cheung's retail rack, the round holes punched by the killing rod clearly visible between the bones, the audience begins their collective in-their-seats squirm-tango. When Officer Lazyboots and his triad buddy start gleefully sucking the barbecued flesh off the bones, the crowd furls shut their snack bags of pork jerky and ponders going veg.

Things spiral downward from there, as Fung indulges her homicidal urges. *Us 2* refuses to get sidetracked, defining its characters and snapping right along. The gore is kept to a minimum of screen time, making it far more effective. Extra credit for Taiwanese bomblet Yeung Fan as the amoral spitfire Kuen, who is as scary as she is sexy—living, dead, or as a head.

Stefan Hammond

In San Francisco during the 1980s, gathering Hong Kong movie-related info was easy. One of the handful of *gwailos* who had caught on would visit Chinatown, check out the lobby cards and marquees, then phone the other *gwailos* with showtimes and film titles, sometimes even actors' names, although more often "the guy in the trenchcoat in the movie we saw last week." There were four cinemas in San Francisco, all showing double bills. We knew there would be English subtitles. Other than that, there was virtually no information in English, until that *Film Comment* issue came out in 1988. It was frustrating, but it was easy . . . because it was pretty much impossible.

Now it's easy again.

The reason, of course, is that pantheon-unto-herself, the Internet. The global superhighway that behaves like an eccentric relative every time you shake cyberhands—bellowing for exotic demons named Java and Applet and even the Imp of adforce.imgis.com. Balky, erratic, as perennially busy as any stressed-out executive but, like a batty aunt, shoving cookies down your throat whether you want them or not.

Nonetheless, the Net has made the search for Hong Kong movie information and software easier than ever. It's estimated that Net traffic doubles every 100 days. In this foaming petri dish, you will find the HK movie resources you are looking for.

It goes without saying that some of these links will have "gone 404" by the time this book gets in your hands. If you draw a blank, search engines are always helpful, and the sites of major distributors like taiseng.com are good places to start.

Meat/pace

Yes, Hong Kong movies can be located in the real world as well. A good video store can be very helpful in recommending Hong Kong films. Nowadays, all cities and most towns have specialist video stores that are hip to HK films. Tell the clerks what kind of films you like and ask for recommendations. Give them feedback.

If you live in San Francisco, check out Naked Eye Video on Haight Street, quite possibly the world's best video store. But don't neglect Le Video on Ninth Avenue, another contender. The staff at these two stores are fantastic, or just browse the HK section.

In West L.A., Vidiots in Santa Monica is excellent. In New York, the place to go is Kim's on Bleecker Street. In Chicago's Chinatown, check out Chinatown Bazaar, Beauty Video & Gift, or 88 Video Shop.

If you live elsewhere, you will likely have a hip video store nearby. But if you get stuck, go have a chat with that muttering aunt. Here's what to tell her:

http://egret0.stanford.edu/hk/index.html
No longer being updated, but (hopefully) still online, this comprehensive searchable database is a silver, gold, and platinum mine of information. Joseph Fierro gets a special HK Film Fan Lifetime Achievement award for this one. A mirror site is at **http://razzle.Stanford.EDU/hk/** and **http://egret0.stanford.edu/hk/links/regional.html** gives you a fantastic page of links to regional sites with a motherlode of HK movie info.

http://www.taiseng.com/
The main distributor for the USA. Their site has tons of info on Hong Kong movies.

http://www.movieworld.com.hk/
This highly searchable database can be extremely helpful. Another good entry point is **http://movieworld.com.hk/moviebase/index.shtml**.

http://www.interlog.com/~kraicer/byplace.html#hongkong
Excellent, thoughtful reviews of many Hong Kong films by Shelly Kraicer.

http://members.xoom.com/GG2HK/
Tauna the Black asks: "How could you not like beautiful young men in wet silk wrestling in mud?" Awesome page.

http://www.slip.net/~redbean/xena/xena_hk.html
Another killer site from Laura Irvine, whose HK-in-SF site (**http://www.slip.net/~redbean/**) is exemplary. This one delves deeply into the Hong Kong movie influence on the *Xena: Warrior Princess* TV show. Irvine created the site as an alternative to "jumping up and down yelling

Hong Kong movie titles at the screen every time I watch a *Xena* episode," and that's a good enough reason to snap your browser at it.

http://www.geocities.com/Tokyo/Towers/2038/
Wolverine's News of the Week, translated into English. Using this as a "newspaper" will keep you up to date on the HK movie scene, though it's in-depth and bound to confuse even knowledgeable HK fanatics. The text links load easily, but the picture-version is data-packed and may crash your browser. If you want the full picture-version, allocate huge amounts of RAM to your browser program, and go make coffee or something while the thing loads. Still, it's worth it. Wolverine gets a gold star for putting this thing up. As does Sanney for his *Hong Kong Entertainment News in Review* at **http://www.hkmdb.com/hkentreview/**

http://www.hkmdb.com/
Hong Kong Movie DataBase is an intriguing site run by HK resident Ryan Law, who contributed a film section to the latest *Lonely Planet* guidebook for HK/Macau/Guangzhou. This database has many useful features, like photos of HK cinemas (**www.hkmdb.com/hkmec/hkcinema/**) and movie posters. You can even see photos of cinemas in Macau at

http://www.hkmdb.com/hkmec/macaucinema/. *HKMDB* has some Chinese content (the RealTime Audio discussion-reviews of HK films are in Cantonese). The *HKMDB* section on HK films in San Francisco doesn't link to Laura Miller's wonderful HK-in-SF page (**http://www.slip.net/~redbean/**) but instead offers e-mail forms that let you contribute the relevant information to *HKMDB*. Free membership is offered, to let you participate in *HKMDB* forum discussions. There's a mirror of Wolverine's News of the Week here at **http://www.hkmdb.com/ hktopten/**

http://www.dvdresource.com/dvdfaq/dvdfaq.shtml
Jim Taylor's nonpareil, continuously updated, DVD FAQ. Don't ask anybody anything about DVDs until you read it.

http://hkmovie.com.hk/
The online address of Hong Kong Movie, a shop located in Mongkok's Allied Plaza (see page 6).

http://www.thedigitalbits.com/
Slick DVD newsletter. Check out **http://www.thedigitalbits.com/articles/titanicboot/titanic.html** for an in-depth dissection of a bootleg boat-versus-iceberg DVD.

http://pages.ripco.com:8080/~oobleck/
The Ng Man-tat for President homepage. Well-designed and hysterically funny

page on HK's comic genius, Ng Man-tat. Two thumbs up for this one.

http://www.heroic-cinema.com
Don't miss this great Australian-based website, described in the sidebar "Honkers in Oz" on page 250.

http://squidmonkey.com
Author Stefan Hammond maintains this website. Check here for updates, rumors, Hex outtakes, squid cherries, and monkeynuggets.

http://www.radix1.demon.co.uk/
For HK movie fans in the UK, Dan's Hong Kong Movies Page is *the* place to go—all the new video releases, reviews, and news. There's even a rundown on whether a new release has been cut or not by the UK censors.

http://www.coolala.com/enter/e003e.html
Coolala has star interviews, "on-location" features, reviews, and a shop selling VCDs at Mongkok prices.

http://china.muzi.net/stars/
Muzi China has put together a fine list of pages, galleries, bios, and links on your favorite stars.

http://www.teleport-city.com/
The realm of Ol' Battlemonkey, reviewer of "films best left unexplained." Check
http://www.teleport-city.com/movies/

reviews/kungfu/index.html for more than a mere fisticuff of kung fu reviews.

http://www.hkmdb.com/mc4/
Reviews and news for fans old and new—handy detailed filmographies of Sammo Hung and Jackie Chan can be located from the front page.

http://home.netvigator.com/~iyoungs/hongkong.html
Another stack of reviews, with an emphasis on the recent stuff.

http://www.chinastar.com.hk/english/movies/main.html
Chinastar not only produces movies but also keeps its synopses and photo galleries at this location. The gruesome *Intruder* picture gallery is exceptional.

http://www.filmcritics.org.hk/
The Hong Kong Film Critics Association

http://www.somethingweird.com
Something Weird Video stocks little from the SAR, and their *The Man from Hong Kong* tape stars Serge Gainsbourg and a French two-girl cabaret act. But they do have kung fu trailer compilations.

game of the name

Gwailo HK movie fans scream with frustration at the complexity of the Chinese language. The official spoken language, known as Mandarin or *Putonghua*, is a tonal language with four distinct tones which vary the meaning of the syllables. Cantonese—or *Guangdonghua*—is the other major dialect, though there are hundreds more. Cantonese originated in Canton (Guangdong) Province and is the *lingua franca* of Hong Kong, and thus Hong Kong movies.

Cantonese has six tones that impart meaning to its rounded syllables. No, it has nine tones. Wait a minute—more than nine. No one can even agree on how many tones there are in Cantonese. Cantonese has been referred to as "pidgin Mandarin" because much of spoken Cantonese cannot be written down in any form. Needless to say, such an anomalous form of oral communication is learned by rote and is prone to a head-thwacking array of homonym-based puns.

Gwailos attempting to sympathize must totally immerse themselves in HK culture. Attempts to get native speakers to explain even simple gags are next to useless; most people don't have the ability (or patience) to detail the complex web of referents required. Compounding this problem is the speed of HK's pop culture. This week's hot gossip is forever supplanting last week's. In-vogue starlets have a shelf life of three to six months, and slang evaporates even faster. You can take classes until you start dreaming in Cantonese, but you'll still get the "*leh ho yeh!*" ("you are great!") thumbs-up sign no matter how badly you mangle the tones. And you still won't be able to understand dialogue. At all.

The bright side to this Sisyphean task is the joy and delight of discovering tiny nuggets of meaning. A slang phrase mastered possesses much amusement value on the street. "No problem" and "I don't understand" are invaluable little weapons, as are "Excuse me" and "I can't speak Cantonese."

the art of cursing

At one point in *Once upon a Time in Triad Society 2*, actor Cheung Tat-ming delivers these furious lines: "Bastard, I tell you. If you stop me from seeing my wife before her death, I will cut you into 19 pieces to feed the worms under her corpse." These powerful words cause his opponent to step aside, and as Cheung passes him, he murmurs: "I don't know I can speak foul language so fluently."

Clearly, the use of Cantonese to hurl invective far surpasses any subtitle. Enjoying the wacky subtitles is our bonus, but we know the native-speaking audience is on a higher entertainment plane altogether. Our hats are off to these masters of oratory, even though we can barely guess at what they're saying.

HONKERS IN OZ
BY MICHAEL HELMS

You'd have to be blind in one eye and deaf in the other to deny the Asian influence on the dog's breakfast otherwise known as Australian culture. To most urban Aussies (pronounced "Ozzies," which is why we call it Oz) it only seems natural to live and work alongside our fellow Asians. Just as in the California gold rush of 1848–1849, the Australian gold rush of 1851 sent residents from southern China's coastal provinces immediately gravitating southward (the dynamic opening sequence of Philippe Mora's historical drama *Mad Dog Morgan* (1976) presents a glimpse of early Australian–Sino relations). The Hammer Films coproduction deal with HK's Shaw Brothers studio *Legend of the Seven Golden Vampires* (1974) was mirrored by Australian film studio The Movie Company's coproduction deal with Golden Harvest—an odd coupling, which begot *The Man from Hong Kong* (1975). *TMFHK* was a butt-stomping, flares-and-kung-fu flick that nonetheless failed to reignite the careers of costars Jimmy Wang Yu or native Aussie George Lazenby.

Nowadays, Asian culture is an integral part of the Australian experience. Ignore that grumpy red-haired frump who forgot that the "White Australia" policy ended in the 1970s. For the Hong Kong film fan, the most important component is the HK films that regularly share screen space with Hollywood product in the major movie houses.

Cinema

Chinese-language cinemas appeared in both Sydney and Melbourne in the late 1970s and early 1980s. A Chinatown circuit soon emerged, with two main distributors vying for Hong Kong product (a third competitor entered the Sydney market in the early 1990s). A screen shortage in the late 1980s saw the second distributor—a Malaysian outfit—rent space on weekends from Greater Union, one of the larger commercial exhibitors in Australia. For a short while, patrons would exit something like *Rain Man* or *Driving Miss Daisy* to be confronted by a packed lobby of rabid film fans eager to catch the all-important midnight screening of *God of Gamblers* or something.

For five years this same distributor took up residence in one of the continent's last great picture palaces: the Capitol in downtown Melbourne. Ironically, the Capitol was vacated a few short months before Jackie Chan put Melbourne on the HK cinematic map by filming *Mr. Nice Guy* (1997) near the tram line running past the venerable cinema. Patronage seemed to vaporize around this time, and the distributor subsequently joined with his competitors in exhibiting at the nearby Chinatown Cinema Complex, a three-screen venue.

This complex on Bourke Street continues to present the latest hits from Hong Kong. Late-night screenings of HK films can also be found at various venues around the country. By the early 1990s, Chinese-language films were screening on a regular basis in all seven mainland Australian capitals. Australia probably has more Chinese-language screens per capita than any other country in the English-speaking world.

Video

Hong Kong movies have been arriving on Australian video shelves in a dubbed (and arbitrary) fashion since the dawn of the video age. Major Aussie labels often inherited Hong Kong films as parts of larger packages and although there was no shortage of Hong Kong titles (mostly Jackie Chan kickfests and Bruce Lee rip-offs) floating around videoland by 1990, they were not released in any sort of organized fashion. Now, thanks to the Chinatown label created by Siren Entertainment—a company that grew out of the local music industry—Hong Kong product can now be found on chain-store shelves across the country. In January 1999, Siren combined with Japanimation specialist Madman Entertainment to release the Hong Kong hit film of 1998—the martial arts fantasy flick *Storm Riders*—on tape.

Chinese-language-only video shops continue to proliferate in inner-city areas and in heavily Asian-populated areas of suburbia. Recently, the Australasian Film and Video Security Office (citing high levels of sex, violence, and other nastiness) has declared war on DVD and VCD importers, which has curtailed the activities of many dealers. However, with perseverance, hundreds of titles are available for rental at any given time. Check out **http://www.china townvideo.com.au** for the Siren website.

The Haunted Fish Tank

The most reclusive shut-in can still inundate herself or himself with some of the finest in Hong Kong film fare courtesy of Australia's SBS TV—one of the more enlightened TV broadcasters on the planet. SBS was established by the government as a free-to-air station in the late 1970s, to cater to Australia's voluminous non-English-speaking population.

The SBS mission includes the provision of a top-quality English translation and subtitling service. As Hong Kong film viewers know, the supplied English subtitles frequently twist the language into all manner of (hilarious) conflict. The further reduction of such product to the small screen is a recipe for eyestrain and headaches. To combat this syndrome, the multilingual crew at SBS prepare each new acquisition by discarding all previous subtitles, then reinterpret the audio script and subtitle the product anew to make it as small-screen friendly as possible. Despite their minuscule budget, SBS's eclectic library of titles (everything from Hindi musicals to stoic Peruvian dramas) includes a wide variety of Hong Kong flicks. Among their offerings are *The Inspector Wears Skirts* comedies, the *Once upon a Time in China* series, and *In the Line of Duty* entries, to *The Story of Woo Viet* starring a very young Chow Yun-fat, and Yuen Woo-ping's *Tiger Cage* films. Another plus for SBS is its ability to show films uncut, as many of its movies aren't screened until 9:30 P.M. or later. This means the *Erotic Ghost Story* series can unfurl in full flesh-baring glory on the flickering TV screens of Oz with no interruptions (the commercials occur at either end of the film). Rarely does a week go by without SBS showcasing several Hong Kong features, rendering Aussie couch potatoes lucky tubers indeed.

More recently, SBS has collaborated with commercial interests to create World Movies, a unique cable channel. Despite an art-film outlook and a reliance on modern European product, World Movies utilizes many of the prints screened on SBS and naturally keeps the Hong Kong quota high. SBS also has its own magazine to keep fans well apprised.

Other Media

As ever, coverage of Hong Kong and Asian film in general remains at the whim of editors and whoever they're trying to impress at the time. Over the years, mainstream coverage of Hong Kong films has been sporadic at best. Chinese cinema advertising in English newspapers has always been tentative and minimal, and underground publications are the source of the most enthusiastic, consistent, and far-reaching writings on Hong Kong cinema. In the mid-1980s, *Crimson Celluloid* and the demented *Violent*

Leisure from New Zealand were the only places you could consistently read locally produced reviews and articles on Hong Kong product. As well as documenting the films themselves, these publications inspired me to create space for Hong Kong films when I began editing and publishing Melbourne-based *Fatal Visions* in 1988.

In the 1990s, one-off publications like *China Blitz* have come and gone and more regularly scheduled publications like *Reel Wild Cinema* continue to cover Hong Kong films via reviews and the odd interview and article.

Currently, the best place to learn about the Hong Kong film scene in Australia is via the website created and maintained by a dedicated guy named Mark Morrison who hangs out at http://www.heroic-cinema.com. It's a neat and complete one-stop chop shop for everything Hong Kong in Oz today.

Nomenclature

Anyone writing about Hong Kong movies in English has a problem: The names of film personnel and the titles of movies are all in Chinese. Although several systems for romanizing Chinese terms exist, they are all somewhat flawed. The best the writer can achieve is consistency.

For example, take the actress Wu Chien-lien. Her family name is Wu (it appears frontside). Ms. Wu is from Taiwan, and the romanization is based on the Mandarin pronunciation of her name (Mandarin is widely used in Taiwan). But Wu is known to her Hong Kong fans as Ng Sin-lin, Ng (pronounced as a truncated "m" sound which can't really be reproduced on paper) being the Cantonese pronunciation. "Wu" is easier for non-Chinese speakers to deal with than "Ng," which is why a well-known director named Ng Yu-sum long ago chose the name John Woo as his *nom de filme*. Are we having fun yet?

Most performers have adopted an English name, which makes things blissfully easier. But not all English names are usable or accurate. Numerous Web pages list Wu Chien-lien as "Jacqueline," but she denies any English name, whatsoever, and there you have it. Many of the pivotal figures in Hong Kong film just don't have an English name, and non-Chinese-speaking fans have to deal with it the best they can. Sometimes, life is just a beautifully lit sparkling-clean bowl of delectable cherry-red cherries, and sometimes it isn't.

For the purposes of this book, English names are used wherever possible. Chinese names appear when no English name is available and when English names are confusing (there are two actors and one stunt coordinator named Tony Leung, for example). The format used here is that used in the *South China Morning Post* and reads "Lau Kar-leung" rather than "Lau Kar Leung," though the latter, as you've guessed by now, isn't necessarily wrong.

If you are researching Hong Kong films, it's essential to use Chinese names. Fortunately, there are searchable databases on the Net. Try http://egret0.stanford.edu /hk/index.html or http://movieworld. com.hk/moviebase/index.shtml or http:// www.hkmdb.com/ with people's names and movie titles in Chinese characters. Joseph Fierro's Stanford site has them as JPEG (graphic) files, which can be quickly downloaded and printed out for reference. Don't trot into your local Chinatown VCD shop and start demanding titles in English—download the characters of the title you seek, print them out, approach the clerks, and *show the printout to them.* Regardless of dialect, they should be able to read the characters. It's the quickest way from point A to point B.

ACRONYM OVERLOAD

VCDS, DVDS, LDS . . . what, more mysterious video technology? Most of us couldn't get that stupid VCR to stop flashing 12:00 over and over and over, so VCR manufacturers finally designed around humanity's basic inability to deal with techno-twaddle. So why must we now worry about what sort of disc dealie to purchase?

Videotape is still popular and is the video delivery method of choice for most HK film freaks. But for one reason or another, many HK films have never been available on videotape in satisfactory viewing condition. If and when they are reissued, tape will be bypassed in favor of the new disc media, which are so popular in Hong Kong and other parts of Asia that they have largely supplanted videotape. Here's a quick guide:

Laserdiscs (LDS)
Big and heavy 12-inch discs. They use analog technology and have been around since the late 1970s. The picture quality is excellent, but their size and weight have made them a bit clunky in the present day. Still, many HK fans are adherents and have vast libraries, as a great number of HK films have been made available on LD.

Video Compact Discs (VCDS)
No entertainment technology has made such an impact in Asia. Using a compression scheme known as MPEG-1, a 90-minute feature film can be digitally encoded onto a pair of standard five-inch CDs. With a double-CD tray, the movie then fits into a

A few that very stink.

Trust Me U Die (1999)

Shot under the title *New Dr. Lamb* and starring Simon Yam as a sawbones. One might expect a shuddering thrill ride like the original *Dr. Lamb* (see Chapter 13). But this torporous disjointed tale starts with Mark Cheng as a sicko doctor, then switches over to Yam as baddie, then sort of runs around like a mangy street cur chasing its ratty tail. There are some inspired bits of business with always-good Sam Lee, but this production's main claim to fame was tarnishing the rep of costar Joey Tan, aka Miss Malaysia Chinatown 1997–1998 (also featured as January cover girl in *Penthouse* magazine's Hong Kong edition). The pageant's organizer said these actions violated a three-year exclusive management contract and were "calculated to bring discredit, disrepute, ridicule, and contempt on herself and the promoter." If only it had brought some life to TMUD as well.

PR Girls (1998)

Certain films are so astonishingly bad that they roar up in agonized triumph, going straight over the top into a new dimension of wildly entertaining superbad filmdom as they provide new realms of jaw-dropping fun. *PR Girls* is not one of them.

Big Circle Blues (1992)

Wow, a Category 3 knockabout starring Mark Cheng and super-buffed head-kicking Michiko Nishiwaki—looks good, right? Wrong! A bunch of uninspiring criminals go to Taiwan, get mad at some banal crime boss, and decide to try to kill him. Cops Cheng and Nishiwaki kill time between fights by arguing with each other. The Category 3 tag is supplied by having some no-name starlet shed her blouse for a few moments. Skip, skip, skip.

Hong Kong X File (1998)

Nobody in Hong Kong cares about UFO conspiracies, so you get a wiseacre

standard CD jewel box. As the CDs are standard issue and mass-produced, costs are low, and VCD players are cheap and readily available. Two audio tracks mean that Cantonese and Mandarin soundtracks can be put on the same disc (if you hear an echo effect, you are listening to both tracks at once and should select either left- or right-channel only). VCD hardware and software is everywhere in HK, including three- and five-disc changers built into component stereo systems with input for karaoke microphones. The profusion of HK movies available is staggering, and old favs are regularly rereleased in this format, invariably letterboxed and almost always subtitled—the boxes usually list "Chinese/English subtitles"; if in doubt, ask the staff. Longer movies can take up three or even four VCDs, but the vast majority fit on two. As a digital format, the quality is not as good as LD, and fast-action scenes suffer from pixelization. Transfers

wiseguy named Horny Keung bobbing his shaven dragon-tattooed head around as he works black magic with purloined pubes from his staff, psychically transforming them into shameless hornbags. And kung fu guy Chin Kar-lok (*Drunken Master 2, The Legend of Wisely*) is sure to whip wicked moves on some baddies! Sounds like great entertainment, a Friday-night bag-of-cuttlefish-and-a-sixpack kind of flick, right?

Ix-nay.

Hong Kong Showgirls (1996)

The opportunity for overripe parody looms large and luscious. Some toothsome starlet (preferably a dropout from the Miss Hong Kong competition) on an overacting jag, stripping off at every opportunity, mispronouncing designer brand names, boning moronic stallions of the entertainment industry, tangling claws with bitchy rivals. A gaggle of hopping child vampires replaces the garlic-scarfing chimps of Verhoeven's unjustly maligned, twisted comedy. One would think that the industry to whom exploitation is a warm fuzzy selling point (see Chapter 13) would take the *Showgirls* ball, run gleefully into the end zone, and spike that orb into a blizzard of seedy shards. Not even close.

Hong Kong Showgirls fumbles along for 90 minutes, never sure what it wants to be or, indeed, if it is still running through the projector. Protagonist and antagonist (Veronica Yip and cleavage-impaired Diana Pang) eschew leotard-peeling in favor of amateurish dance routines—Pang can do the splits, a stunt that fixates the filmmakers. The other one either can't or won't do the splits, but *Hong Kong Showgirls* doesn't suffer from this. It suffers from everything else, including some sort of quarter-baked ghost story about a masked figure who wants to dance with our brace of plucky showgirls. Ghost effects include a smoke machine and a 99-cent Woolworth's skull-on-a-stick popping up from a bathroom stall. Oh, oh, such a stinker.

also vary, and there are some shabby-looking VCDs out there, though most are OK.

Digital Video Discs (DVDs)

The medium of the future. Using a standard CD-sized disc, a 90-minute film can be put on a single DVD in MPEG-2 format, which is better quality than MPEG-1. In fact, properly mastered DVDs look better than any other home-video format and can also offer multiple-language soundtracks and a wide variety of subtitles. You must check carefully as not all discs offer these features—unfortunately, some offer little more than their tape or VCD counterparts save a higher-quality picture and sound.

Companies that have made the effort to craft a value-added DVD package are worth tracking (Media Asia, Tai Seng, and Criterion are good examples). Want to watch *Beast Cops* with an English-dubbed soundtrack and Spanish subtitles? You got it. Some DVDs even offer audio commentary as a soundtrack option; listening to Terence Chang and John Woo yak about *Hard-Boiled* (or hearing Herman Yau and Anthony Wong explicate *The Untold Story*) while you're watching the film is the type of thing you will only find on DVD, and an incentive to buy the film so you can watch it again and again. Other goodies include switchable aspect-ratios (letterboxed vs. pan-and-scan), original theatrical trailers, and behind-the-scenes stuff like production stills and/or storyboards.

You need these incentives because DVDs are relatively expensive (though rentable— try http://www.dvdpost. com/rental.html or http://www.netflix.com). Also, there's a region-coding deal, which splits the world into a bunch of zones; zone-specific DVDs won't play in other zones. Whatever brainiac came up with this scheme managed to put Hong Kong and China in *two separate DVD regions.* This sort of nineteenth-century isolationism hasn't married well with twenty-first-century technology, and many people have avoided buying into DVD because of the region coding. Fortunately, HK releases have so far been uncoded, which means they should play on any DVD player. But don't assume anything: The situation is fluid, and you should check www.dvdresource.com/dvdfaq/dv faq.shtml for Jim Taylor's fantastic DVD Frequently Asked Questions (FAQ), which will give you more info than you could possibly want. Other good HK-ON-DVD sources are http://www. taiseng.com and http://www. mediaasia.com/dvd/index.htm.

glossary

Cantopop: An entertainment business that is at least as big as the film biz in Hong Kong, it consists mostly of syrupy pop tunes sung in Cantonese dialect. Film stars usually have Cantopop careers on the side; celebs like Andy Lau and Aaron Kwok are far better known for their vocal resumes than for their film appearances. Few stars break out of the mold unless they go over to Taiwan and start doing, wait for it, Mandopop.

Category 3: This is the adults-only category, reserved for films with nasty sex and/or violence. A few films have been slapped with a Cat 3 tag solely for inventive abuses of Cantonese, which is pretty impressive.

chop: This verb means "to attack someone violently with a machete or other large-edged weapon, referred to as a 'chopper.'" Chopping attacks are gruesome and bloody affairs, and the most skillful machete wielders aim to cripple their victims permanently rather than kill them.

DVD: Digital video disc, or digital versatile disc (see "Acronym Overload," page 253).

Fatty: Anyone not as thin as a straw can be referred to as "Fatty" in the HK movies. Peter Coe and his friend Dave, Thirteenth and Fourteenth *Sifus* of Dumpling Thunder Fist, insist that the "Gang of Fatty" referred to by Michelle Yeoh in *Butterfly and Sword* must be an elite cabal of HKers. Coe swears that being down with the Gang of Fatty attests to one's HK film savvy or proves that you were at a banquet with portly HK actor Kent Cheng.

feng shui: This was a popular Stateside fad in the late 1990s, sandwiched somewhere between kabala and tae-bo. Literally "wind and water," *feng shui* is the ancient science of arranging architectural elements, furniture, and other objects to ensure that cosmic elements remain undisturbed by earthlings. *Feng shui* can be quite complex and lyrical, but not all masters agree on what exactly should be moved where. The most influential *feng shui* guys get to pick airport opening dates and things like that.

fist game: This noisy guessing game is played in hostess bars or at banquets or other gatherings. Opponents throw out a number of fingers as they chant in ritualized fashion. Basically, they are guessing the number of fingers their opponent will display. Loser has to slug down a glass of something alcoholic, which is the point of this rather silly game. If you see characters in a HK movie shouting and gesticulating with their fingers, then drinking, now you know what they're doing. Amazingly, a brief English-language version of this game appears on the English soundtrack on the *Beast Cops* DVD.

gai: Literally, "chicken," but also slang for "callgirl." The punning possibilities are myriad and obvious. The word for "duck" is used to refer to working boys rather than working girls. Some people like chicken, some people like duck.

"give it a damn": This translates as: "What the hell, I don't care." When HK movie characters have their blood up, they will declare: "I won't give it a damn!"

Grand Guignol: Established in 1897, Paris's Theatre du Grand Guignol was notorious for its repertoire of horror plays, plays so horrific that a doctor was stationed in the lobby to revive fainting spectators. The theatre's fame was such that Parisian guidebooks used to list it among the city's most popular attractions along with the Louvre, the Eiffel Tower, and legalized brothels. The phrase "Grand Guignol" became synonymous with bloodletting and gore.

gwailo: Literally, "foreign devil," but used to refer to Caucasian types. In recent years, the term has been assumed to be pejorative, and the more politically correct term *sai yan* ("Western person") has been substituted. But Hong Kong is not politically correct, and there's really nothing wrong with *gwailo*.

ICAC: The Independent Commission Against Corruption, founded in the mid-1970s. A watchdog organization that keeps high-level corruption to a dull roar in the SAR. The ICAC story was made into a 1993 film, *First Shot*, starring Ti Lung, Maggie Cheung, and Charles Heung.

"it's funny": Neither funny-weird nor funny-ha-ha, this means that something is fun.

"it's peanut": This means that something is not a big deal. Just take it as peanut.

Macau: The tiny Pearl River Delta community is 60 kilometers from HK and its successful gaming industry has made it a known haven for goodfellas. Its fascinating blend of European roots and Chinese soul (Macau was a Portuguese colony for four centuries) has given it a character far different from that of nearby HK. On December 20, 1999, Macau returned to Chinese rule for the first time since the sixteenth century, becoming (like HK) a Special Administrative Region (SAR).

the Mainland: the People's Republic of China, founded by Mao Zedong in 1949. After Mao's death, new leader Deng Xiaoping created a series of Special Economic Zones designed to ease the country into the modern age. The SEZs of Shanghai, Beijing, Shenzhen (bordering Hong Kong), and Zhuhai (bordering Macau) were established in 1979. Although China has made far greater strides than the former "evil empire" of the USSR, many Westerners still view the PRC with suspicion. See "Blood! Thunder! Handover!," page 138.

mahjong: The Hong Kong equivalent of bridge, this four-player table game is a noisy and fun way to lose money. Rather than flimsy playing cards, plastic tiles are slapped on the table as players blister their way through four- or five-hour *mahjong* sessions. The combatants noisily criticize their fellow players' gutless, sure-to-lose strategies as the tiles flip belly-up. Characters in supernatural films sometimes end up in a ghost *mahjong* game, which is not a pleasant sort of contest.

"pull off a stunt": Any type of trickery can be denoted by this odd phrase. Hong Kong film characters frequently deliver subtitles like: "Bastard, you want to pull off a stunt?"

SAR: Special Administrative Region. In today's People's Republic of China, some regions are more equal than others. The "SAR" concept was created to allow Hong Kong to be reunited with the PRC while simultaneously retaining a high degree of autonomy. Macau became the second SAR upon reunification in December 1999.

SDU: Special defense unit, the Hong Kong equivalent of the SWAT team.

sifu: Master. Teacher. *Sifus* are male or female practitioners of martial arts or Taoist technique. They are usually dedicated, elderly, and masterful, and they expect total obedience from their students.

swastika: A four-armed symbol with right-angled endpieces. It is a Buddhist symbol which has been used for over eight centuries and still denotes vegetarian restaurants and food products in Asia. Misappropriated several decades ago by a frustrated Austrian artist.

tael: Ancient unit of measurement, still used for gold. In the old days, it was used for everything, except for the catty, another eccentric measuring unit used for foodstuffs.

VCD: Video compact disc (see "Acronym Overload," page 253).

wai gor: Literally "Brother Wai," this is the Cantonese term for Viagra.

wushu: A form of martial arts that has evolved into a competitive sport. Not an Olympic sport, though—more like beach volleyball or something.

XO: Expensive cognac packed in ornate bottles. In HK films, it's usually consumed in large snifters by underworld characters anxious to show off how tough they are.

yakuza: This Japanese wiseguy syndicate has been the source of countless films and film characters in Japan. They also appear, usually in cartoony fashion, as villains in Hong Kong gangster flicks.

yau mo GAU cho wah!: Cantonese phrase heard at least once every single day on the streets of Hong Kong. It means: "You gotta be kidding me!"

index

Italicized page numbers refer to photos or photo captions.

about the author and contributors

Stefan Hammond is coauthor (with Mike Wilkins) of *Sex and Zen & A Bullet in The Head: The Essential Guide to Hong Kong's Mindbending Films*. He lives in Hong Kong.

Jeremy Hansen is a New Zealand journalist who fled that tranquil nation for the madness of pre-handover Hong Kong in March 1997. Before that, he worked as a producer for the BBC World Service's New Zealand outpost and spent three years writing feature stories for *Metro* magazine. He currently writes features for *Post Magazine*, the Sunday magazine of the *South China Morning Post*.

A graduate of UCLA Film School, **Wade Major** is a Los Angeles–based entertainment journalist and independent filmmaker. His work has appeared in *Entertainment Today, Boxoffice Magazine, Transpacific, Face*, and the online magazine *Mr. Showbiz*. Major is coproducer of the 1999 documentary feature *Splitscreen: The Secret History of American Movies*, and the author of *Jackie Chan* from Metrobooks.

A teacher of English and film at Virginia Tech, **Michael Bliss** has written books on Brian De Palma, Martin Scorsese, Sam Peckinpah, Jonathan Demme, and Peter Weir. Bliss's favorite non-Woo Hong Kong films are *Supercop, Project A*, and *The Iceman Cometh*; and although it defies rationality, he will watch any film that features Anthony Wong.

Hong Kong–based actor and stuntman **Jude Poyer** has appeared in Hong Kong films and international productions shot in HK. He is a member of the Hong Kong Stuntman Association and reviews local films on RTHK's Radio 3 channel. Poyer has had his butt kicked by Yuen Biao, Takeshi Kaneshiro, and Donnie Yen. Jet Li, Jordan Chan, and Jean-Claude Van Damme have killed him.

Chuck Stephens sleeps with one eye open, just in case a Jay C. Flippen film comes on the TV late some night; he has, as well, never forgotten the movie Elvis Presley and Kurt Russell made together. A film critic for the *San Francisco Bay Guardian*, and a recently reinvigorated filmmaker of no official distinction, Stephens keeps an apartment in California, but lives in Bangkok, where he is currently at work on his first feature—a feminist musical.

David Chute is a freelance journalist and film critic based in Los Angeles. He writes as often as possible for *Film Comment*, the *LA Weekly*, the *Los Angeles Times*, and the video server at amazon.com. His favorite movie varies on a daily basis, but *Seven Samurai*, *The Killer*, *Kiss Me Deadly*, *Sword of Doom*, and *Two Tars* are never far from the top of the list.

Dave Kehr is a New York–based film critic whose work has appeared in many anthologies and publications, including the *New York Times*, *Film Comment*, and *Entertainment Weekly*. He worships at the shrine of Maggie Cheung.

Bey Logan is the author of *Hong Kong Action Cinema*, editor of *Impact* magazine, and screenwriter of Hong Kong films *White Tiger*, *Ballistic Kiss*, and *Chinese Heart*. He currently works in the Hong Kong film industry as a writer and producer. Logan, wife Ponnie, and son Ryan are kung fu experts, and are working hard to perfect the Logan Family Slamdunk Iron Head Style.

Andy Klein is a Los Angeles–based film critic who went bananas over Tsui Hark's *Peking Opera Blues* in the summer of 1989. He has subsequently written extensively about Hong Kong cinema for *Variety*, the *Hollywood Reporter*, the *Los Angeles Reader*, *Bikini*, *New Times Los Angeles*, and *Martial Arts Movies*.

Karen Tarapata is a diehard Shaw Brothers fan and tape collector who lives and writes in Nyack, New York. Favorite films include anything with Alexander Fu Sheng in it, *Mad Monkey Kung Fu*, and *Mr. Vampire*. When not glued to a video monitor, Tarapata studies Yang-style tai chi.

Tim Youngs is a writer/editor based in Hong Kong. He can be found most Saturday mornings in Mongkok, salty/buttery buns in hand, eyes fixed on big screen. He will watch soap operas in Cantonese for the merest glimpse of starlet Ada Choi.

Michael Helms has been sipping chrysanthemum tea in Melbourne Chinatown cinemas since 1980. He still has the Bruce Lee/kung fu scrapbook he created as a 12-year-old and still publishes *Fatal Visions*—the mag he's been producing since 1988 to yammer on about Asian cinema among other things. He expects to watch *A Bullet in the Head* a few more times before complete eyesight failure.

Ross Sit is a Hong Kong–based illustrator and graphic designer who has been published in numerous local publications. He holds a visual communications degree from the University of Kansas and specializes in conceptual editorial illustrations.